BY U.S. BONDS

that's my story

GARY U.S. BONDS
and Stephen Cooper

Foreword by Steven Van Zandt

By U.S. Bonds
That's My Story
Gary U.S. Bonds with Stephen Cooper
Copyright © 2013 GLA Music Group, LLC.

All rights reserved. Except as permitted under U.S. Copyright Act of 1976, no part of this publication may be reproduced, distributed, or transmitted in any form or by any means, or stored in a database or retrieval system, without the prior written permission of the publisher.

WP
WHEATLEY PRESS, LLC

Wheatley Press US @ Apple Direct
225 Varick Street, New York, N.Y. 10014
www.wheatleypressUS.com

Library of Congress Cataloging-in-Publication Data (filed)

Hardcover (color photos): ISBN-13: 978-0-9887063-0-9
Hardcover (black & white photos): ISBN-13: 978-0-9887063-1-6
eBook: ISBN-13: 978-0-9887063-2-3

Printed in the United States of America

Book Design by KarrieRoss.com
Edited by Samantha J. Brand
Photos Edited by Mark Weiss

First Edition:
10 9 8 7 6 5 4 3 2 1

Disclaimer: The Publisher makes no representations or warranties with respect to the accuracy or completeness of the contents of this book and specifically disclaims any implied warranties of merchantability or fitness for a particular purpose. Neither the publisher nor author shall be liable for any loss of profit or any commercial damages.

CONTENTS

FOREWORD BY STEVEN VAN ZANDT V

CHAPTER 1
    A View from the Road: Watching Gary Bonds 1

CHAPTER 2
    Before I Forget 11

CHAPTER 3
    But He Can't Dance 23

CHAPTER 4
    Beginnings of a Young Turk 39

CHAPTER 5
    A Hey, Hey, Hey, Yeah 51

CHAPTER 6
    Past a Quarter to Three 65

CHAPTER 7
    Happy for the Rest of My Life 79

CHAPTER 8
    "City Jail, City Farm" 91

CHAPTER 9
    That's All I Got 105

CHAPTER 10
    Time to Re-Tire 119

CHAPTER 11
    A Guy From Jersey 128

CHAPTER 12
"One More Time, Mr. Gary U.S. Bonds" 139

CHAPTER 13
On the Line 153

CHAPTER 14
Perpetuity is a Very Long Time 165

CHAPTER 15
No Beef with Ali 181

CHAPTER 16
Fooled 'Em Again Bro' 192

CHAPTER 17
Invited to the Ball 205

CHAPTER 18
Another Bruce 219

CHAPTER 19
Blow Daddy 225

CHAPTER 20
That's My Story 231

DEDICATION 235

INDEX 239

FOREWORD BY STEVEN VAN ZANDT

I DISLOCATED MY FINGER PLAYING FLAG FOOTBALL SOME '72.

In the great big scheme of things, another kid from New Jersey going through life with a crooked finger wouldn't have meant too much. Except it was how I met Gary U.S. Bonds.

I had quit playing guitar two years earlier, totally disheartened. I felt like we'd missed it. The Renaissance had come and gone, 20 years of the greatest music ever made-and ever will be made-and we had watched it from the sidelines.

I had a bad feeling the '70s was going to be the first of many decades to come where those of us who loved and depended on Rock and Roll would be forced to tolerate its inevitable slow slide into irrelevant mediocrity. I just couldn't stand there and watch it. So I quit.

I was right by the way.

Anyway, in an effort to exercise what would be my forever bent finger, I took a gig as a piano player in a bar band. Turns out the drummer was a cousin of one of the Dovells and they needed a band and he said the magic words that closed the deal: Las Vegas!

The Dovells had made two of my favorite records, "Bristol Stomp" and "You Can't Sit Down," which helped, but I had been a big gambler as a kid and if there was a chance to visit Mecca I was gonna grab it.

So began my adventures on "the oldies circuit." The British Invasion had ironically put all of its own heroes out of work, so a network of venues formed for the pioneer artists of the '50s and early '60s that resembled the Senior Tour in golf (I think that's been changed now to the more appropriate and less demeaning "Champion's Tour") financially successful, but unintentionally no less demeaning, this became known as the "oldies circuit."

Oh how they all hated that name. Keep in mind most of the first generation Rock pioneers were only in their late 20s, early 30s when they were put out to pasture!

They not only hated the term "oldies," but were permanently pissed they'd have to spend the second halves of their lives playing nothing but their five or whatever hit records instead of making new ones.

So there I was meeting all my heroes and man were they not in a very good mood (except for Gary who always seemed to be in a good mood) but I was having a ball!

They were all personality-plus characters magically transported directly from my little turntable, come to life before my grateful eyes.

I met Gary, Bo Diddley, Chuck Berry, Lloyd Price, Little Richard, Fats, Frankie Valli, Dion, the Shirelles, Chubby Checker, Ben E. King, all the legends.

After a wonderful year of doing that, I formed Southside Johnny and the Asbury Jukes with Southside. When I produced the Jukes' first two albums I brought back as many of those mentors as I could to guest on the records and show everybody how great they still were.

Lee Dorsey, Ronnie Spector, the Coasters, the Drifters, the Five Satins. About three/four years later Bruce, sharing the same impulse, decides to do a record with Gary Bonds. Frankly, I thought it was an odd choice.

Gary, along with his Producer Frank Guida and sax player Gene "Daddy G" Barge, had invented Garage Rock, literally, with his party hits sounding like they were recorded in a garage, but the weird way his voice was recorded, while perfect on those records, didn't exactly showcase any promising golden tones if you know what I'm saying.

I said to Bruce, "What about Ben E. King, Chuck Jackson, Wilson Pickett?" I named a dozen others. "No," said Bruce, "Without Gary we maybe wouldn't be here."

Okay baby, it's your funeral! (Same thing he said to me by the way when I told him I was going to produce local misanthrope Southside Johnny) Bruce started the project by himself.

He wrote two songs and the E Streeters played on them, but while Bruce was one of the greatest Co-Producers you'd ever want to work with, back then he was not a great Producer.

Bottom line, the record kind of sucked and he couldn't get Gary a deal. I get the phone call. I went in, re-mixed them, made one call and got him a deal, but I optimistically promised not just the single, but an album as well. So now of course Bruce is busy doing whatever, so Tom Sawyer tosses the album to me ("You guaranteed it!"), with him visiting now and then. I needed some kind of concept so I figured let's just stick with Gary interpreting the greatest writers on earth and see where it goes. Lennon/McCartney, Dylan, Jackson Browne. And it is here that I discover Gary's voice.

In a word, it is spectacular. Again, quite a shock for those of us only familiar with his hits. How Bruce knew what Gary was capable of I will never understand but that's what makes him The Boss.

We hurried through the recording, the record company was in a panic because the single was taking off (it would go Top 11!), and I thought we were done but Bruce suggested I write a song to complete the album.

I looked at what we had and knew it was a great re-introduction to Gary, but felt the record could use one song that was really personal. Written just for him. Something biographical and relevant right now.

That was "Daddy's Come Home." It turned out to be one of my favorite compositions and the song that really showed what Gary could do vocally.

We would use that performance as the jumping off point for the second album.

This time, all of it would be personal, almost all of it written by Bruce specifically for Gary, and this time I'd take my time with the vocals and the mixes. The results are some of the greatest vocals ever done by anybody ever. The whole album (On *the Line*) just sounds amazing and I'm really proud of it.

One never knows what's coming, but my creative chapter with Gary, for the moment, closed strong with "Standing In the Line of Fire," the title of the third "comeback" album which he recently performed at the Little Kids Rock event, blowing everybody away.

Along with "The Last Time," written specifically for Gary for the *On the Line* album, the three songs I wrote for Gary are three of my favorite songs, three of my favorite performances of my songs, and three of my favorite productions.

Everyone knew he was a legendary pioneer, but with those records Bruce and I did, he proved himself a master interpreter and truly one of the great singers of all time.

I am proud to call him my friend.

Steven Van Zandt
Lillehammer, Norway
February, 2013

BY US BONDS

that's
my
story

One

A VIEW FROM THE ROAD...
WATCHING GARY BONDS

They sat shoulder to shoulder in the theater lobby, still wearing their sweat-soaked stage-clothes. It was just minutes after completing the first half of their show, billed tonight and most nights of the tour as the *Great American Soul Book*, and by chance or error other nights as the *Great American Songbook*. Gershwin and Sondheim were absent from the proceedings, but tonight's 50 minute, 16 song first act summoned among others, Messrs. Redding and Pickett, Sam and Dave, Jackie Wilson, Ray Charles and the great vocal groups of the '50s and '60s whose contributions comprise the American soul canon. Some liberties were taken with the song selection, and the bounds of soul music were indeed stretched, but for a good cause: the delight of 400 predominantly Welsh patrons of the unpronounceable, at least to visitors, Theater Brycheinoig. It was accomplished respectfully and knowingly by the enduring artists, two men of soul who had taken their places behind a laminate table.

Their table is one that we all see during the holidays. It's the one grandmothers have grandfathers bring up from the basement so that honored guests and second cousins might all partake in a single sitting. But this was no banquet. Forty minutes into the show's first half, two gentlemen, theater volunteers, brought two tables out from behind the box office which was within the theater lobby, between the auditorium and a pub which served simple fare and beverages pre- and post show. The volunteers set the tables at a 90 degree angle to each other, and two folding chairs were placed behind each table. Then they disappeared into the pub and returned with two unmarked boxes which they placed on one of the tables. Taken from the pub freezer, the boxes held a frozen confection. One box held vanilla and the other chocolate. A change basket was located and each volunteer took a seat and braced for commerce.

The auditorium emptied in a fashion as orderly and measured as was the mid-show applause. Some patrons headed for the restrooms and an equal number went outside to smoke. The balance was split between the pub and the two laminate tables. From the men's room line I heard someone, surely a Welshman, try to whistle the "outro" from "Dock of the Bay" as Gary just did in tribute to "Otis" just one of his many friends both "dear and departed." The Welshman failed where Gary matched each plaintive note still vividly remembered though 40 years had passed since Otis Redding's posthumous hit.

Vanilla sold briskly. It was nearly sold out by the time Benjamin Nelson (Ben E. King) and Gary Anderson (Gary U.S. Bonds) entered the lobby from a side door which allowed artists to exit the backstage area. By this time, about a dozen people milled about the empty table behind which Anderson and Nelson took seats. Anderson carried a plastic takeout sack from which he removed a handful of his CDs and two black razor-point Sharpies. He gave one to his friend of 50 years. They were open for business. This was a half-time "meet and greet," open to all, more custom than contractual obligation, a chance to meet the fans, sign pictures and sell what the trade refers to as "merch," logo t-shirts and caps (they had none) and CDs (just a few). The dozen lined up half in front of Gary and half in front of Ben. It was confession time at the altar of soul in Brecon, Wales. The theater program revealed the altar of soul saw infrequent use, at least this season which featured a variety of children's choruses and tribute shows paying homage to various local favorites. Each patron praised the half completed performance, and informed one or the other feature as to when they had first heard their music or last saw them perform. The majority of patrons were in their mid-sixties, with the eldest few in their eighties. Each of the admirers was graciously acknowledged and thanked when they admitted to being the greatest fan of one or the other or both of the costars. They brought pictures, LP jackets and old photos which were all cheerfully and freely signed, "You're the Best," by Gary or "Stand By Me," by Ben. Ben took a picture with a fan and then served as photographer for another fan who wanted a picture with Gary. A request came for Ben to sign a much yellowed picture clipped from a local paper announcing an upcoming show circa 1964. A fan at the adjoining table asked Gary to change a bill so he could buy some chocolate. Gary apologized and said he didn't carry a wallet when performing. Ben told Gary the yellowed picture was of Jackie Wilson.

Chocolate outsold the CDs and the pop-up store was closed for the night as time for the second half approached. The evening's work was not yet complete. Gary returned his unsold CDs to the bag along with the Sharpies. Appearing a half-foot taller than a somewhat slumped Ben, Gary stood and asked Ben how he was feeling. The inquiry went unanswered and possibly unheard, but Gary couldn't tell. Unnoticed by the crowd, the pair headed backstage through the side door, Gary first, with Ben following at a slower pace.

I did the math later that night while staring at a Brecon sky so clear I was able to pick out constellations the actual existence of which to that point I seriously questioned. Beginning with a glide path that starts out modestly, ascends to more than a hundred nights a year for a long stretch, then recedes to perhaps 50, but increases for tours like this one (50 shows over 70 days) and my guess was that over their combined hundred plus years doing this they had amassed between them six or seven thousand shows.

Though Ben did not say it, Gary had no reason to believe that his friend, like him past 70, was not up to his best. Despite age and health, or boredom, or the thousands of miles that separated Ben from his wife Betty, or Gary from his beloved "Big Mama," or the preceding 40 shows in 40 cities, or the 10 yet to follow, Gary knew that when called upon, Ben would "own" the sold out theater before tonight's bassist completed the intro to a much anticipated "Stand By Me."

Soul singing is a high stakes calling in which these two are outliers, if only for having survived. These men are victors for having done this for a collective hundred years, with enough desire and talent remaining to levitate 400 Welsh from their seats. The soul fathers are mostly gone now, and their remaining sons have grown slow of gait. Recall one, and it is likely that their names have gained prefixes like "unforgettable" or "immortal." But not these two tonight. A planned 50 minute second half ran to an hour-twenty and none of the three encores was given grudgingly. It was 1964 again. The set-list was dispensed with, the band struggled to keep up with meter and key, and the two sons of the South paged through the soul book singing flag-less anthems to love and joy, hurt and redemption.

Gary let Ben pace himself during the closing set, and after three hours Gary saw that Ben was done. With each having done this for 50 years, there was shared satisfaction in knowing that they had given all, and done all they could to send 400 fans home satisfied. Ben led Gary off the stage and they were both followed by "Little Mama" and the rest of their band.

While Ben and Gary were family figuratively, Little Mama was family literally. She is Gary's daughter, and for the *Soul Book* tour she is road manager, comptroller, map reader, caterer, supervisor of communications and technology, and most vitally, back-up vocalist and musical director. Little Mama followed the two back to the dressing rooms. Ben had his own and Gary and Little Mama shared.

It is here, when the applause has stilled and the crowds go out to rejoin the night that rock and roll stories inevitably veer towards the tragic. And it is not for lack of imagination on the part of the storytellers, or the common failings of their subjects that they go there. They just do. Whether it be the price for singing the devil's music or just an occupational hazard, the two know that few have managed to escape.

Imagine the aged star alone, barely remembering his last brush with celebrity, or for that matter the lyrics of his "money" song, ducking into what passes for a dressing room. He flips the door latch unnecessarily, inasmuch as handlers and hangers on have been scarce for some time. A single nail on the dressing room door holds a wire hanger and his street clothes. He opens a duffel bag on to the table and two packs of Marlboro and a Mennen Speedstick tumble out. He lights a smoke, curses the night, the crowd, his manager and publisher, omitting just for tonight, two wives, two near wives, various children, three record labels, a crooked accountant and an uninformed, unappreciative public unworthy of his performance. In the cliché rock and roll storyline it ends here. When it does, what follows is the brief obligatory mourning by his few remaining fans, the reissue of a "greatest hits" CD, public reminiscences from those he influenced, and finally a modest headstone, the gift of a guilt-wracked label head. But sometimes they linger for another chapter or two, when finally at a Veterans' hospital downtown, the body is discovered to be that of a tortured man, who long ago had his day, and it lasted just two minutes twenty to the fadeout. His roommate is quoted as not knowing that the strangely quiet man with whom he occasionally shared a room did have two charting singles.

But Gary will not veer and take us to that place. He knows there's still one more party that needs starting, and that is his calling and mission. "Rock and roll is what I do. It's what I know, and the only thing I've ever done. Can't drive a truck, can't play baseball and I don't want to. I'll go wherever it takes me, as long as I can."

Gary's dressing room was neat and clean, oversized, and I suspect a rehearsal studio between shows. There was a full length mirror bisected by a shelf for requisites, flanked by two folding chairs, part of the set that Gary and Ben used during the meet and greet. There was one soft sided roll aboard, the smaller of two pieces of luggage that they brought for the 50 night tour. Little Mama opened one and took out a bath towel that resembled the collection found at the hotel.

"Daddy, here, take this," she said as she put the towel around Gary's shoulders and neck which glistened with a well earned sweat. Gary had already opened the buttons of his black stage shirt which was liberated from his trousers by the time he reached his dressing room.

"Thank you sweetheart, why don't you sit down," he suggested gripping the towel and motioning to the other chair as Laurie unzipped the padded case which protected her laptop. She powered it on and placed it on the ledge of the mirrored wall.

"Was okay," Gary offered, and I took that as part question and part statement to his daughter from whom he sought confirmation that the show was well received.

"I think they liked it," she said with a combined modesty and indifference for a performance which must have been the high point of the Brecon cultural calendar.

By now her focus was the laptop on whose keyboard she delicately and rhythmically tapped. Vocalists learn to modulate, but for Little Mama, actually Laurie, this was not a key change, just a routine job change fluidly executed. Daughter Laurie was stage left for the entirety of this evening's affair. For each show she joined additional vocalists hired for different stops on the tour. Laurie knew her Dad's songs and Ben's too. Before leaving for the UK, with her mom, Big Mama, she mapped out the needed vocal fortification required for the *Great American Soul Book*.

The laptop displayed a silhouette that conjured images of Jackie Kennedy's televised White House tour. Big Mama, like Jackie, was at ease in her surroundings, the suburban ranch house considerably smaller, but no less tasteful than the First Lady's home. She projected the same welcoming ease, confidence and grace. Big Mama, Laurie Anderson as well, adjusted her monitor so her designated audience of two would have the best possible view. I kept a respectable distance from the post-show Anderson family "Skype."

I was beyond earshot, but the 15-inch screen allowed me to view discreetly. Big Mama was comfortably seated on a sofa framed by two pull-up chairs in what appeared to be the Anderson living room or den. A gold record visible over her right shoulder, Big Mama faced her monitor which revealed her to be not all that big, but the beneficiary of superior genetics. Viewed digitally from 20 feet, with good resolution, mother and daughter might pass for sisters of the variety that share additional siblings between them. Big Mama sat erect with her right leg crossed as if anticipating callers to discuss the upcoming Junior League tea. Confident, black pants and turtle neck fashionably snug, her look dared the admiring viewer to hazard a guess as to age. Had her cheekbones been any higher, the two slits from which her dark eyes peered might not have been visible at all. Mother and daughter shared complexions with nary a blemish, a combination of butter pecan and bronze powder.

Big Mama is pure-bred Puerto Rican, birth-name Cedeño, raised in Williamsburg, Brooklyn. Her hair was revelatory, straighter than Jackie's, shades darker, with some altitude which must have required work in advance of the Skype. It was an appropriate daytime coif for the ethnically ambiguous, silken background vocalist of whom you are certain the headliner has designs well beyond vocal harmony. She's the one your eye returns to three songs after her solo. This is how she looks late afternoon, digitally, when her daughter and husband check in 40 shows into a 50 show tour. Checking in had progressed since Gary's first tour, when operators would tell those at the bottom of the bill that charges for their collect calls had been rejected. But the Skype was brief, and the conversation consisted mostly of show highlights and where the troupe was headed next. I gathered this was an Anderson family routine.

Once ended, with an exchange of much "love" and "sweethearts," Gary found a clean shirt in the roll aboard. Little Mama remained in her stage clothes, a black printed t-shirt, black jeans, and boots which rose above her ankle, an ensemble which read, "If I were not the star's daughter I'd be out with the leader of the pack." Little Mama's goal was a hasty exit from the venue, to locate some food other than Indian take-out, (seemingly the only late night fare on the tour), and then to head back to the hotel. Tomorrow they would loop back south about 300 miles to another secondary theater, not far from their last show before Brecon. Knowing that the trip would take another five or six hours in the back of a much abused SUV belonging to the actual road-manager, a large man allegedly descended from the wildebeest, Laurie knew the best way to prepare was to make sure that Gary and Ben were well nourished and rested. Her efforts would be thwarted.

The band, three rhythm players, two horns and Laurie's co-back-up vocalists, had their own dressing room adjacent to Gary's. Laurie knocked and entered to check and see which players were traveling to the next show. Indian take-out loomed.

The band was hosting a visitor of some renown, who along with a friend, wished to extend courtesies to the headliners. They traveled some distance to be there. Not only had they anticipated enjoying the evening's entertainment, but they surely anticipated the "stop and chat", that would follow. A show of respect was in order.

The visitor entered the business about five years after Gary, and he, like Little Mama, was destined to remain "Little." Steve Winwood, circa 1967, the multi-instrumentalist and Hammond B-3 prodigy sealed his future with the opening bars of Billboard #7 charting "Gimme Some Loving," a song he wrote as a member of the Spencer Davis Group. He went on to stints with Traffic and Blind Faith, remained relevant, and tonight aside, avoided brushes with the nostalgia circuit. His visage had that weathered veneer now common to second wave British Invaders. Laurie looked at him but could not place where they had met. For the moment, she overlooked that it was the second wave that finally banished her dad to semi-regular employment at hotel lounges and on package shows during the waning days of AM hit radio.

Following a round of hugs and kisses, Laurie brought Steve into the dressing room she shared with Gary, and Ben followed soon after. The band filed in as well. Half seemed to have some vague notion of Winwood and the others were too young to fake it credibly. Winwood lived a distance from the venue and Gary was flattered that he came out for the evening. The three spoke shop: Gary's take on Arthur Conley's "Sweet Soul Music," and Ben's reading of John Lennon's "Imagine," which rarely makes its way into soul programs. The remarks were sincere, solicitous, and well intended, sons to fathers, pupils to teachers, comrades revelling in tales of the road, rejoicing at having never veered to that dark place. Gary was accustomed to this.

The unpaid tour photographer, also known as the bass player's girlfriend, captured the reunion with assurances that she would e-mail pictures to everyone. But Ben didn't use email, or his cell phone. The visit ended long after the last Indian takeouts were shuttered. Unfed, but otherwise satisfied, Gary and Ben reached the hotel where they were greeted by the desk clerk who said Ben's wife was calling on the house phone. In his sonorous baritone Ben wished us a good night and went to his room to tell Betty the same.

Stephen Cooper

Brecon, Wales
March 2011

Two

BEFORE I FORGET

Rock and roll is loud, fast, and impatient, served up three minutes at a time. If they like it, they'll play your song again, and if not there's another one just seconds behind. There's no ponder in rock and roll. Do it well and you'll be doing it again before your last song is done. Miss once and they take your soul. Miss twice and you get it back, but you're the answer to a trivia question that nobody bothers to ask. It's a profession for the big, the bold, and the peculiar, because rock and roll thrives at the extremes. But it lives in the middle, with more misses than hits and more fade-outs than supernovas. This is a story from the middle, a small story about rock and roll, my story, remarkable in that it continues, and for those who have made it possible.

Some of the story has been forgotten and some is best not remembered. My memory, like my life, is far from perfect. So forgive these sins of omission, and the omission of sins. That's my story and I'm sticking to it.

In his song "Promised Land" Chuck Berry sings about the "poor boy" who left his home in Norfolk, Virginia aboard a Greyhound bus to find riches and opportunity in the Golden State. Chuck never tells us whether the "poor boy" had plans for a career in rock and roll, but when I left Norfolk I did. I left Norfolk looking for a chance to entertain, but I didn't leave alone. I went with my mother and my buddy "Slow Drag" in Grandpa Newkirk's Crown Victoria, probably a 1956, but it looked older. It was 1961 and I had just turned 22. We skipped the bus and headed by car for a three hour drive to Washington, D.C. As my third single, "Quarter to Three" started to get strong airplay nationally, I was signed to join LaVern Baker, the Drifters, my "homegirl" Ruth Brown and headliners Sam Cooke and B.B. King on a package show. But after that first show, and a teary hug from my mother, just like the "poor boy" I was expected to ride the bus with most of the acts and the band we shared for a tour of theaters and clubs that welcomed African Americans as both entertainers and patrons.

Months before, when my first record "broke" there was no tour, no picture sleeve 45, or album cover with photographs which would have revealed my race. My label shipped more of my records to stores which were in white neighborhoods than black neighborhoods, and my radio play was greater by disc jockeys at the white stations. After listening to my sound which was unlike any before it, many black deejays sent my records back not knowing what to make of them. But following my second charting single which went to #1, there were albums, fan magazines, and national television. Despite the fact that white teens continued to buy most of my records, early on I was signed to tours which did not stray far from what the previous generation of performers called the Chitlin' Circuit, theaters and clubs which served an almost exclusively black audience. In larger urban areas we appeared at theaters which had mixed audiences and a few which had recently ended their policy of racially divided seating.

LaVern Baker, the Drifters, B.B. King, these were all people that I thought were bigger than life, and those girls, especially the young ones, they loved Sam Cooke. I had two songs and one suit and they were the professionals. When the shows worked their way south we would play the Royal Peacock in Atlanta and the Carver in Birmingham. When we went north it was usually the Uptown in Philadelphia and the Apollo in New York, and in Chicago we would play the Regal.

On that first tour I stayed back, did my two hits, and then I borrowed "Rockin' Robin" from Bobby Day, and "Let Them Talk" from Little Willie John to fill the 20-minute, four-song slot I did for as many as six shows a day. I kept to myself and watched the legends, saw how they did it, and how they moved and worked the crowd.

I met a lot of the headliners when they played Norfolk. Most of the black performers stayed at the Plaza, Bonnie McEachin's hotel, and Mom knew Bonnie and took me there when I was a kid. But working with them was different. They were making a lot of money and as their opening act I was fearful. I didn't want to ruin their show by trying to do what they did. I was cautious. I had not yet developed a stage personality and I probably looked uncomfortable to the audience. This was a theater with a thousand seats, not a Norfolk lounge with 30 drunks. I restrained myself. But as I tried to learn by watching Sam and B.B. from the wings, I found out quickly that they were watching me. I remember Sam telling me, "Do something Bonds, you got a nice voice and the girls love you."

After I disappointed B.B. by failing to connect with the audience on our second or third stop, he said, "Tomorrow when you go out there talk it up, let people know what you're doing and how you're feeling. They'll make you a friend if you let them. Backstage you're talking up a storm. When you get onstage you shut up. What the hell is wrong with you? Do a little more." By that time B.B. had already been touring for 20 years, had a dozen hit records and a following in every city we played, but his advice did not penetrate and his friend Sam had seen enough.

It may have been at the Regal theater where I stood behind the curtain watching Sam close the show. He did six numbers, just some of his hit singles, and the crowd wouldn't let him off. There were two encores and I could feel that every girl in the audience would have liked to take him home. I wanted to be the first to congratulate him backstage and when I approached him and tried to pat him on the back, he smacked the shit out of me with an open palm on my chest and head. It wasn't the assault that hurt, it was his words, expressed as tough-love, something my mother and grandmother had never used. "I told you when you go out there, this is what you're supposed to do," referring to his thirty-minute, knee weakening turn which closed the show. Sam "killed," and saved me professionally at the same time. I needed no more encouragement than the fact that he felt I might be able to do what he did on stage. He told me from that moment on I was off the bus and that I would ride with him.

The headliners had their own cars, and sometimes they'd share. For the rest of the tour I rode in the car with Sam. Sometimes he had a valet who drove, and sometimes Sam took the wheel, but I was always beside him. Some nights B.B. rode up front as well, when Sam's wardrobes and our luggage and instruments filled the trunk and back seat. Thank God B.B. was smaller then and so was I, probably no more than 120 pounds on my five-foot-ten-inch frame. I spoke to Sam and B.B. and to me those rides were college and I had the best professors. Defying age, B.B. is still touring, and "Professor" Cooke, I may have been one of his last students, but he was generous to the end which came tragically just a few years after that first tour. I started talking to my audiences and haven't shut up since. Now they say I talk too much.

I was off the bus and unafraid. I learned how to handle a crowd and get a ride from the headliner no matter who it was or where we were appearing. But I haven't stopped learning.

My buddy, Sirius XM deejay and rock historian, Norm N. Nite nailed it when he told me, "As a performer, it's all about the stuff you learn after you think you know it all."

Sam gave me the courage to reach an audience by opening up and telling them how I feel. This is the first time I'm trying to do that on paper, but I'll do it just like Sam taught me on stage at the Regal.

They say you never can go home, because when you do its not the same. The people have changed or fled, and the places are either gone or forgotten. But I can go home, and I've been doing it every year for the past 40-plus years since I packed the car and took Big Mama and a very little, Little Mama away from my childhood home.

My mother, known to everyone in Norfolk as Miss Irene, together with her mother, Mrs. Margaret Newkirk, brought me to Norfolk in the summer of 1942. My father did not make the trip, and my parents separated for reasons that Mom and Pop never discussed with me. Their separation remained a mystery for most of my youth. I used to imagine that my dad, John Henry Gary Anderson, might not have received sufficient attention from his wife since my arrival. To me, his only son, he would give his name, but to me, his wife and mother-in-law would give all their attention. Or perhaps my mother could not sufficiently distract my father from his studies long enough for them to forge a successful working marriage. My father never met a subject he did not want to study to mastery and he remained a student well into his 40s. After earning a Bachelor of Science degree from Morehouse College in 1932, he taught and then enrolled at Hampton Institute (now Hampton College) where in 1943 he earned a Master of Arts in Industrial Science. He then continued graduate studies in Occupational Guidance and Economic Problems. I learned from my stepsister that he was a Doctoral candidate at Penn State University. He served as Principal of Northwestern Senior High School in Jacksonville, and taught Science and Mathematics at Edward Waters College. It was rare for African Americans to attend college in the 1920s and 1930s and I suspect that only a small number pursued graduate education. He continued to indulge his passion for diverse subjects and expressed himself artistically through his hobbies, woodworking and upholstery. I remember my mother telling me that he even took credit for designing and building the electro-mechanical time-clock which was in use at Hampton College basketball games for decades.

Miss Irene was raised in Jacksonville, but born in Georgia where her family, the Durhams, can be traced as far back as 1837. I guess I got my love of music from Mom. Mom studied piano, gave lessons, and no matter where we lived we always had a piano in the house. My father was born in Allendale, South Carolina where he was orphaned as an infant, the product of a racially mixed marriage. His father was white, of middle European descent, and his mother was African American. He was adopted by the Reverend Atkin Anderson and his wife Savannah. They brought my father from Allendale to Jacksonville where the Reverend preached. It was there where he met Mom and they married in 1937. From pictures I could tell they were a handsome couple. Pop was a pipe smoker, athletically built, with broad shoulders, medium brown hair and light green eyes, quite unusual for a black man. He looked more like a linebacker than a professor. Mom was light skinned, attractive, and like me an only child. We were both spoiled by our mothers, and once I was born Grandma challenged anyone who did not consider me to be the center of the universe.

Mom was 19 and Pop 32 when they married. They met in school when she was 16. He was her teacher. Grandma was not prepared to part with her daughter, and I would learn much later that she considered the union scandalous. Even though Grandma had married a much older man and gave birth to Mom at 15, I guess she felt times had changed and she didn't want her only daughter to repeat the mistakes that she had made. Grandma wanted Mom to leave her mistakes behind; her influence resulted in us picking up and moving to Norfolk.

There were many reasons for a young black family to make the northerly trip up the coast. Norfolk, a city of a quarter million, bordered on the West by the Elizabeth River and to the North by Chesapeake Bay, was a major beneficiary of the build up and eventual entry of the United States into the second World War. The war effort swelled the population with the influx of enlisted men and émigrés from the north and south filling the high-paying positions in the shipyards and aerospace factories.

Norfolk was diverse, but there was no mistaking the black and white neighborhoods or the black and white clubs that were plentiful on Church and Granby Streets. Another important reason we relocated to Norfolk, was that Grandma planned to remarry.

Grandma met a retired Navy mess officer. Newkirk might have been the most popular man in our neighborhood. As a retired Navy mess officer and cook, he was welcomed at the kitchens and storerooms aboard every class of ship which made its way to Norfolk. With me at his side, Newkirk would visit his friends on board, and we would leave with arms full of meat and groceries courtesy of Newkirk's buddies and the U.S. Navy. Not only were we well fed, but we often had enough to share with the neighbors.

Mom also met a retired Navy man with a government pension. His name was Eddie Mimms. Mimms was a chef from Macon, but Mom met him in Norfolk. My grandmother had one sister, my Aunt Louise who remained in Jacksonville. Her husband David owned a dry cleaning plant. David and my Dad knew each other and did business. Although my father was primarily a teacher, he had opened a small hotel in downtown Jacksonville, and he became David's best customer. Aunt Louise and Uncle David looked after me during the summer. As soon as I was old enough to travel alone my summers started when I would board a southbound Seaboard pullman at Portsmouth and mother would ask the porter to make sure I was safe and well fed during the overnight trip to Jacksonville. Aunt Louise would meet me at the station and I would stay with her. But while I summered in Jacksonville, and eventually learned to accept Pop's new wife and my new half-sister Joyce, home was Norfolk and to tell my story I traveled back to where it all started.

Some say my career started when Norfolk deejay Jack Holmes of station WRAP decided to play a new record by a local talent who was rechristened "U.S. Bonds." But my career started earlier, at the moment when Miss Lucille took one of my first publicity photos, a Gary

Anderson head-shot, and taped it on her "Wall of Fame" to the left of the bar at the original Mark IV Lounge. At that time, around 1958, barely old enough to order a beer, my picture began its ascent to the top of the wall where it hangs today. At that time it deserved to be closer to the bottom. Stars like Ruth Brown, Ella Fitzgerald, and Pearl Bailey were on top, but maybe Miss Lucille knew something. Although it was my goal, I still had not recorded, and my professional career consisted of some solo work at local clubs, school dances and talent shows that my group, the Turks, did mostly for free. I was excited when I got my first pictures. Confident but practical, I ordered a box of either 25 or 50, not knowing whether they would last a week or a lifetime. I gave Miss Lucille Seals one of the first ones not knowing whether she would display it, and that decision proved to be one of the best of my new career.

Miss Lucille and her husband opened the original Mark IV Lounge on Church Street in 1952. It has operated continuously since then and has successfully competed against the other black clubs for 60 years. It's at its second location on Church Street and Miss Lucille has run things on her own since her husband's passing. Mark IV Lounge, or just the "Mark IV" to its regulars, is a jazz club, a bar, a clubhouse, a meeting room and the center of Norfolk social life for a great many of the city's old-line African American families. When Miss Lucille holds court, women and men, accompanied or not, are welcomed along with the young and old, straight and gay. Always feeling at home there, they have partied, celebrated and mourned there, surrounded by lifetime friends and those they've just met.

My mother took me to the original Mark IV for the first time while I was still a teen, and going there has become a habit. Currently it seats about a hundred, mostly around three rows of long banquet tables which run parallel to the bandstand. It's a shallow room, with no more than 20 feet from the bandstand to the front wall which faces the parking lot. The stage is slightly raised and narrow. It's a stage I've played many times at different points in my career, sometimes planned and sometimes not. Miss Lucille has offered her stage to the aspiring and retiring, the unknown and the famous, and those hoping for enough singles in the tip jar to cover their bar tab.

The regulars know that for the past few years the Mark IV has had no regular hours, or days for that matter. Miss Lucille opens the club when she cares to and on special occasions, and that suits the regulars just fine. Many of them are as old as Miss Lucille, but not her equal when it comes to state of preservation, and most have cut back on their nights out. They have a sixth sense about when the Mark IV is open, and when it is they gravitate to the Church Street Square Shopping Plaza, a strip mall of red brick where the club is situated on the corner where Virginia Beach Boulevard meets Church Street.

For Miss Lucille the Mark IV is a labor of love. With modestly priced cocktails, ample credit, and a kitchen that's given way to buckets of supermarket fried chicken, the lounge is likely a money loser most nights. If you didn't know better you might think the widowed owner is struggling, but Miss Lucille's modesty and attempts at innocent grandmotherliness are a head fake. At an age when her peers had already taken to scrapbooking and knitting, Miss Lucille bought the land upon which the shopping plaza sits and built a strip center, now home to 20 businesses. She remains upbeat and energized, looking like she only recently stepped off the chorus line at the Cotton Club. She's admired for her entrepreneurship. Looking decades younger than she is, Miss Lucille still manages to turn heads.

I called Miss Lucille and told her I was coming to town, and I knew I could count on her to take care of things as usual. This meant rounding up the usual suspects, my oldest friends, many of whom I've had since childhood. Miss Lucille knew that every member of my old crowd would find out that I was in town, so it was important that word got out to "Little Walter," Ba-Bee, (pronounced "Bay-Bee") and Duchess, JB, Curtis, Westbrook and Fat Rat, as well as LuLu, and Frissell. Great names, all of them. When a nickname holds up for 60 years, it was well chosen. And when you can't remember someone's "Christian" name, it was very well chosen. About half are very well chosen.

Miss Lucille wanted to know if I was working in the area or just visiting. I told her this trip was a bit of both, I was working, but not performing. It was June, and she was curious. Summertime is when our nicknamed friends pack their bags for their customary visit to the "Hotel Anderson" in Long Island, where we have lived for more than 40 years. With the exception of "Little Walter" who is respectfully provided private accommodations, it's wall-to-wall cots for two weeks.

As Curtis said to me, "Big Mama wouldn't have it any other way," and he is right.

I told Lucille I needed her help, and that I would be working, but not singing. The work would be on my book, something I had considered doing for years, but always resisted. Despite numerous offers, I always thought it was too soon, or too late, or I was too busy, or fearful that not enough people would be interested. My thoughts changed during my last visit to Norfolk.

My previous visit was in January 2012, when I performed twice at a weekend celebration of the life of Norfolk's beloved "Big Man," Clarence Clemons. Listen to my music and you can tell that I'm partial to horn players and I never do a gig without at least one. I missed him dearly and wanted to help. While it was more than 35 years since Bruce Springsteen wandered into one of my shows, I actually knew my "homeboy" Clarence before. Although I'm a few years older, and we lived in different parts of Norfolk, (he went to Crestwood High in Chesapeake and I went to Booker T.) as youths our musical paths crossed. Since we were re-introduced by Bruce we had worked together with and without the E Street Band dozens of times. We grew up in the same part of the world and had this mutual admiration thing going. I was really flattered in 1989 when Clarence did an album called *A Night with Mr. C*, an obvious reference to my favorite sax man "Daddy G" who had a big impact on Clarence's style. Reviewers said the best cut on the album was his version of "Quarter to Three," which he frequently did in Bruce's shows.

The first show was a co-promotion, with the City of Norfolk joining Bill Reid, owner of music venue, The NorVa, and Jersey Shore transplant Doc Holiday. Holiday operates a recording studio in nearby Newport News. They all knew that the Big Man's hometown was an appropriate place to celebrate his life. Bill, who would be hosting the second show at his club, convinced Norfolk officials on the idea of doing a free, seated show at the city-owned Attucks Theater. The second one, a "club show" with standing room for more than 1000, would be at Bill's place. Both shows would benefit a family youth center named after Clemons.

With Clarence's son and nephew performing, and other Clemons family members planning to attend, both nights needed to be appropriately staged. The shows needed to be a respectful celebration, just short of a party, with emphasis on the honoree's music and life. The first night's performers needed to be mindful of the venue. The Crispus Attucks theater was named for a courageous African American who successfully served with the colonists and fought the British in the war for independence. His name was given to the theater by its developers, African Americans, who designed, financed and built a theater which became known as the "Apollo of the South." The first show would host Norfolk Mayor Paul Fraim and other dignitaries. Bill suggested that I not only perform, but serve as emcee for both evenings.

I met Bill 20 years earlier when he was running the Cellar Door operation in Washington D.C., a chain of live theaters. From just one club in Georgetown, Bill and his two partners grew the company into one of the largest operators of concert venues in the country. Bill left the company in 1997, and since that time he has owned and operated two venues in Virginia, The National in Richmond and The NorVa in Norfolk.

Bill is a country boy, a jock, and a promoter since his college days when he booked shows for his frat. But the thing he most loves to promote is Norfolk. The NorVa was a movie theater, a classic one, that was gutted and turned into a health club, complete with a hot tub and racquetball court. With Norfolk's people more in need of jobs than Pilates, the operators failed, leaving another sad reminder of the city's many unsuccessful efforts to reverse its poor economic state.

Bill and his partners acquired the health club, kept its best parts, and returned the former movie palace into a state of the art multi-media entertainment space that has everything but seats. Bill presents a diverse program of national and regional talents and his commitment to the arts is the best way he feels he can help my home town. Bill worked with the city to designate part of Granby Street, near The NorVa, Norfolk's Legends of Music Walk of Fame.

We had taken refuge in Bill's private office, an interior space within The NorVa's 50,000 square feet. First, I was told to ask him whether James Brown had ever used the hot tub. I learned he did, but he did not submerse his hair. Bill's office is standard issue for a music mogul with an over-sized desk hidden under mounds of CDs, unopened mail, and half-filled coffee cups. Flanked by gold records, we sat exhausted but confident following a run through of the first Clemons show.

"Gary, we couldn't do this without you, it's your town, they respect you," Bill said referring to the various musicians who turned out to support the events. "Southside (Johnny) respects you. They all know what you've done. But the Saturday show will be kids. They figure you worked with Clarence and Springsteen, but do they know why and how? When I tell them and sell them on the Norfolk Sound that story revolves around you and the fact that you've never really left Norfolk and don't plan to. Someone's got to get the story down before you forget."

Three

BUT HE CAN'T DANCE

I DIDN'T THINK MUCH ABOUT BILL'S words during the weekend. I was too busy keeping egos in check and making sure we delivered two high quality shows. With the City of Norfolk opening the Attucks to do the first night, and Mayor Fraim and other officials planning to attend joined by members of the Clemons family, we could not forget that this was both a celebration and a memorial. With the club atmosphere at The NorVa, the second night's music and presentation would likely be less scripted, and we would benefit from having the first show under our belts. Though many of us had played with one another, we had never played together as a group, so Friday's opener would require some care. Joining me would be Southside Johnny, Bon Jovi guitarist Bobby Bandiera, John Cafferty, E Street Band bassist Garry Tallent and original E Street Band drummer Vini "Mad Dog" Lopez. Also appearing would be the late honoree's son Nick. The Attucks show ran for more than three hours to the finale which brought everybody back on stage.

I felt good leaving the Attucks. We were respectful and entertaining. Bill tells me that the Mayor appreciated it. We pleased the crowd, honored a beloved townsman and raised some money for a good cause. I thought about my bandmates for the weekend, and how long I had known each of them and all the recordings and shows which connected us.

Springsteen scholars who track this kind of thing calculate more than a dozen performances when I have worked with the E Street Band. Clarence and Garry Tallent both got credits for their work on my *Dedication* and *On the Line* albums which included many players from early versions of Southside's band, the Asbury Jukes. These same players can be heard on the Steven Van Zandt produced title track of my album *Standing in the Line of Fire*. I have routinely appeared on Southside's albums, most recently joining him in a duet on "Umbrella in My Drink" off his CD, *Pills and Ammo*. "Mad Dog" Vini Lopez has also joined me for some of my shows. I wondered if they were thinking the same thing I was. Nothing like a memorial service to put you in touch with the dwindling days of your own life, and when the departed is younger than you are, as Clarence was, you start thinking about a lifetime of "what ifs." Maybe Bill was right. Get it down on paper before I forget, and a book could introduce a lot of new listeners to both my old and new work.

B.B.'s words came back to me, "Bonds, let the people know how you feel."

I would, and I would do it the same way I write songs. I am proud of my songwriting. Even though I have more than 200 numbers in my catalog, including co-written million sellers on both the pop and country charts, I have never been tagged a "singer-songwriter." I have written a few alone, but most are collaborations, the earliest with "Daddy G," Gene Barge and later on with "Swamp Dog," Jerry Williams, Jr., and most recently and frequently with "Little Mama," Laurie Celeste Anderson. I can't be impartial; Little Mama is my favorite. She is a talented lyricist, and having formally studied recording and production at the academic level, she can envision her words within a finished piece. When I am under pressure to find a rhyme or capture a complex thought within a four measure phrase, I can turn to her. While I have written at the keyboard where I am limited to a few chords, and backed myself with some fundamental rhythm guitar, my preference is to sit with a member of my band who is familiar with my work. I have them accompany me with frequent pauses to jot down both melody and lyric. I write as a vocalist, and as I sing a phrase or scat a wordless melody, we have developed a type of musical shorthand. With partners I am able to capture my musical thoughts and put them in a form which can be expanded into arrangements suitable for my shows or recordings.

Like all songwriters, not only do I have the 200 finished songs, I've got the many hundreds that remain in various stages of completion, ranging from couplets in search of melodies to scraps of ideas that will never be sung. I don't remember writing many of them, but I do remember where I keep them, and I am sure if I get around to it, there's probably another "Quarter to Three" somewhere in that mess. But that's not my style and habit. If a song is going to be finished, I will likely finish it the day I start it. But I take comfort in the fact that another "unknown" songwriter, my pal Ben E. King (co-writer of "There Goes My Baby" and "Stand By Me") has his own 50-year collection of unfinished masterpieces hidden away in something he calls his "green books" which so far remain unpreserved and uncataloged, a project which he says, "Maybe someday my grandchildren will get to." I was glad to learn that the Songwriters Hall of Fame has finally recognized Ben E. as one of its own with the 2012 Towering Performance Award, for "Stand By Me," and I urge his grandchildren to start that project now.

As I have failed as a songwriter just working by myself with a tape running, I knew an attempt to write my story that way would not result in a finished work of any value. I own some very lightly used tape recorders to back up that claim. I need human interaction. I need feedback. I need someone to tell me when they think I am getting off track, even if I know they are wrong. I have a fan who writes and he offered to sign on for the book project. We agreed on some simple rules: my life, my story, my voice, and when it's not, the reader will know. His job is to listen, keep track, watch carefully and forget what he's already read or heard. I asked him to understand that I have lived the past 73 years without taking notes. I promised myself and him that I would do my best to tell it as I have lived it.

I didn't think Lucille would have difficulty turning out the Norfolk crowd. But I was surprised when I pulled up to the Mark IV and found all the closest parking spaces already filled. Entering, I counted at least 20 friends awaiting my arrival. I didn't bring my band to the Mark IV this time. I was traveling with my co-writer, a photographer and a videographer. Again, I need human contact whatever I am creating, be it music, or in this case a book. I could have called my friends, but I knew it would lose the intimacy that I wanted in my story. You can't ask a friend of 50 years to "phone in" the story of our friendship, especially since each relationship is still living and breathing. These were not people I knew "back then." These were and are my friends. I also knew that the sum would be more interesting than the parts, and that if we were all together, one recollection would lead to another.

Frissell Coleman sang with me on the street corners of Norfolk in 1956, and we're still buddies. I considered calling him and interviewing him on the phone, but the thought of asking him about our first group, the Turks, "And could you please speak up the tape's running." That's not what I wanted. But when I walk into the Mark IV to see Frissell sitting with Westbrook and Frank Wilson, and Purcell, LuLu and Fat Rat, add some liquid inspiration, start with hugs and kisses, add a chicken dinner and we are all back in 1955. The cameras disappear as memories sharpen and words start flowing from the head and heart.

Going back to Norfolk to see them made me think about why these friendships had lasted despite the differences in our lives. I think the differences made these 50-year friendships thrive. These friendships pre-dated my career in the music business, and if I do have some fame, the friendships certainly came first. If anything, what I do has given us all something to root for, but it's just what I do, and nothing more. I never gained or lost a friend in Norfolk because I'm an entertainer. Unlike so many of my later relationships, my celebrity did not bring us together, and the tough times did not separate us.

They're fine people. They're people I trust and people I grew up with. What more could you want? These are people that are not out to do harm or trade on my name or reputation. They didn't resent me on the way up, or quietly take pleasure when things got tough. If some are jealous of me, I just have not seen it. If I can help them, I will, and I have, but I do so quietly. And there have been times when they took care of me and mine.

These are the friends that would look in after Mom and Grandma when I first went on the road. I'd call home and find there was a party going on, but it was in my house and everyone would be sitting with Mom in our kitchen. If they weren't at my house, I'd track them down at some club. I'd call them at the Blue Nile to find out how everyone was doing, and let them know how our show was going. And when I called from the road between sets to find that my friend "Jelly's" sister had died, I apologized to my audience, dressed, and drove the 400 miles back to Norfolk. I know the saying is, "the show must go on," but sometimes it just can't. Maybe my priorities are not the best ones for an entertainer, but they're the best ones for me.

Differences never got in the way of our friendships. As a young man I was able to cross the racial lines of Norfolk, and the shops and clubs that catered to Norfolk's white residents were open and welcoming to me most times, but some of my friends were not as fortunate. And amongst our friends there were not only rich and poor, dark skinned and light skinned, and a few whites, there were gays as well with some who were open and a few who struggled. Being African American in Norfolk was at times difficult, and as one of my friends once explained it, being a gay African American man in Norfolk "puts another bullet in the gun." We didn't see a need to celebrate our preferences then, but we sure as hell accepted them and respected them.

At age 13 or 14 I rounded up some buddies who liked to sing. We all did it for the usual reasons. We sang because it was cool and it attracted girls. These are the same reasons given by every man who has ever sung from Caruso to Dylan. I'd bet the first song man ever sang had some variation of, "Baby, I need you," or, "Baby, come back." We sang and tried to copy what we heard on radio. We sang the songs we heard our idols sing. We sang in church, but check that last one. Mostly my buddies and I sang outside of church, beyond the back door. We weren't looking to ease our way into a deal with the Lord, but more a deal with the pastor at the Shiloh Church. The pastor knew our preferences came from a hymn book of covers we did of the Moonglows and Spaniels, and I did my best to learn all that Clyde McPhatter did. Pastor knew the best way to keep his parishioners happy was with some smooth harmony. He also knew he could find it just outside the church doors, especially on Sundays. With the promise of a modest gift in the name of the Lord we could be persuaded to join his service for a number or two. The gift was well intended and precious and after our walk with the Lord we would share the offering with a needy woman down the block who did a brisk business in whiskey on the Sabbath day because the state regulated package stores were closed. Amen.

Bessie was the lady who sold the whiskey and Bessie was going to be my back up if singing did not work out. When I got my first car she asked if I could do her a favor, "cause the regular guy didn't show up." Bessie was an important lady in town who provided a valuable service and in the black neighborhoods everyone knew what she did. One Sunday, she asked if I could take a drive to North Carolina. I had this 1948 Ford Coupe that had what we would call today a hatchback. It didn't open but it sloped down sharply. It was black and beat up when Mom bought it for me and if the odometer worked we would have known how beat up it was. Bessie said she needed me to drive about three hours south, a little more than a hundred miles from Norfolk. I didn't have the car that long and a road trip sounded like fun. Bessie gave me three dollars for gas and told me how to get there. I hadn't given it any thought when she said she needed two crates picked up. I knew I was going to be hauling whiskey, but I didn't give it any thought or consider that it might be dangerous. I think I did the trip in less than six hours and when I got back she gave me $15. Fifteen dollars was a good day's pay and I don't think I used up the gas money. That trip turned into a three times a week run and Bessie could work with my schedule, whether it was school or singing.

As it turns out, other than singing, running whiskey was the only job I've ever been able to handle. When I left school, Mimms had me come to work as a busboy at one of the restaurants where he worked. He had me wake up and open the place with him at around nine. From nine to 11 I argued with him about why I needed to be there so early when there were no dirty dishes until after 11. He never woke me up again. I lasted longer at Lerner Shops, a women's store where I was a stock clerk. I think that ended in about a week, and Mom was just as happy to have me home and doing my singing jobs when they came up.

Although I couldn't keep a job, I still earned money. When we lived on Granville Avenue we were near the municipal Norfolk Community Golf Course. My friends who had full-time fathers never bragged about their dad's short games, or their ability to drive long and straight, and golf did not play an important part in our lives. Similarly, I don't recall that any of my friends' moms took up the sport. But we would walk the course and find golf balls and sell them back to the pro, Clarence Underwood, who was a golf traditionalist. He was not alone in thinking that blacks should be serving in the clubhouse, polishing spikes or carrying bags. On one of my walks over the course I found an eight-iron, with a slightly bent shaft and some rust, indications that it had been abandoned in anger some time ago. I took it home and went to work on some of the cut balls we found on the course. I knew that clubs came in sets, but I was at a loss as to why you needed more than one club to play. I taught myself to hit both long and short, and if you hold the club-face perpendicular to the ball you can even use it to roll a straight putt. I would sneak onto the course around sunset and as evening approached I learned to make an eight-iron do more than ever intended. I didn't know that my night golf game was being watched by the club pro.

I learned that Clarence Underwood was one of very few "Master Instructors," and how he wound up at a public links in Norfolk I'll never know. He not only took a liking to me, but he also loved introducing children and women to the game. He introduced me to the game formally by hooking me up in games with his friends and students. I guess I was a novelty, still in my teens, playing with a single club, using beat up golf balls, and I was black. Underwood would let me play the course with his friends and unbeknownst to me Underwood was betting his buddies that I could outplay them with the single club. There was no shortage of takers and soon enough Underwood was cutting me in for 25 percent of the winnings. This lasted for a while until my game improved, and when I acquired a full bag of clubs there were few takers for Underwood's bets. Golf has continued to be an important part of my life and I am still a regular on the music celebrity pro-am circuit with enough equipment in my attic to start a pro-shop.

While later on I will credit my musical influences for inspiring my singing career, I need to credit some golfers as well. At the time my first record hit the charts, still unsure that I could make a living in music, I went to Richmond to play in a qualifier for the old United Golf Association. The U.G.A. sponsored tournaments and was the governing body for professional African American golfers who were barred from membership and competition in P.G.A. events until 1961. I didn't win, but I qualified and was now able to compete. I was counseled wisely by both Ted Rhodes, who was at the end of his career, and Charlie Sifford who was the personal instructor of singer Billy Eckstine.

Sifford eventually became a P.G.A. member and was the first African American to win a tour event. Rhodes, who introduced Joe Louis to the game, explained to me that there were only four tournaments that really offered prize money, and that he saw no way that the tour leadership could share any of that with me. To survive on the tour the top black professionals found it necessary to pool their winnings from week to week. Rhodes went on to sue the P.G.A. for its discriminatory practices and prevailed, which resulted in most P.G.A. tournaments going the "invitational" route with no particular requirement that invitations be extended to African-Americans. Singing offered better opportunities.

I sang because I could. I was untrained and sang effortlessly, and I discovered that I could convincingly sound like many different vocalists. I had a great musical memory. I would learn how important this was later on, when I could overcome the limitations of single track recording by overdubbing my own voice with successive takes that were perfectly synched with my original.

My first stage was at the corner of Olney Road and Brambleton Avenue. My immediate inspiration was a show my mom took me to see at the Attucks. It was a twin bill, the year was 1955 and Ivory Joe Hunter (his real name) was at the top of the charts with his Atlantic single "Since I Met You Baby." Opening for Ivory Joe was Bullmoose Jackson, not his real name (actually Benjamin), whose career dated back to the mid '40s when he toured with Lucky Milinder's band. Bullmoose played sax-driven dance music that fit more comfortably in the preceding decade, but a series of risqué jump blues ("Big Ten Inch Record") found interest as novelties then and now.

My mom loved Ivory Joe and I loved both performers. I wanted one of those sharp suits, a driving rhythm behind me and those pretty dressed up girls who used to rush the stage to touch the hems of their idols. Let them at me. I could do that. I could sing a bit, and amongst Bullmoose, Ivory Joe and me, I think those girls would rather be touching my hems—certainly then. Mom was watching them and watching me. Somehow after the show she would get me backstage and I would tell Ivory Joe, or Jackie Wilson or Clyde McPhatter that I wanted to do what they did. They saw I was serious, and she saw it as well.

At 6'2" Frissell Coleman was a great asset on the basketball court. He appeared older, wasn't bad looking and had a better than average baritone. I drafted him when I played hoops and asked him to become a Turk along with Dee-Dee and Moose. For most of our short singing career the Turks were all guys. This changed in 1958 when we heard Jerry Butler and the Impressions do "Your Precious Love." We needed a high tenor to do the Curtis Mayfield part.

As Frissell explains it, "The guys could hit the note, but they couldn't hold it."

We found a female Turk, Hermione Gross, but she only stuck around long enough to do one show with us at Norfolk's Towne Club.

We played church dances, sock hops, and small clubs for small change, places like the Petite Ballroom and the Bachelors' Club. We performed with the Showmen, a local group that was starting to break out, and a men's glee club at the Norfolk Naval Base. We struggled when we were added to a holiday show at the Norfolk Arena for an audience of inmates from the local prison. The prison officials wanted us to do spirituals, but the prisoners got the Turbans and the Drifters, Pookie Hudson, and the Moonglows. We did our best to make "Hushabye," and our Coasters-inspired signature song, "Zing Went the Strings of My Heart," sound sacred.

Maybe it was the fact that we never won a talent show that sent us all our separate ways. Despite the quality of our vocals, the Turks always wound up as runners-up in the school and community shows. We would consistently lose to General Norman Johnson and the Humdingers, a predecessor of the Showmen. Their lead would go on to be a fixture in Carolinas beach music circles and successful with his group, The Chairmen of the Board. Their #3 hit in 1970, "Give Me Just a Little More Time," showcased Johnson's distinctive "stuttering" lead.

As much as my friends sang my praises that night in Norfolk, there was no shortage of ribbing about my shortcomings. Ba-Bee, like Frissell, needed to remind me that we never won those school talent shows, "Gary, you know you can't dance, that's why General won all those shows."

"But, I sang better than all those guys together," I countered.

Out of the back of the Mark IV an unidentified "friend" yelled out, "He dances like a Caucasian, everyone knows that," which started a round of laughter and high fives.

You think you're at home and here they go tearing me down and going all "racial" on me.

But Duchess came to defend me, and Duchess can dance. Speak to Duchess for more than 10 minutes and she will tell you, "I was the first African American 'go-go' dancer in Norfolk and maybe the whole state." I don't know where you can look it up, but Duchess (actually Joyce Moore) was a great dancer, and if she still has the dress with the fringes and the boots with the chunky heels, she can probably still do it, though fear of physical harm prevents me from disclosing her age. "Gary, had that curl, and he had swagger," said Duchess.

To which Lucille added, "And he could sway."

But swagger and sway only got us to be runners-up.

Purcell needed to let everyone know that my dancing may have been limited, but it got better, "Gary, you were doing the Apollo, I was with you, and you had that white suit on and you were singing Little Willie John's, 'Let Them Talk.'" It's a ballad I've done for years and recently recorded. Purcell continued, "They put that spotlight on you and you did a high jump on top of the piano and got down on one knee and you sang (Purcell doing a Gary U.S. Bonds imitation), 'Let them talk, if they want to...' I never saw Norman Johnson do that."

Neither did I. It reminded me of a review I got from a British fan who saw me on a 1986 tour, "When performing, Gary is not very extrovert. He doesn't move much and tries no fancy foot steps or gymnastic gyrations.... And yet the moment he walks on the atmosphere is charged. He has a certain indefinable (sic) presence." (James F. Cullinan, *Norfolk Echo* No. 2, December 1986).

I didn't know that the late General Johnson had British fans, but it looks like the reviewer saw what the Duchess saw years earlier. But the history stands, the Turks were runners up and my dancing is suspect.

Dee-Dee went to the Army, and Frissell to an Air Force career in which he spent many years touring the world singing, and keeping us safe and comforted with his baritone. Frissell was stationed in Florida when his sister wrote him, "Remember that Gary you used to sing with? He's got a hit record." Frissell said he wasn't surprised to get that news.

Then he reminded me that he was with me on the corner that day in 1958 when the owner of a Norfolk record shop passed by to tell us he had just purchased a recording studio. It didn't mean much to us. We knew Frankie from Frankie's Birdland, the store that carried all the latest R & B records. He said he wanted us to make a record. We just wanted to sing. Frissell never got to record with me or anyone else. Too bad, cause he could sing.

Discussing the great singers with Ben E. King one day, Ben E. asked, "Gary, you know who the greatest singers are? They're the ones who never made a record and never made it into the studio. That's why I feel so lucky." Ben E. went on about the greats when he mentioned Sy Palmer. I never heard the name before. "We sang together; Sy was great," said Ben E. He explained that Sy was a "pre-Drifter" and a "post-Five Crown," who never made it to the studio. I asked Ben E. what happened to Sy and he shrugged clueless, like there were a hundred Sy Palmers he could have named. Ben E. wanted to emphasize how lucky it was for the few like us who got to record successfully.

Frissell Coleman may not be available on record but he was available to me on a recent July night. He laughed when I asked him if he was ready for a Turks reunion and maybe a road trip, "Can't do it Gary, nothing but two of us left."

"Little Walter" Johnson did not record with me either. He did not sing, but his contribution to my career and popular culture for all time is now secure. Walter's contribution cannot be minimized or overlooked and I had no particular reason to keep this a secret for so long. Maybe this is what Bill Reid was thinking about when he urged me to get my story out. This revelation comes more than 50 years after the fact.

The visual aspects of my act have always supported the musical. My look has evolved over the years reflecting changes in fashion and maturity, mine and my audience's. I spend time on my look, and as my sound has inspired others, so has my look. Years ago I picked up on the "loosened skinny tie, white shirt and dark suit" look and it was not long after that Chubby Checker and Billy Joel started wearing it.

Online there is no shortage of photos of me at various stages in my career, but those most closely associated with me, some say they are "iconic," are the earliest ones used on my album covers, publicity pictures and record sleeves. These have been memorialized in numerous books celebrating album cover art and '60s pop culture.

Walter's contribution took place in the upstairs bathroom of his home in the Brambleton section of Norfolk which was across the street from where we lived with my grandmother. Armed with a box of Silky Straight, Walter helped execute my concept of what is known as a "kiss curl," prominent on my forehead in those early photos.

The occasion was my first appearance on *American Bandstand* in 1961 during which I lip-synched "Quarter to Three." Up to that point I had never gotten my hair processed, straightened, "conked" or "gassed" as the most popular straightening processes were known to African Americans. Using these products required training and preparation and a strong stomach, things neither Walter nor I had. We were not prepared for the odor of lye and chemicals which quickly spread from the upstairs bathroom to the downstairs of his house. Ignoring questions from Walter's mom who must have known what was going on, Walter went to work and I directed. We both discovered that there was nothing silky about Silky Straight. My curl was front and center as we planned, and it would stay there, immovable, along with every other hair on my head. It was like my hair was chiseled from a slab of marble. It was hard, and it lasted through *American Bandstand* and probably for a month after that.

The curl was controversial. Some fan magazines said it was recognized as a sign of leadership by Norfolk street gangs of the '50s. Others gave credit to my label head who supposedly thought it would be a great gimmick and a way to promote crossover airplay by bringing attention to my light complexion with a hairstyle associated with whites. Not true. I liked it, Walter accomplished it, and the fans responded.

But many questioned if the idea was original. Did I borrow the look from Bill Haley? No way. I got to know Haley later on when we both performed at a 1969 Richard Nader revival show at Madison Square Garden. Haley was a country artist at heart, older, shorter and blond in those days with about a 50-pound edge on me. Back in Norfolk I would have heard his early hits, but a fashion idol, hardly.

Bobby Jay, former WCBS FM (New York) disk jockey who does service on both sides of the microphone as a part time Teenchord and previously with Frankie Lymon's Teenagers, shared his opinion on the subject. "Gary, you had it all, the package, looks, talent and the spit curl. You had sex appeal oozing from your pores. Haley just had the curl."

Haley and I talked backstage at the Garden. He was ailing and his hair had thinned. His curl had suffered and mine was long gone. He didn't ask me where my curl went and I didn't ask him if he ever used Silky Straight.

But give Walter credit for helping deliver my vision and thank Dick Clark. Walter reminded us all that Dick Clark's show was actually an hour long, but the Norfolk station which carried the syndicated program only played the first half hour. Dick would turn out to be a lifelong friend, and it started the first time we met. Dick made everyone in Norfolk his friend when he put me and my new Silky Straight curl on during the first half hour of his show.

While Walter was reminding me about our adventures in hair straightening, he did not hesitate to remind me of certain other habits I had when it came to wardrobe and grooming. All the neighborhood kids took notice that my clothes were always meticulous, freshly pressed and spotless. Walter agreed with Frissell that I always looked better turned out than all the kids in school, and it was not unusual for my buddies to come to our house looking for me, only to be told that I was still in the shower and not yet dressed. They would be in my bedroom waiting and they saw that Mom or Grandma had laid out my clothes on my bed, color coordinated, and wrinkle-free. I think this went on till the time I got married. To this day Big Mama calls me "Lord Fauntleroy." That's a name borrowed from a 19th century children's novel about a scruffy American youth who discovers he is the heir to a title and wealth. He takes to wearing elegant suits which became all the rage for young boys. This was the benefit of being an only child with a very devoted mother and grandmother, but I did not lack for male role models outside of my dad where contact was limited to my summer visits.

The Gault-Page family lived in Brambleton, and my buddy was Ba-Bee. "Ba-Bee" was Richard Gault-Page. He came from a large family. We grew up together, and when we moved from our first house on Middle Street to Brambleton, the Gault-Pages moved as well from Middle Street to a well kept house on Sheldon Avenue. I was happy the Gault-Pages moved to Brambleton not only because I could still be friends with Ba-Bee, but also because of his uncle. Ba-Bee's uncle was the favorite of all the neighborhood boys. Many of us did not have full time fathers and Ba-Bee's uncle Gwendell filled that void in our lives. He taught us to play ball and he had a boat. In summers he would take us out on the boat and tell us stories and teach us lessons we needed to become men. We were approaching our teens and Gwendell was a positive male influence on all our lives.

Ba-Bee left Norfolk and joined the military around the time it looked like I might have a recording career. He was overseas when he learned that I had a hit record. He told the guys that he wasn't surprised and gave great credit to Mom and Grandma. He recalled, "They always kept him dressed proper and in school, and were always supportive of his singing. Gary was determined to make it and they believed in him. I knew he was going to make it. Gary had talent, nerve and compassion."

We sat around and the long table at Lucille's filled. We tried to keep it light. With all the refreshment and no shortage of tributes, I had to remind my friends that this was not a send off. I had them all laughing.

Norfolk Mayor Fraim was kind enough to meet with me when he heard I would be visiting to do some research for my autobiography. I met briefly with the Mayor when we did the Clemons show, and when I visited his office I found out that he, like Bill Reid, sees the benefit of preserving the history and music of Norfolk. He's also a fan and has been one for quite a while. I told Mayor Fraim, "A few years ago when I left Norfolk they were locking me up, now I'm shaking hands with the Mayor." Sadly, this was true, but my leaving will be handled in a later chapter.

The Mayor said that my career gave the city an uplift and a continuing source of pride. "What was happening in New York,

Philadelphia and Chicago musically, connected to what was happening here. The Norfolk Sound has traveled. Gary still lives here and we love him as a favorite son." Nice words from the Mayor who still digs Jerry Butler, the Shirelles and the late Solomon Burke. Mayor Fraim worked as an usher at the Center Theater for three dollars a show and got to know all the acts as they passed through town.

Westbrook agreed with the Mayor about my not leaving town, "He followed his dream and took us with him. But he always came back."

Four

BEGINNINGS OF A YOUNG TURK

FRANKIE FROM THE RECORD SHOP had not yet delivered on that promise he made on the street corner, and it was too late anyway. The Turks had moved on, to parts unknown or to defend our country. One of those departed Turks, Frissell Coleman, asked the crowd at the Mark IV whether they remembered Sleepy King. Some combination of age, fatigue and an excessive number of heartfelt toasts found the groups' memory to be faulty and they fell silent except for me. Frissell knew I would remember Sleepy, but it really surprised me that he did. My meeting Sleepy came at a turning point, when I started to do what I've done every day since. He was a piano player who hailed from Greenville, North Carolina. He was a passable player and a better than average rhythm and blues singer who continued to perform into the '70s when I last heard of him. He had limited success on the charts, with perhaps one charting record, but he was talented, with a voice that could handle standards and was big enough to work against some raucous horn playing. Today we'd call him a soul singer and despite being from the South, his style leaned to what we call today, "Northern Soul."

In the late 1950s he would pass through Norfolk and pick up local musicians to join him as he searched for jobs at clubs and juke joints. With nothing more to claim than 20 or so headshots and my suit from the Turks, I considered myself a singer for hire. Mom was not happy, but I convinced her that I was just putting my education at Booker T. Washington High School on hold. Sleepy must have seen me singing for tips on Church Street during one of his scouting trips. He offered me $25 to join him on a club date, but he also expected me to help load and unload the instruments and set up. I convinced myself the $25 was for singing. I don't know what he paid the two other men he hired. They would figure prominently in my early recording career. Gene Barge and Earl Swanson were both formally trained jazz saxophone players with impressive resumes even at that early date. Like me, Gene would soon get a new name courtesy of Frankie from the record shop. Gene was playing in Norfolk and shuttling to New York where he was doing session work and dates with Chuck Willis. At Atlantic Records he would forever put his imprint upon rhythm and blues with just one of his many signature sax solos.

As Gene tells it, he was a friend of Chuck Willis and doing club dates with him. Chuck was a reluctant performer, more of a songwriter (he wrote a #1 for Ruth Brown), and he had some success on Okeh Records before being signed mid '50s by Atlantic. While riding to a New York City session Gene suggested that Chuck do a remake of "C.C. Rider" which was a Ma Rainey tune from decades earlier. They cut a demo which Atlantic bought, but they wanted no part of Gene for the recording, as Atlantic already had some house players who were among the best of New York's session men. Attending the session as an observer, Gene was drafted when Sam "The Man" Taylor was unable to come up with a solo. Gene took Sam's chair, and that is his solo you hear which led to turban-wearing Chuck Willis becoming the "King of the Stroll." Atlantic started to use Gene but the label was still struggling and it was costly to fly him in for sessions. They found a young player locally, a transplant from Fort Worth who could play a moanin' barnyard sax just like Gene, the late King Curtis. King Curtis was not only less costly, but his "Barge-like" attack perfectly complemented Leiber and Stoller's compositions for the Coasters that would help Atlantic become a hugely successful independent.

Gene was educated at West Virginia State University and settled his family in Norfolk where he taught high school civics and directed the band. Before traveling to New York, Gene played sax for the Griffin Brothers. The Griffin Brothers were from Norfolk and along with Gene they had Emmett ("Nabs") Shields on drums and for a few years Margie Day on vocals. Nabs and Margie would also wind up working for Frankie from the record shop.

Earl Swanson, like Gene Barge was a tenor man. Before he worked for Sleepy, Earl had recorded with those same Griffin Brothers when they were signed to Chess, and before that he backed Little Richard on his earliest RCA sides in 1951. When I met Earl he was married to Ruth Brown who was from Portsmouth and she had already been recording at Atlantic for almost 10 years. Her output for Atlantic Records, which during the 1950s included many high charting singles, is widely regarded as having saved the label which went on to be known as "The House that Ruth Built." Ruth's husband Earl, Gene and Nabs would soon help me increase my nightly fee substantially from Sleepy's $25.

With an upright bass strapped to the top of Sleepy's, car, we would drive the 100 miles to Scotland Neck, North Carolina, not far from where he was born. Scotland Neck had two kinds of people: the poor and the poorer, and they came mostly in different shades of black and brown. I still had my one suit from the Turks and Sleepy told me that in his band you needed to keep your coat on when entering the club, but I could remove it if we started rocking. The coat would come off quickly. It was my first road trip, and one of the few paying gigs I ever did as Gary Anderson. I sang rock and roll; I sang slow blues. I sang ballads, and whatever was popular on the radio at that time. When we were finished, we would put the bass back on the top of the car and the instruments in the trunk. We rode the three hours back to

Norfolk with the amps in our laps. When all you want to do is sing, and you're still in your teens, $25 is not so bad.

Sometimes the gigs were better, especially when I appeared with Ruth Brown. I remember an evening about a year later when we were booked into that same club in Scotland Neck. Route 13 would take you part of the way from Norfolk to Scotland Neck and it was famous for state troopers who cosidered any carload of blacks as a threat to the peace, especially if they were entertainers. Although we were being careful of the speed limit, our car was pulled over on the trip home. Earl talked to the officers, but despite the fact that there was a bass strapped to the roof and horns in the trunk, they could not be convinced that we were in fact a band, and a famous one at that, returning home to Norfolk. Sadly, they were not popular music fans either, so they were not impressed that Ruth Brown was riding in front on the passenger side. It was three in the morning and the only way we were allowed to pass was after we did a short acoustic set roadside for the trooper and his partner. "Alright you can go now; don't let me catch you again," was all we got for our encore. Whatever it was, we never did it again and from then on we would spend the night and travel home in the morning when a carload of black entertainers had a better chance with local law enforcement. We repacked and drove on.

The Sleepy King jobs were a start, but the work was not consistent and while the pay was adequate for singing a set, it was short pay for singing and serving as a "roadie" and equipment manager. I worked locally as well at small places like the Queen's Lounge, getting a little more confident of my skills each time. It was at the Azalea Gardens Club that I showed that I was quite naïve as far as taking the best steps towards building an image and reputation as an entertainer. At the Azalea Gardens Club I met James McCleese. In 1958 I would make certain decisions that would lead to James' ascent to the top of the rock and roll food chain in a few years.

The Azalea Gardens was what we called a "shotgun club." It had a long narrow bar on the right side going from the front entrance to the rear, with a narrow row of tables in back of the bar stools and a small group of tables by the rear entrance. The Azalea Gardens was a black club, a rugged black club, and I went there to see the current attraction, "The Wonder Boy." "The Wonder Boy" was the stage name of James McCleese, and he got that name while serving the Lord as a boy preacher. He went from the pulpit to the stage as part of the Nightingales, a gospel group which toured out of Portsmouth. He moved further away from the sacred when he departed gospel for rock and roll and signed on to the Azalea Gardens Club for an extended engagement. James told me that he was starting to get some attention not only for his singing, but for his wild show. Jimmy and I decided to work as a duo, and inspired by his own name change, I billed myself as "Nature Boy" to his "Wonder Boy." I don't recall whether my name choice was influenced by Nat Cole's earlier hit, but you would not have needed to see more than our entrance to know that Cole's melancholy ballad had no influence on our act.

The "Nature Boy and Wonder Boy" duo gained a lot of attention due to our acrobatics and outfits. Both McCleese and I donned loincloths and our entrance called for McCleese to go to the back of the bar as I went to the front. Each of us held tightly to ropes which were suspended over the center of the shotgun bar. As our band stationed in the rear started to vamp, we would each swing in Tarzan-style and start singing when we met at the center of the bar. After that kind of entrance, the singing really didn't matter.

This story will dispel any notion that James and I were one and the same, a rumor that seems to have spread from the UK to the rest of the Commonwealth. In preparing the book, I stopped by the *Late Show with David Letterman* to speak with Paul Shaffer, whose autobiography, *We'll Be Here for the Rest of OurLives*, sets a high bar for the rest of us who've decided to write memoirs. I wanted to test his memory and talk about some of the work we've done together including *Blues Brothers 2000*. Paul is authoritative about all things rock and rhythm and blues and when I told him I was finally getting my story down he raised a question.

"Gary," Paul started, "tell me. Up in Thunder Bay [Paul's hometown], there was a rumor that you and Jimmy Soul were one and the same. True or not true?"

Not true. In a few years McCleese would learn that he would no longer be a "Wonder Boy" or Jimmy McCleese. He would be known forever more as Jimmy Soul, singer of the second #1 for Frankie from the record shop. Years before, the authoritative Brian Walsh, a British fan and contributor to the *Norfolk Echo* wrote:

"It is worth noting that around this time in England the music press carried various pieces which indicated that record buyers believed Bonds and Soul were one and the same person!" (*Norfolk Echo* #1, September, 1986).

If Walsh or Shaffer had seen our show at the Azalea Gardens they would have known that it just was not true. More about Soul later on.

Frankie's Birdland was Frank Guida's record shop and the start of one Sicilian-American's dream. When I strip away a half century of complications, ignore the business and listen to the music, I see now that his dreams and mine were simple and the same. We both wanted to make music, we both wanted to entertain. But there were differences. He pursued that dream blindly, and I did so innocently. He charged forward with courage and an ignorance of failure that I understand and appreciate now. He was fearless, and loyal only to that dream and he would chase it at my expense when he needed to, and leave the nasty details to his lawyers. To him I would always be that kid he took in from a Norfolk street corner. I was replaceable, disposable, and never quite grateful enough. Frank said he would take care of things. I admired and trusted him. My questions were answered, but less truthfully as our success grew, and no matter how simple, they were interpreted as a show of disloyalty. But we succeeded together, two outsiders. I respected him then and he respected what I could do, as he knew firsthand what it took to perform. The impact of what we did has lasted longer than either of us would have guessed. Frank told me and anyone who would listen that what we were doing was important. It did not take 50 years for me to see that he was right.

Frank portrayed himself as a father, protector and creative genius. But he could not sing. For that, he needed me, but I never heard him say it. He was never shy about his success. He took credit when it was due and credit whenever he could float an argument, no matter how flimsy. He found strength in victim-hood, and played the part of a solid gold little guy from a two-bit town, fighting for his life against the larger independents and major labels. He was the kid who got his ass kicked in the school yard, but wound up for a brief time with the bully's best girl. His imagination was boundless and grew more bold with age. Frank would hear his handiwork in every hit record he ever heard, and saw thievery in everyone going back to when old Tom Edison first dropped a needle on a cylinder of wax.

One competitor responding to a charge that he had borrowed too freely from one of Frank's records remarked, "Frankie was suing the angel Gabriel for taking a horn lick off one of his records."

Francesco (Frank) Joseph Guida was born in Palermo in 1922, the son of a hairdresser who immigrated to the Fordham Road section of the Bronx when Frank was a tot. But for Frank, life started in 1942 when he married Carmela "Millie" Adesso who would be his wife for 65 years. Soon after marrying he was drafted into the Army. Private Guida served in the Army Air Corps Medical Administrative Unit which relieved medical personnel from having to perform non-medical duties. His service started on an outer island off Trinidad in 1942 and soon after he was transferred to the capital, Port of Spain.

I learned little about his Army life other than it was there that he formed a G.I. Calypso group which performed at a USO club. Calypso had not yet made its way to the East Bronx and that would not happen until the middle 1950s. So it is safe to assume that his first exposure to the sound happened in Trinidad. As for the popularization of the music usually credited to another New Yorker, Harry Belafonte, Guida argued that Belafonte had lifted his repertoire when they both performed at small clubs in New York's Greenwich Village. Guida loved the music he heard during his service years and upon his return to New York he sold canned goods by day and Calypso by night, fronting a group which continued doing the songs he learned in the service. The demand in Harlem for a Sicilian Calypso singer supported by a black band may not have been huge, but Frank did not have much competition.

Frank argued that he provided the Andrews Sisters with their big hit "Rum and Coca Cola" through his messenger, the comedian Morey Amsterdam, whom he claims to have met in Trinidad. With several versions of the song popular in the West Indies, Guida said he met Amsterdam at a servicemen's show and asked him to take a version back with him, sensing that the song would work for the trio. According to Guida he did, but not before Amsterdam took a writing credit for the song which would eventually lead to a lawsuit. As for Harry Belafonte, Guida felt there was no greater injustice than the legend's rendition of "Matilda," which Frank popularized in the clubs of Harlem as a tribute to his sister of the same name. As for his failure to score as a performer, Guida never considered that it was due to any lack of talent or the oddity of a Sicilian wailing, "Day-O, Day-O," in front of a black combo. He blamed discrimination. While Guida boasted that he was beloved in Harlem, he blamed his failure as a performer on the reluctance of white audiences to accept "mixed" acts especially on television. In the song, Matilda went to Venezuela with her ex's bankroll. In life, sister Matilda married a Navy man and relocated to Norfolk. Her brother followed, with wife Millie and newborn daughter Anne in the winter of 1953.

At the Mark IV there were reminiscences of Frank Guida. They recalled Frankie's Birdland which opened at 817 Church Street when Guida took over a struggling record store which was called The Groove. At the time there was no specific reason why Frank was going to be any more successful than the previous owner.

Frankie would admit to borrowing the shop's new name from the famous New York jazz club, and his plan was to expand the selection of music he offered primarily to Norfolk's black population to include jazz. But Guida's desire was to entertain, even if it meant he needed to retail first. To stimulate the sales of jazz records, Frankie hosted a local TV show called *Frankie's Jazz Workshop*, and a similar radio program, *Frankie's Jazz Hour*. He also branched out into wholesale distribution, representing a number of labels in the mid-Atlantic states. The opportunity to get closer to the microphone presented itself when a local group known as the Five Pearls walked into Frankie's Birdland and asked to record. He recorded them. Frankie knew the Five Pearls and thought they were talented and he arranged for them to do a demo at a local radio station.

When talk at the Mark IV turned to Frank's first shot at recording a group, Fat Rat was quick to remind everyone that his brother Raymond was a Sheik. What do the Pearls and Sheiks have in common? When Frank's recording of the Five Pearls was played locally there was a good response, so he immediately released the record on the first of his many labels to come, EF-N-DE. As a retailer he understood the need for distribution which was unavailable to him outside his own shop, so he sent the record to Atlantic. They promptly signed the group and had them record one record for their Cat division. But before putting the record out, Atlantic would discover another Five Pearls group and the Pearls would become the Sheiks. Fat Rat's brother Raymond would later join the Sheiks and they would again record for Frankie in 1961.

Frank was encouraged by the success of the Sheiks. It was not that their record on Cat sold (it did not) but rather that he was now doing promotion, production and retail. Additional recordings followed on new labels. Guida formed the Guide label as well as Pepe Publishing to collect his income as both a writer and publisher. He was becoming fully integrated. He could not sing the songs but he could co-write, publish, record, distribute and retail. Guida seemed to be following a path first taken by an equally unlikely label head, Syd Nathan of King Records in Cincinnati. Nathan, who failed as a drummer, started a number of labels and he recorded an odd mix of country, hillbilly, and "race" records and is remembered most for his long and stormy relationship with James Brown. Like Guida, but on a much larger scale, Nathan owned the label, took writing credits, handled distribution, but he also owned his own pressing plant and printed his own labels and album covers. By 1959, Guida, like Nathan, would shift his focus away from retailing and concentrate on the creative side of the business.

Again, he thought he could succeed where another man had failed. In July of 1959 for $1,757 he purchased the bankrupt Norfolk

Recording Studio at 408 West Princess Anne Road. When asked by Lloyd Story whose business had failed why he wanted to buy the studio Guida reportedly said, "I'm going to have a hit here in three months." In October his record was added to the Billboard Hot 100.

Gene Barge remembers the studio as not being much of a studio at all. As part of the studio deal, Guida acquired a two-track Ampex and a monaural Concertone recorder. The toilet doubled as a vocal booth but some thought the vocal booth doubled as the toilet. But as important as the studio and the equipment, it was the addition of Frank's first recording engineer that made this time especially significant. Joe Royster was a country boy from Granville County, North Carolina. He played some guitar and wrote songs but mostly he sold men's clothes at Schulman's on Granby Street in Norfolk. This is where he met Frank Guida.

Royster, as a musician, would have been aware of Frankie's Birdland, and he must have been impressed when Frank told him that he was going to open a studio. Despite a lack of any previous experience as an engineer, Guida gave Royster a shot which allowed him to keep his day job. Royster would also collaborate with Frank on his label's first hit, and it was an unusual record. It would be issued on the newly formed Legrand label, Guida's most significant, and the one both he and I will always be identified with. The initial label was purple with silver lettering.

Frank had an idea to do a record which would have as part of its lyric the names of all the high schools in various parts of the country. One song with multiple versions was brilliant. It provided multiple opportunities for a local hit and if you didn't succeed in one city, there was always another. It was 1959 and he traveled to New York and researched the school names and pitched the idea to Jerry Wexler at Atlantic Records. Wexler thought it might work for Bobby Darin. Frank had already dealt with Atlantic when he sent them the Sheiks, and although they were an independent, to Guida and Legrand which had not yet released a record, they were a major. It is possible as well that on this trip he offered the idea to the newly formed Laurie Records which had just broken its first hit for Dion and the Belmonts, "I Wonder Why."

Back in Norfolk, Guida turned to Royster for a suggestion as to who should record the Norfolk version of "High School U.S.A." Royster suggested Tommy "Bubba" Facenda who had been a member of Gene Vincent's Blue Caps from Portsmouth, Virginia. Tommy was a Blue Cap during their successful European and Australian tours, but by early 1958 the group had their last charting single. Facenda entered the studio with Royster playing guitar and my fellow Sleepy King bandmate Earl Swanson on sax. The flip side was "Give Me Another Chance," a "Leader" composition, one of the names used by Guida and the same name he used on the "A" side for his Royster co-write. The record did well locally. Atlantic folded on the idea of letting Bobby Darin do it and agreed to have Facenda do the balance of the "cities" of which they released 28 in total. The 29 versions posed a difficult problem for Billboard on its rankings, but in the aggregate Guida had a high-charting hit, with Legrand #1001 entering the charts in October of 1959 and then peaking at #28 with a total of 13 weeks in the Billboard Hot 100.

While Legrand #1002, "Tiger Rock," was an Earl Swanson instrumental of a Guida and Royster composition, inspiration came in part from the first "Daddy G," Bishop Charles Manuel "Sweet Daddy" Grace. Grace, a former pullman cook, was the founder of the United Church of Prayer for All People, and possibly the prototype for all the flamboyant, high profile preachers that have followed. Daddy Grace's fold numbered more than 50,000 at its height, and his more than 130 congregations occupied buildings they referred to as "heavens." Grace's personal trademarks were his fingernails and hair. Both were grown exceedingly long, and his colorful garments were costly and luxurious. Grace was acquisitive when it came to both cars and real estate and he amassed the finest of both in large quantities. The Norfolk "heaven" was at the corner of Church Street and Princess Anne Road, not far from Guida's store. Fresh in Guida's mind must have been the sound of the "shout bands" which were an important and festive component of church services and figured prominently in a church parade which made its way down Church Street every July 4th. Shout bands featured trombones and horns which could mimic human expression with squeals of joy and hearty laughter. The double bass and snare drums carried an upbeat, happy rhythm and the "shout" was a bit of call and response found at the end of a selection. Shout bands rarely were confined to what was written on a music sheet. The music was improvised, and tunes would run as long as the players felt they should run. In Norfolk the House of Prayer was popular as was Grace, and the Norfolk branch thrived. At that time the music of the shout bands was in the streets and our minds.

Joining Earl Swanson on "Tiger Rock" was Junior Fairley on bass, Willie Burnell on piano, Leonard Barks on trombone and Nabs Shields on drums. They would become my first band. Purcell remembered that Frankie saw me outside of Birdland. He came out and asked if I would come to the studio to do a record. Without fussing with pen and paper, Frankie told me and others that I was signed exclusively to Legrand. I didn't know what it meant to be "signed." I told Mom and Grandma I was going to make a record for the guy who owned the record shop. I also told Bumpsie, Jelly Belly and Frissell that I was going to make a record for Frankie and that we'd go down to the studio together.

Five

A HEY, HEY, HEY, YEAH

I CAN'T RECALL SEEING A SIGN THAT said Legrand Records at the original studio on Princess Anne Road, but I do remember driving there. It was January 1960. The day started as most did, and if it was unusual to still have your clothing laid out for you when you are 20, then it was an unusual day, but not for me. Mom must have ironed my outfit the night before and it was Ivy League done Norfolk style with khaki colored chinos and a striped rugby style shirt. I told my Mom the night before that I was going to see Frankie that afternoon and we were going to record. I didn't make a big issue out of it and neither did she. It's not that she didn't want me to be a recorded singer, to her it was more important that I accomplish it because it was what I wanted to do. If it happened fine, and if not, my freshly ironed clothes would still be waiting for me.

I was driving a Ford at that time, and like the first car I drove at 16 when I got my license, Mom and Grandma helped me buy it. I found it and they helped pay for it. I may have picked up Jelly Belly on the way. I didn't give it much thought and I wasn't nervous.

I remembered that a couple of years had passed since the Turks were singing on Olney Road and Frankie said he was going to record us and that he was planning to open his own studio. He kept his word. At this point Frankie was a successful guy around town. Birdland was doing well and Frankie turned the store over to his brother-in-law so he could concentrate on making records that his brother-in-law could sell. I knew he had that "high school" record he did with Earl Swanson and some of the other guys Earl played with in town.

I walked in and saw Joe Royster for the first time. He must have gotten off early from Schulman's. He was neatly dressed, as was his boss. Frankie looked over Joe's shoulder as he sat at the console. They both had ties on. I didn't have one on and I wondered if there was a studio dress code. There wasn't, and Royster told me that he had to dress at Schulman's. Frank was a presence, and the failed Calypso singer was clearly in charge. Although he'd lived in Norfolk for six or seven years, he didn't sound like us. He didn't speak Southern, he spoke New York, and he spoke it quickly, and his Bronx-Italian dialect was detectable. He looked authoritative, taller than me and Royster, and when he looked your way his gaze went through you. Frank's hair was wavy and neatly trimmed and Joe's was darker with prominent sideburns. Also in the studio was someone they called Slow Drag, my age or older, black and actually another Walter Johnson, but he discarded that name years earlier. I had seen him in Frankie's once or twice. I never figured out how he got that name, or what exactly he did for Guida, but Frank said he was good to have around, intelligent and dependable.

I had never been in a recording studio before, but from the look of things I figured that this was not what they were all like. I saw two tape machines on racks and they appeared to have high mileage. Frankie had walked away from the console to set up the two microphones. One mike was for keyboard and bass, and the other one was for vocals and horns. A drum kit was in a corner and some horns were sitting in stands. The bass was laying on its side and two guitar cases were leaning against a stack of folding chairs. Except for Royster, I knew all the guys, Earl, Barks, Junior, and Willie. The guitar player may have been Wayne Beckner. Bunchy (Leroy Toomes) and Frissell filed in as well.

There were no music stands, but if you have no music they just get in the way. Some of the chairs were opened, although I found most of the guys stood when recording. The floor was littered with coffee cans that were half-filled with cigarette ash. At this point I'd been smoking for a few years. Royster handed me a piece of long yellow paper. It wasn't music, it was a handwritten lyric sheet. As opposed to everything else which was made up on the spot, this looked like something he prepared before. He said it was for a country song he had written that they planned on giving to Bunchy, (who had already done a song for Guida) but Frankie said he wanted to give me a shot first. I asked Joe to tell me how he heard it and he turned to get his guitar; it was an archtop acoustic. He told me it worked in "E" and he strummed "New Orleans," or at least a form of the song which would change much during the next four hours. He sang it country, and we could have done it Dixieland style and it would have sounded like Earl's, "Tiger Rock." But I could not be convincing with a country number at that point and Frankie said he was looking for something else, something harder. I rolled up the lyric sheet and walked over to the bathroom/sound booth where the band members were standing. I saw no ready evidence of liquid refreshment but I might have found some if I looked carefully. From what I could tell, they had already been there for a couple of hours.

I read and reread the lyrics and they were pretty straightforward, an ad for New Orleans written by someone who had never been there. I had never been there either. Guida would tell you he'd been everywhere at least once. Earl Swanson and I were going to share one microphone and I would stand in front of him. I told Earl, that I would start with some kind of Cab Calloway thing, some kind of intro, not a count off, but something like Calloway did to get the audience involved. Thinking back, having never recorded before, what I had in mind was something that was really geared to live performance. I scatted my take on Calloway's "Hi-dee-ho," and it turned into a bunch of "hey yeahs." Earl followed with a sax riff which trailed my singing the first line of the lyric. Barks fell in behind Earl. It was no longer country and the lick proved infectious. But Frankie needed it to be perfect and with everything going into the two mikes, and a pants salesman for an engineer, we would start over more than two dozen times. I thought that was how it was done, but reading the musician's faces I sensed not. Swanson was getting frustrated. As a jazz player he knew it was impossible to repeat the stuff we liked when everyone was improvising. So again and again we took it from the top. But Earl hammered away with the sax riff, just nine notes, a six note question with a three note answer, over and over, with every needle on the console pushing deep into red. We all loved it.

Three hours into the session my buddies were dancing and the cocktail hour had begun. We had an unpaid chorus and the party had started. Then Frankie heard something. The instruments were pushed to a maximum volume as was my voice and the instruments were winning. He emptied out the sound booth and gave me a microphone to take in there. I sang along with my own voice. I could duplicate what I just sang, and with a slight manipulation of speeds my double tracked voice could be heard. The chorus moved out of the john but kept on singing and sound was leaking everywhere. Whether it was Daddy Grace's shout band or simply the sound of money, Frankie heard something he liked. Royster was quiet. He could barely recognize his song and not because he was drinking. It was glorious. Exhausted, we did the "B" side in three takes. "Please Forgive Me" was a conventional ballad I hastily wrote and only one of more than 30 I did for Frank where he did not take a co-writing credit. The session was fun but I did not know it was important. It was important enough to have Frankie make a master and press the record. He told me he would put it out.

I was the one who told Frank about Wonder Boy, and he may have even gone to the Azalea Gardens Club to check him or us out. Frank had wrapped up my session and he told me that he was going to be doing a session with Jimmy. I felt good about it and thought Frank appreciated my advice. He gave Jimmy a song, another one he wrote with Joe Royster that he would have me do a year later called "One

Million Tears." Frank was still experimenting with different labels, and the McCleese records he put out on the Marco Label, which meant by this time he not only had Legrand and Marco, but also Guide, Norva and Jaro. He would not only try to build a slightly different sound for each, he would also sign different distribution contracts for the labels. Legrand would be distributed by Laurie Records and their name would appear on the Legrand label. Guida's distribution deal with Laurie, and then later their Rust subsidiary, did not deter him from suing the company for being too liberal in their "borrowing" from my biggest record.

Mom asked me how the session went when I got home and I told her we did a song called "New Orleans." There was no discussion but I told her I wanted to do it again, not "New Orleans," but another record. The "New Orleans" session faded from memory. I continued to perform my little act in Norfolk and I didn't hesitate to let everyone know that Frankie from the record shop cut a record with me. I didn't have a record to show, and I didn't know if I would ever do it again, but I did start singing the song in my act. No one knew it, and it didn't get much of a response. Nothing happened with the record by summertime, so I planned on going to Jacksonville to see Pop.

When I did the record we were living on Granville Avenue in the Brambleton section. Mom and I were sitting on the front porch late one morning and the radio was on inside the house. It was tuned to WRAP 850 (now WTAR) and the morning man was "Daddy" Jack Holmes. "Daddy" Jack played rock and rhythm and blues and he would not only play the big records by stars like Sonny Til, Billy Eckstine and Ruth Brown, but he would also play and promote the popular acts from the Tidewater area like Ida Sands, the Showmen (with General Johnson) and Noah Biggs. I joined the list that morning when "Daddy" Jack played my song. But I wasn't too sure when "Daddy" Jack said "New Orleans" was a new release by a local boy, "U.S. Bonds."

I turned to mom as she turned to me, "Someone stole my record!"

Then "Daddy" Jack explained that U.S. Bonds was Gary Anderson, a local young man headed for a big career. "Daddy" Jack put the record into rotation but I doubt whether it played much outside of our part of Virginia.

Nearly six months after we recorded the song, Guida told me what he did. He retold the story to a Norfolk newspaper:

"I wanted to send the record out to deejays across the country, but this record is different. I knew if they heard it, they would play it, but I needed to get them to open the envelope." (*The Virginian-Pilot & The Ledger Star*, October 9, 1994).

As much as he would have liked to take complete credit for the idea, some credit must go to a patriotic man by the name of Elias Codd. Codd's Delicatessen was on Church Street next door to Frankie's Birdland, and Frank would stop by Codd's often. Codd was a proud American. He looked like a deli man, very round and balding. Inside his shop he displayed an enlarged replica of a savings bond, a flag, and in his window there was a large cut-out figure of Uncle Sam proclaiming, "Buy U.S. Bonds." During the second World War Codd was recognized by the Treasury Department for having sold $1 million of War Bonds. At the time that Frank came up with my stage name, Codd was 65 and would have lived long enough (he passed in 1967) to see his patriotism help me and my family. Frank's idea was to deceive deejays by making them think that the envelope contained a public service message. He stamped "By U.S. Bonds" on the envelope. He went further. On the Legrand label the song "New Orleans" was indicated as being performed by "U.S. Bonds." There was no clue as to whether it was a person or a group. Once the envelope was opened, it wasn't necessary to play the entire record to tell that it was not a public service announcement. Sorry Mr. Codd, the only "bonds" being sold was an unknown singer with a new name and a song which sounded like a party captured on vinyl. It was deceptive and clever. Many played it and many did not like it.

Frankie got records back from deejays. They said they didn't know what to make of it; they didn't like the quality. They said it was too raw, too noisy, too distorted and unfinished. More records were returned by black stations than white stations. But they did not all come back. Frank told me the record was being played by Porky Chedwick in Pittsburgh at WHOD. Porky was a white deejay who sounded black to many listeners and played classic Doo-Wop and R & B for a rugged steel-town listenership. Porky played my records and was also helpful to Bo Diddley and Little Anthony. Frankie also said Dick Clark was going to play the record, but we needed to go to Philadelphia first.

Frank and I drove in his car to Philadelphia, where at the *American Bandstand* studio Dick maintained an office. It was the first time I would meet the man who would be a good friend for more than 50 years. I owe my popularity to him. I was nervous when I entered the studio and I sensed Frank was as well. Dick was the kingmaker. Boyishly handsome and well spoken, he was non-threatening and made this new music palatable to the parents of teens who bought the records. He played my song and introduced me to a national audience. I worked for him for years on his *Cavalcade of Stars*, and I rode his tour bus with Bobby Rydell, Fabian and Freddy Cannon. I appeared with his first multi-act show at a Las Vegas hotel when we played the Flamingo. I introduced Dick to his second wife, Loretta Martin. She worked as an assistant to singer Jo Ann Campbell and traveled with us on the tours when she worked at Frank Barsalona's agency. When my career had a resurgence in 1981 I was back on his show with almost 20 years between appearances.

I was crushed when Dick suffered a stroke and I stayed in touch with him throughout his courageous recovery. We would get together whenever I was on the West Coast and we shared a love of his two favorite things, rock music and fine wine. I found out he passed when the East Coast media needed interviews and I was one of the guys they went to. When he passed I lost someone dear to me and my family, and I didn't mind telling people about it. Dick started putting black acts on his show when they could not otherwise be viewed by a national television audience even though they were selling carloads of records. My first business trip was a success. He said he would play my record and we spoke about a future appearance.

"New Orleans" entered the Billboard Hot 100 on October 17, 1960 at #71. That same week Ben E. King, leading the Drifters, was at #1 with "Save the Last Dance for Me," and my future teacher, Sam Cooke was at #3 with "Chain Gang." My records were selling and Frank started giving me some small checks, the same amount every week with assurance that he was looking after the rest. He let me know that he had paid for the musicians and the promotion.

A second session was scheduled after the visit with Dick Clark, but once it was scheduled Frank gave me some papers to sign. He was kind enough to refer me and my Mom (I was not yet 21) to his lawyer who would represent us and answer any questions we might have about my records and what I could expect to make. I don't think we ever met the lawyer and Mom looked at the papers and signed them. She wanted to make me happy and wasn't going to let any lawyers get in the way. Black families in Norfolk in 1960 didn't have lawyers. I just wanted to sing and I never thought I'd make a living selling records. I wanted to sell audiences and Mom just wanted her boy to be happy. Grandma never said much about my records. I was doing more local shows and having an easier time getting booked, and now I could point to my record. Nationally my records were on the charts, but I was still unknown. No one knew what I looked like and no one seemed to care if I was black or white. There were no fan clubs and no television appearances, yet.

Sometimes it works to your advantage when they don't know what you look like. First, my popularity in white radio markets might never have happened if deejays knew I was black. Black records were for the black stations which catered to black listeners. I could also get some extra bookings while I was still unknown.

Around this time Aaron Neville had a minor hit and he was booked into a small club in Norfolk. At least I think he was booked. Either way, a club was promising an appearance by Aaron Neville. A week before, I got a call from a deejay who asked if I was available to play a club. The deejay said the job paid $500, but I needed to be Aaron Neville. The deejay told me not to worry. No one knew what Aaron Neville looked like and no one knew who I was, Anderson or

Bonds. I told him it bothered me that Aaron Neville was worth twice what I was getting at that time. He told me Aaron Neville only got $250 when he showed up, "So if we got a deal, learn the record."

I went to the club and things were going fine until I was recognized by a friend from my neighborhood, "Gary, you ain't no Aaron Neville."

"Tonight for $500, I am," I replied, and I begged my friend to dance away and shut up.

It's happened to me, and I have shown up more than once at clubs to find impostors doing my show. Usually they're white, not very good, and they always blame their agent.

My agent was Frank Guida. He was also my manager. He owned my label, sold my records, wrote the songs, published the songs, and lent me his lawyer. He also changed my name. I call that full service. He would also lend his name to most of the songs I would write and this was the case with "Not Me," the single that would come out of my second session. "Not Me," had a catchy refrain, a scatting intro, a prominent sax riff and a mention of the Everly Brothers' 1960 #1 "Cathy's Clown." When writing it I kept in mind the elements which made "New Orleans" click. It also captured the beat of all the Cameo-Parkway dance songs that followed. The song was about a Romeo who chases attached women in a number of cities, but claims he's innocent when caught. The record was selling well in early 1961 when it was dropped by Billboard after failing to crack the Hot 100 (it "bubbled under" at #116). Guida explained that a reference to "having fun" was being interpreted as something other than innocent fun. Others have said that when the Romeo threatened physical harm that the record was not suitable for airplay. These were innocent times, but these times would pass quickly and the record made it to Philadelphia where the Orlons scored a #12 hit with it in 1963.

The second session had the same cast as the first, with one major exception. Earl Swanson was out and Gene Barge was in. Both were great tenor players and I never learned whether Earl left on his own, not wanting to play four hours without charts, or the chemistry just wasn't there and he was invited to leave. As a jazz player who liked rock and roll, Gene might have been better suited. Again, Royster was at the switches and everyone fell in behind Gene Barge. It took half the number of takes and the lead-in worked like "New Orleans." I left the studio once I completed the vocals for "Not Me," but the players stayed to cut another number. Frank must have figured our session would have taken longer and he probably paid the band for some additional time. When Gene Barge, Barks, Junior, Nabs and Willie Burnell left the session, Frank had a single by a new group, the Church Street Five, and Gene Barge would have a new name, "Daddy G."

The single, "A Night with Daddy G," was a Barge, Guida, Royster composition, and the title and the group was more clever marketing by Guida. This was a variation on what he did with my name on "New Orleans." Was "Daddy G," Daddy Grace? Was this new song by one of Daddy Grace's shout bands? Daddy Grace's House of Prayer was on Church Street and wasn't Nabs a drummer in a shout band? Was the song about this very colorful spiritual leader somewhat sacrilegious? He didn't repeat the trick with the envelopes going to the deejays. The record sold in and around Norfolk. It was wilder than "New Orleans," but while it was highly rhythmic, it didn't have a vocal "hook," a catchy phrase that makes you anticipate the entire melody. Instrumentals generally don't sell anyway. When the record broke, I was on my first road trip. We played multiple cities around Norfolk, nothing more than a few hundred miles away, mostly small clubs with some high school dances added. I was out promoting "Not Me," but by this time crowds were asking for "New Orleans."

Guida scheduled another session in March of 1961, my third. I was disturbed by what happened to "Not Me," and somewhat discouraged that I could not repeat the success of "New Orleans," but the pay I was getting was increasing along with the number of dates. I am puzzled to this day as to why the record was removed from the charts as I learned that royalty statements indicated more than 200,000 records being sold.

This time I didn't need to let the guys know I was doing a session. That responsibility was assumed by Slow Drag, and we were becoming inseparable. They were already there when I arrived and I walked into the session with nothing prepared. I figured Guida would have something, or maybe Daddy G. I don't know if the phrase "one hit wonder" was around at the time, but I did not want to be the first singer to be called one. The players were setting up and they started playing "A Night with Daddy G," and I started singing some nonsense and it occurred to me that maybe I could add some words to the song. It was a shame the song didn't sell, but we all knew that Guida wouldn't waste any money plugging an instrumental by some faceless group. I grabbed the back of a tape box and started scribbling. It took about 20 minutes. This was more of that important stuff Guida said we did. I sat over with Royster who was ready at the controls and we went over what I was going to do. Again I needed a count off, it worked for me, like practice swings. I told him I would sing an intro and then the band and lyric would start. I walked over to Gene and told him we were going to slow it down a bit and Guida really wanted Gene to come forward when he did the solo. This session started past cocktail hour and the chorus had expanded. Royster was not a one take engineer and with the equipment he had it was another 30 takes to get what I was now calling "Quarter to Three." With Guida, Royster and Barge already on "A Night with Daddy G," my lyrics got me a quarter of the song. I spent a fair amount of time in the bathroom on this one too, but my ability to overdub was turning Royster into a sonic genius and giving Guida a formula that would bring him closer to that microphone and closer to being very successful.

Not everyone agreed that Royster was a sonic genius. Some were conflicted about "Quarter To Three." "The record is fuzzy, muzzy, and distorted. According to present day standards it is appalling.... However, for my money the disc is not just good, it's sensational and revolutionary." (Jack Good, *Disc*, July 15, 1961).

Good summed up what many people said at the time, and still say today, not only about "Quarter to Three," but about our records in general. I wound up working for Good in later years, and as a TV producer both in the UK and United States, Good, like Dick Clark would bring quality production values and international exposure to dozens of acts. He would later film the Beatles, and bring *Shindig* to the U.S. on which I made several appearances.

Guida wanted me to do a few more songs before I went back on the road, and I did some homework. I also told Pop that I was not going to be able to make it to Jacksonville again that summer. Gene Barge helped me with my homework and Guida said that if we were lucky with "Quarter to Three" a follow up would be needed for the summer when radios were a requirement on every blanket at the beach. We were doing "happy sounds" and we came up with a happy theme. It was fitting for me in that it had been a few years since my last class at Booker T. Washington High. "School is Out" was made to order for the summer months and my shout out to the Yankees was guaranteed to get me play in New York, especially if the Bronx Bombers continued to win American League titles. On the flip side I did the song Frank tried with Jimmy Soul, "One Million Tears." I was established as a personality and my looks and name were known. Once "School is Out" was released I would get back my first name. The newly designed Legrand label would read, "Gary U.S. Bonds."

"Quarter to Three" started to get national airplay as soon as it was released. My friends in Pennsylvania jumped on it and young Jerry Blavat was all over my record. After a release sometime in April of 1961, we broke into the Hot 100, but just barely, on May 28 at #99. Guida was now doing the things he needed to do to compete with the big boys. He set up distribution for all of Legrand in the UK with Top Rank records, he got a label in Canada, and turned me over to a full time agent, Frank Barsalona. Barsalona was starting his legendary career at General Artists and I was one of his first acts along with Timi Yuro and Jimmy Clanton. Barsalona, since inducted into the Rock and Roll Hall of Fame, changed the way rock music was presented and the economics of the business both for performers and promoters. Barsalona was responsible for booking me and a short two years later he would put the Beatles on the *Ed Sullivan Show*. I started to do interviews with the news services. Frank set up record hops in the northeast and put pressure on the teen music magazines both here and abroad to write features about me. He leveraged my name, my hair and my commitment to God and country and promoted my personal image to be the opposite of my music. Where the music was untamed and unrestrained, I was well mannered, impeccably groomed and a model citizen. Mom was proud.

Dick Clark called. We were ready to do *American Bandstand*. "Quarter to Three" had swiftly moved up the charts. In two weeks we moved up to #33. Walter did my hair and we did *American Bandstand* on June 16th. The power of Clark and *Bandstand* was huge. The record had moved up to #9. Ben E. King's "Stand By Me" was ahead of us at #4. The next week Ben E.'s song stalled at #4 and we jumped ahead to #3 and went on to be #1 for the next two weeks.

Mom helped me pack and we headed for Washington, D.C.

Six

PAST A QUARTER TO THREE

SLOW DRAG DROVE MOM BACK FROM Washington, D.C. in Newkirk's Crown Victoria, and I joined the tour at the Howard Theater. I have already explained that I was awestruck and still learning my craft, but if the only considerations were record sales and radio play, I had earned a place on the same stage with my idols. By July, when "Quarter to Three" hit #1, Sam Cooke was on the charts with "Cupid." "Cupid" was at #36 heading as high as #17, and when Sam's record got no higher than #17, my summer release "School is Out" was above it at #16 and heading higher. Guida was too conservative with his timing, and he underestimated the potential of "Quarter to Three." For two weeks it remained in the top 20 together with "School is Out." Mantle and Maris dominated the sports pages that summer while Norfolk's Legrand label became the center of the rock and roll universe. The school yard bully was getting his ass kicked by a wannabe Calypso king.

Competitors were not content to watch. My first four records sold in excess of two million singles and Guida's name and Legrand were being whispered at all the larger independent labels, and I suspect the majors as well. No one had more information on what we were doing than the people at our distributor, Laurie Records. My buddy Dion, and we go back to the early '60s, was Laurie's first and biggest star, and he is always quick to remind me, "If there was no 'Quarter to Three,' there would never have been a 'Runaround Sue.'" He should know. He co-wrote "Sue" with Ernie Maresca. I don't remember if he first said that to me when we were doing shows back in the '60s, but with the biggest of grins he reminded me just recently of my song's influence while we were prepping for our performances at a dinner in New York honoring Steven Van Zandt.

Musicologists would agree with the statement, as well as musicians who have had to play behind Dion and me. The common elements are the scatting and the sax riff, but I give the nod to Dion's song for the narrative about the mythic "Sue." That's all his and Ernie's. Imitation is flattery up to the point when record sales are involved, but I can't blame Dion's hit for knocking us off the charts. Our songs never overlapped, with "Quarter to Three" dropping off on September 3, and "Runaround Sue" "bubbling under" on September 24 and then climbing to #1 on October 29. In a way, "Quarter to Three" in one form or another was at the top twice in 1961.

Guida wasn't pleased, after all, Laurie Records as Legrand's distributor, shared a common financial interest in the Norfolk Sound. Guida was none too subtle when he re-released the Church Street Five single "A Night with Daddy G," as a "B" side, called "I'm Gonna Sue." This was not insignificant even if it was just a "B" side. It was an answer song, but not aimed at the record buying public. It revealed a growing preoccupation Guida had with playing the victim. Months earlier he glorified in the fact that his shoestring operation, working outside the music mainstream, had become the envy of many. That motivated him and Daddy G and me to write and create records which were fresh and innovative, although we were not always in agreement with every decision. He was now content to press records to irk the competition. It satisfied only his frustration and his feud was meaningless to the record buying public and my fans. While the legal records cannot confirm it, in a 1994 interview in the *Virginian-Pilot*, Guida said that there was an out of court settlement for copyright infringement.

Guida heard "Quarter to Three" everywhere, especially in Chubby Checker's 1962 hit "Dancing Party," and from the intro to the theme, he was not wrong. But a lawsuit was hard for anyone to take seriously for two reasons. First, Guida himself was shamelessly borrowing from others. The "Twist" bandwagon started in mid-1960 when Cameo Parkway had Chubby record a version of the Hank Ballard dance tune which was a "B" side out on King. Chubby's version went on to chase Hank's version off the charts. Guida wanted a part of the Twist franchise (with Calypso overtones) and he had me record my own string of Twist records starting in late 1961. Second, Chubby and I were good friends and we still are. We were competitors at that time, but Chubby was clearly on top of the dance record business with a global craze he worked hard to popularize with a series of great vocals and a live act that is still one of the best.

Guida was not intimidated and ignored his own poaching. Lawsuits are inexpensive, and even when you lose, the publicity is often priceless. But Frank was generous, without asking my permission he let me personally join with his companies in a lawsuit against named defendants Cameo Parkway and composers Kalmann Cohen (known as Kal Mann, a Cameo principal) and David Appell (of Cameo Parkway house-band Dave Appell and the Applejacks) who were sued for $100,000. This too would be settled out of court (though I would receive nothing) with Guida suggesting that Cameo Parkway agreed to record another song from his catalog. Whether this resulted in the Orlons doing, "Not Me," cannot be confirmed, but the biggest benefit to Guida was the three-inch headline in Norfolk's black newspaper, the *New Journal and Guide*, "U.S. Bonds vs. Chubby Checker, Norfolkian Suing 'King of the Twist.'"

I was 22 and had been recording for less than two years. I had only been in a recording studio four times. Two million of my records were sold, and I had a hand in writing some of them. I had my first LP, I was touring the major black theaters and had just signed to do a *Dick*

Clark's Caravan of Stars after an appearance on national television. I was suing the "Twist King" and every other song on the radio had elements of what we were doing. But I still could be found hangin' at the Blue Nile with the guys. When the guys asked me whether it was true that I now had a fan club, I told them I did, but the things that were important to me had not changed much.

Walking in to meet Dick Clark I was the same Gary Anderson, and walking off *American Bandstand* I was still the same guy. There were no new friends. I didn't need new friends to hang with. I had old ones and I brought them with me and we went home together. At different times I had either Slow Drag, Purcell or Jelly out on the road with me and to them I was the same guy, because I was. I didn't take whatever level of precious fame I had too seriously, and I still don't. Big Mama has heard me say time and time again when we finish a show, even if it's a big one, "Now it's time to go home and settle down with some neck bones and beans."

I knew I was selling records, but what mattered to me was what I did in front of an audience, and the size of the audience did not not matter. I wanted to send people home happy, take them away from their cares for an hour or so, and let everyone have a slice of the pie. That's my idea of a good deal. My friends didn't need anything from me and didn't ask. Growing up we were more comfortable than most of them and Mom took care of me, and we helped my friends and that wasn't going to change. When my career accelerated, we ate a little better and drank a little better, but their main concern was being there for me. Their loyalty was to Gary Anderson, not Gary Bonds.

Performing is mostly down time. It's getting to a city and waiting, getting to a theater and waiting, and then performing and once you are done you're too charged to shut it off quickly. My friends were there for all of that. They were looking out for me and protecting me mostly from idleness. I didn't need new friends for that. They would look out for the prettiest girls or lose one when necessary, and we'd support each other if one of us had too much of a good time. But that's what we did before. They would share the driving or ride the train or plane and make sure I got paid. Promoters could be difficult and not every show was a sell out. Some of the club-owners were characters and not intimidated by my 125 pounds and limited boxing skills. I wanted to share with the same guys I shared with when we had much less to share.

I hadn't been able to make it to Jacksonville to see Pop, or my stepsister Joyce and aunt and uncle for a couple of summers, so when I found that I was booked into a club in Jacksonville Beach I was elated. I told Joyce, who had just entered high school, that I was coming to town. While I was looking forward to visiting Joyce and going to school with her as she had planned, I was more anxious about having my dad see me perform. It would be the first time. I was traveling with Daddy G and drummer Melvin Glover and at this stage we were still recruiting local talent to save on travel expenses. Melvin knew I had some anxiety about my father being at the show. I told Melvin, "My father is a scholar, two masters and working on a Ph.D. He ain't no rock and roll guy."

"They're gonna pay you to do that," was Pop's comment a couple of years ago when I told him I was singing at some clubs. They were paying me to play Jacksonville Beach and that night they paid me to sing for an audience that included my father.

"He wasn't the most nurturing person, but Daddy was so proud when you came to the Beach." Joyce remembered that, but I don't know how she knew. He didn't say much after the show and just wished me well and asked where I was off to next. A man who never left school couldn't appreciate, "School Is Out," even if his son was singing it. I told him I was off to Indianapolis with Dick Clark.

Caravan of Stars was Dick Clark's take on barnstorming. He would load up a bus with the youngest and hottest acts and we'd do a show a day for two or three weeks. It didn't pay much, but the exposure was great and we all benefited from having our records played on *American Bandstand*. Some of the acts stayed on the route, playing dozens of shows a year, and others would sign on as headliners when they had an especially big record. Tom Jones, the Supremes and Sonny and Cher all toured with the *Caravan* and built national followings courtesy of Dick Clark.

I met the tour in Indianapolis where we did the state fair, and after two shows we moved on to the Michigan State Fair in Detroit. In Indianapolis I appeared with tour regulars, Bobby Rydell and Freddie Cannon. I believe Freddie did more *American Bandstands* than anyone else. Chuck Jackson was on that bill stealing the show nightly with "I Don't Want to Cry," which had done well earlier in the year. Chuck showed that he learned a lot from his mentor Jackie Wilson. Chuck moved on with me to Detroit where Chubby Checker headlined and the Shirelles joined us from another tour.

Legrand was a smooth running hit factory, but still conservative when it came to estimating how long my records would chart. "School Is Out" was still a respectable #45 on October 8, and after not having a record on the charts for two weeks, I was back on at #59 with "School Is In" on October 29, but it would get no higher than #28 on November 19 and then drop off the charts a week later. "School is In" was not recorded at the same time as "School is Out." It was actually the first song we would record at a new studio on Sewells Point Road. This one wasn't much of a studio either, but Frank did buy Royster a new second hand mixing board. But I was not yet finished for the year. Frank Guida would get his beloved Calypso on the radio and high on the charts.

Frank could justify his copying others as sweet revenge, and as he got older his list of artists who had appropriated his music grew beyond Morey Amsterdam, Harry Belafonte, Chubby Checker and Dion. The Beatles, Phil Spector, Motown and beloved Ben E. King (Frank claimed he "gave" him the gospel track that became "Stand By Me") were accused of lifting his ideas and production techniques if not his copyrighted material.

In late 1961 Guida saw the singles charts overflowing with Twist numbers and the album charts dominated by Belafonte's million selling "Calypso" and "Jump Up Calypso." He came into the studio with the idea of combining the two. I didn't like the idea of going into the Twist business, but it was hard to overlook the charts. As for turning public domain Calypso numbers into Twist records, it would have been Guida's wish to do straight up Calypso, but Belafonte had a lock on that (though purists said Belafonte was not actually doing Calypso). Calypso remained Frank's passion and his instincts had kept us on the charts for two years. I couldn't argue with him even though I would have preferred a different direction. The plan was to do a Twist/Calypso album and Frank looked to the man he "inspired." From "Jump Up Calypso" Frank derived "Twist Up Calypso," an album known as much for its music as for the outfit I wear on the album cover.

"Dear Lady Twist" was initially issued as "Dear Lady" and when it placed at #65 on the charts for its first week, I had been off the charts for only three weeks. That week there were six Twist songs in the Top 100 including three by Chubby Checker and two versions of "Peppermint Twist." Not knowing if the Twist/Calypso hybrid would work for me, Guida hedged his bets with my former partner from the Azalea Gardens Club, James McCleese. Now called Jimmy Soul, Frank took the song he "popularized" as a performer, an homage to his sister Matilda, and put it out on his S.P.Q.R. label as "Twistin' Matilda." Guida's adaptation found Matilda taking her man's money to Las Vegas rather than Venezuela as in the original. Frank's bet and his hedge scored. "Dear Lady" finished the year on the charts and stayed on until March 31, 1962. That was the same day that Jimmy Soul's "Twistin' Matilda" entered the charts at #97. But I was not off the charts. That same day "Twist, Twist Señora" entered at #68. Frank had three charting Calypso numbers, and as he wrote in the liner notes to *Twist Up Calypso*, "This album is the fruition of a dream of 15 long years."

I mentioned the man and his dreams earlier and how his dreams would take priority over mine and occasionally the truth. This was the case in our financial dealings. While to this point I had managed to avoid most of the clichés people have come to associate with the careers of early rock and roll performers, I did not avoid the financial ones. Frank kept me on an allowance, gave me some expense money, and allowed me to keep what I made when I arranged to work locally. When I was booked on tours he was paid, and he had some arrangement with my agent, John Barsalona. I had not seen any real money from recordings until I was in Norfolk to do the Twist sessions.

I knew we were selling records, but the only money I was sure of was in my pocket.

Frank's office was now at the Sewells Point Road studio, and he called me in to give me a check. I was no longer a minor. Without any explanation he handed me an envelope. The check was substantial, in excess of $50,000, but as to what it represented I didn't know and didn't care. We are all familiar with the story about the label owner who buys the Cadillac and "generously" gives it to his financially innocent star. I got a check, and tried to cash it at Norfolk Cadillac. I bought the beige Coupe deVille on the floor, the first of many. The check arrived just in time because I remember that day and not having enough money to fill up my old car. Once seeing the check the dealer arranged for me to open a bank account, which I did not have, and he even had his salesman drive me to the bank. I took Slow Drag with me. I gave my old car to Mom. There was a substantial sum left and that enabled me to help Mom and Grandma, who by this time had closed her beauty salon. I picked up the car and drove to Fine's Menswear and we suited up.

With a new Cadillac paid for with "cash money," and our new suits in the trunk, there was no shame in flipping the keys to Slow Drag and telling him to point the car towards New York. We headed to the Apollo and there was no need to bring a band. Reuben Phillips had taken over the house band at the Apollo, and I was sure he would not find my three songs too challenging. I had never been to New York before. I had been to Philadelphia, but my best frame of reference for New York was that many people back home referred to Norfolk as "Little New York." They should have referred to it as "Very Little Like New York."

We did four shows a day and seven on the weekends. I wasn't the headliner, and I still couldn't dance, but I played to the girls in the front row who were familiar with my songs that had charted consistently for the last two years. For my week at the Apollo I was getting about half of what the headliners were getting, less than two thousand dollars, and I spent a good portion of that at the New York Sheraton. While most of the acts stayed uptown at the Theresa or the Braddock which were near the Apollo, I decided to stay midtown at the Sheraton which had just opened on 52nd Street near Times Square.

On the bill with me at the Apollo were the Platters, Chuck Jackson and the Miracles with Jackie Wilson headlining. As Sam Cooke took me under his wing at the Howard, Jackie had been a mentor to Chuck. Jackie taught Chuck the ropes when he came in from Pittsburgh for his first appearance and part of his education was shopping for clothes at Phil Kronfeld. Kronfeld was located on 49th and Broadway and not far from where I was staying at the Sheraton. Kronfeld was known as a place where entertainers, fashionable pimps and wiseguys could go to find clothes that they couldn't find anyplace else. Phil would take care of you, and if he didn't have what you needed or you were a little bit short, if you sang or danced or told jokes, you had come to the right place.

Chuck took me to Kronfeld's when I checked into the Apollo and he told me he learned not to be careless with his belongings following his last appearance.

"We had just come in from a tour and I had this guy driving me. We got to New York on a Friday. He unpacked my wardrobes and I did the show. We came back on Saturday and everything was gone, even the portable television I brought. The only thing they left was this one suit I had with a short red jacket. I used to tell everyone I got it from a matador. If I would have worn that at the Apollo they would have laughed so loud they wouldn't have heard me singing. So Jackie tells me to call up Phil Kronfeld who made all our suits. I tell Phil I'm in a jam and he asks how long I have before the show. I tell him an hour and a half and he said, 'I have your measurements, come down.' I get down there and he has something for me all ready to take back to the theater. Sure enough it looks just like one of my suits and Phil told me it should fit. Damn thing fit perfectly. I hurried back to the Apollo for the show. The next day I called Phil and thanked him. He said to come down because he's got four more just like the one he sold me. I get down to Kronfeld's and I find out he's selling me my own suits. Turns out some sharpie sold him my wardrobe." Chuck recalled it all vividly, but he added, "I'm still looking for the TV."

I learned to take care of myself in New York and through it all Slow Drag was by my side. We went from the Apollo to the Uptown in Philadelphia to join the Isley Brothers and then we flew to the Regal in Chicago. We returned to New York and checked back into the Sheraton. Guida said they had a song that they wanted me to cut in New York. It was a song supposedly written for me by "professional songwriters," as contrasted with Guida and Royster who did a lot of things and also wrote songs. Doc Pomus and Mort Shuman were hot, but I was puzzled that Guida wanted me to record a song which he did not write or publish. He had good reason and Barsalona explained it to me. If the session went well, I would be singing the song in a film distributed by Columbia Pictures with a release in both the United States and Europe during Spring Break. Barsalona also handled Gene McDaniel and Gene would be doing a song as well. Gene would also be in the movie. Neither Frank nor Barsalona knew the name of the film.

Doc Pomus was legendary. You could not have invented a more soulful fellow with the heart of a bluesman trapped in a body that childhood polio nearly destroyed. But Doc's heart was too big to still, and he was a very talented lyricist who together with his partner, classically schooled composer Mort Shuman, would have hits with everyone from Dion to Ray Charles and Elvis. Two of their many hits for the Drifters may be the groups' best, "This Magic Moment" and "Save the Last Dance For Me." I am really liking New York at this point. I liked the hum of the city, the clubs nearby, hanging out at the Brill Building, visiting publishers and meeting the other acts as they came to town. Barsalona invited me up to his New York office to let me know that he had set up my first tour of the UK, Scotland and Wales, a two week trip with about 20 shows.

I was not surprised that I would be co-headlining with Gene McDaniel, and I was starting to understand how the entertainment business worked. Barsalona said that we needed passports and that his office would expedite them for us. I called home and told Mom, and this was big news. The news was I was going to England. The fact that

I was going there to sing was secondary. I forgot to tell her about the movie. Barsalona told me that I would fly on Pan Am to London where I would meet the co-headliners including Johnny Burnette and the rest of the supporting acts. Based on my record sales and the release of "Twist, Twist Señora" which would happen at the start of the tour, the European promoter decided that I would close the show. The show would be billed as *Rock'n Twist U.S.A.* and the three American headliners would be joined by four or five supporting acts of which one would provide backing for all the acts.

The plan was to meet at a studio in London for a day of rehearsal and then take a bus to Glasgow, Scotland for the opener. We would do two shows a day at most of the theaters which held from 400 to 1,000 people. Johnny would start it off for the American acts with "Dreamin'" and finish with his hit, later recorded by Ringo Starr, "You're Sixteen." Gene had "Chip, Chip," and "Hundred Pounds of Clay." I would do 20 minutes and finish with "Twist, Twist Señora." We would leave for London after we shot the movie.

The movie was made outside London by first-time director Richard Lester, an American. Lester must have impressed the critics because three years later he would direct *A Hard Day's Night*, and then *Help!* for that other group. The movie was set for spring holiday distribution in the UK and United States. The theme was more British than American and centered around "Trad," the traditional Dixieland jazz craze which started on English college campuses and was going mainstream. It wasn't quite the mania that the Twist was, but the Twist was showing some age at this point and the Twist movies had already been done in the two previous years. These movies were just quick ways to promote record sales inexpensively, and flimsy plots were the rule. Dialogue was typically, "Hey (insert singer's name) why don't you do a song?"

The plot was innocuous. The teens at a fictional town in the UK want to convince the "square" city officials that they are unjustly suppressing this music. The teens plot to put on a concert and seek the help of a sympathetic deejay. They think a show is the best way to persuade the elders that Trad music is respectable. The old folks do their best to stop the show and in the end the teens are victorious and the elders see that the music is actually quite wholesome. In my scene I am performing at a British charity gala and I am introduced to the nightclub stage by a British emcee who refers to "Quarter to Three." Recall, this is 1962. The movie was shot in black and white, with Chubby Checker, Gene and myself accounting for all of the black. To gain from the Twist's continued popularity into 1962, Chubby was added to the cast to do "Lose Your Inhibition Twist," which was written by the defendants in my lawsuit over Cameo Parkway's theft of "Quarter to Three." Chubby, Gene and I lip-synched our new singles as did added cast members Del Shannon and Gene Vincent. Trivia buffs will note that I appear with a group that is actually Gene Pitt and three members of the Jive Five who had a #3 hit the previous fall with "My True Story."

I did not go "Hollywood." I went Bronx. The American artists each performed at a sound stage in the Bronx, and the movie was assembled by Amicus Pictures at Shepperton Studios in Surrey. Prints of surprisingly good quality have survived and are available on DVD. Young Richard Lester proved that he could work effectively with a limited budget, and for what the movie is, it is not the worst of the genre. To me, the scene of half-shadowed, cigarette smoking Gene McDaniel singing Burt Bacharach's "Another Tear Falls" is worth the trouble of finding a copy. Also appearing are Kenny Ball and Mr. Acker Bilk who had hits in the U.S., however the rest of the cast were primarily British jazz players and the American artists were dropped in so the movie could be released stateside. The Trad craze never crossed to the U.S. and the movie borrowed its U.S. title, *Ring a Ding Rhythm*, from a Sinatra album of the same period.

I was a movie star for about three hours. Half that time was spent getting my hair done and the curl was cut from the movie. It took over an hour to light the scene and about 10 minutes for the choreographer/ director to get the blocking for both me and the four Jive Five. The song took no more than 10 minutes and since I was adept at dubbing my own voice, lip-synching was not a challenge.

We drove back to Manhattan and I packed for London. I packed light for the trip and came back with much more stuff than I took. I bought an excessive number of British cashmere knits and my plan was to give them to the guys when I got back to Norfolk. Gene McDaniel and I became close during the tour. Gene could have crossed over and played any nightclub in the country. He was a strong, expressive singer, and if given the choice his preference would have been to sing jazz and standards. He read music, composed, and told me that he trained to be a horn player. He made his point when he sat in with the band toward the end of the tour. Gene was comfortable in the UK and he let me know years later that he was planning on relocating to middle Europe. The shows were sold out for most of the route and the highlight had to be Gene learning that his wife had given birth while we were finishing a show in Birmingham. Returning to the States and connecting to Norfolk, there was little down time.

"Seven Day Weekend" was released while I was overseas, and it joined the Hot 100 when I returned. Frank had high expectations for the record, but I always felt he would not have been bothered if it did not do as well as our Norfolk product, particularly the songs he wrote or co-wrote. The Pomus/Shuman song would get no higher than #27 and fall off the charts after just seven weeks. The movie did not reach theaters until the fall, and when it did the box office was dismal. By then my song had faded. Frank wanted me back in the studio, and with Pomus and Shuman coming up short, I thought for sure we would go back to what we started with. I did not want to do another Twist number, or worst of all a Guida adaptation of a Calypso number. I did not think Pomus and Shuman gave us their best work, but I thought it was time to try something else, maybe a ballad, but it was not to be.

Frank came to the studio prepared, with a song he did with Royster and a new collaborator, Patricia Matthews. I never met her or saw her. The lyric sounded like a deposition, and he wanted it sung to a Little Richard beat with a shrieking female chorus. It was as if Frank had his lawyers put together an indictment against all the singers Guida accused of stealing his sound. It was for Guida a protest song, and Frank had me sing it upbeat. There are many songs which reference other singers, but this was different. This wasn't poking fun or drawing inspiration. This is a plea from a man who has run out of ideas. "Copy Cat" is about a man who has "thrown in the towel" and stopped creating because his creations would only be pilfered. Chubby is mentioned a number of times along with Freddie (Cannon?), Leon (did he mean Dion?), Curtis (Lee?), and Bobby (Rydell?). There was a paranoia in the song and I started to see it in the man.

"Copy Cat" was another turning point. I saw it when I returned from Europe. Frank was focused on what our competitors were doing rather than on what we could do to stay fresh and vital. Our music was like none before it and now we were copying those who copied us. It was a continuation of "I'm Gonna Sue." Frank's priorities came first, and his priority was nurturing his victim-hood. Having taken the school yard bully's girl, he was content to let her go and wallow about "what might have been." This was to be the beginning of the end of my relationship with Frank, and my career with Legrand. But Guida would have one more colossal, improbable win before his descent and I would have no part of it, other than as an enabler. He would become the lord of an empty empire, left to stew in his cinder-block bunker, surrounded by a security fence. I sang "Copy Cat" and boasted that I was invincible because of Daddy G. But Daddy G would not be a hostage to his talent. "Copy Cat" topped out at #92.

I would not sell records again for a very long time, but for the moment my string of hits gave me the expectation of ample club dates and concerts for a very long while. They say a single hit record can feed you for 20 years. I would find this not to be true.

Seven

HAPPY FOR THE REST OF MY LIFE

"My parents were not happy when they heard my agent had booked me into the Bamboo Lounge for a 10 week run," Big Mama recalled. "I was hired for a revue. They needed a girl singer and I could do English and Spanish songs which were popular at the time, but my background was group harmony. In fact, I could even do some songs in Yiddish and Hebrew. But being away from our home in Williamsburg, Brooklyn was not something my parents were comfortable with. I started singing professionally at 15 while I was in high school when the mayor gave me permission to miss school so I could rehearse for our group's first date at the Apollo. My father didn't like it when I needed to take the subway to go sing so he would come with me. If I was going to Atlantic City, my parents decided it would be best if I took someone with me, so they found this guy who said he used to look out for Leslie Uggams. She was a couple of years younger than me, but she started her career before she turned 10.

My chaperone's name was Leroy Collins, and I wound up taking care of him, and eventually packed him up and sent him back to

Brooklyn. When I got the Atlantic City job I found out that landlords were not so anxious to rent me a place. I was a singer, young and not white, and that was enough for real estate agents to tip off wary property owners. I wound up finding a house which was only a short bus ride from the club. After paying for Collins and the rent and the cost of being away from home, there wasn't much left, but I was singing. Atlantic City in 1962 was not what it is today. The hotels were rundown, of another era. The neighborhoods were still divided, with black streets and white streets. Some of the clubs had black entertainers and catered to a mixed crowd, and some clubs would never hire a black act and were restricted. There were gay clubs for gays and gay entertainment for straights. The entertainment district centered around Kentucky Avenue and the clubs, many of which had hidden gambling operations, still attracted top name entertainment and a fair number of wiseguys as well as the women who loved them for the night, and sometimes longer."

I got lucky in Atlantic City. I met my wife Laurie there, and in March 2013 Laurie, who would become known to everyone as Big Mama, and I will be married for 50 years. She was the most beautiful woman I had ever known then, and she still is today, and she sings better than anyone. Laurie tells me that Slow Drag told her right after I met her that I would marry her. He was right, and I didn't pay him to say it. He had been around me for a while and he knew. She wasn't the first girl I kissed. Having recorded and worked clubs for a number of years and traveled extensively I had ample opportunities and took some, but they weren't worth writing home about, then or now.

I dated a girl named Dorothy back when we were 13 and 14. She lived around the corner from us when we lived on Granville Avenue. There was about a two year period when we were boyfriend and girlfriend, but once I hit 15 my attention turned to music, it was the Turks and traveling to do shows. If I saw a girl twice it was exceptional. I tell people now I was a "player," but mostly to defend the fact that I have had few meaningful romantic relationships.

Grandma used to remind me about the whipping she gave me when I was caught in the backyard with Ba-Bee's sister. I was nine or

10 and so was she and for the whipping I got I should have been doing something, but Grandma could not be convinced that it was all very innocent. Even though I was now 23, I was still well tended to by a doting mother and grandmother. They were still making sure my clothes were clean and pressed, and if money ever got tight for them or me, we handled it.

Other than running liquor as a teen I had never had a job other than singing, and no one at home wanted any of that to change. It would take a special woman to compete, and I found one. Mom, Grandma and I were close, and at the time I played Atlantic City, Mom, Mimms and I were living in a luxurious brick home on Sedgefield Drive, a white block in a section of Norfolk called Green Hill Farms.

Although I finished the year without a charting record, I had no problem getting good money at the Hialeah Club on Atlantic Avenue, around the corner from where Laurie was singing. I took Slow Drag with me. At that time Atlantic City had so many clubs, The 500, the Jockey Club, the Paradise and the Club Harlem, and many of the acts were booked for extended runs. That made downtime anything but boring. Many of the clubs were still doing variety shows with chorus lines, and Slow Drag enjoyed making new friends and introducing me as we went from club to club after my show was over.

Laurie recalled the time she was visiting a friend of hers who lived in Roxbury, Massachusetts, "My friend and some of hers were playing records up on the roof where they lived. I joined them and we were dancing, just girls. I had already been singing for a few years, and they asked me if I knew Gary U.S. Bonds because they were playing one of his records. I told them that I had heard of him, but I had never met him. I had already done the Apollo twice and knew Earl Lewis, the Flamingos, Chuck Willis and Frankie and Lewis Lymon. I told them I had seen pictures of Gary and they had as well. My friend said, 'Isn't he cute.' I agreed, and one of them had a year old fan magazine that she showed me. It had a picture of Gary with that curl. I hadn't given that visit another thought until I went to work in Atlantic City. I saw that Gary was working at the Hialeah and one night as I got on the bus to go home I could see a bunch of girls surrounding him on Atlantic Avenue. Even from a distance I could see he was still cute."

It was after my third show at the Hialeah that Slow Drag came back to the dressing room to tell me that there was a guy who wanted to introduce me to a girl in the audience. You would hear that a lot in Atlantic City and I didn't know what Slow Drag meant. Then he clarified himself. He said the girl was a singer who worked at the Bamboo around the corner. We left my dressing room and we came out and found Laurie and Collins at a table. Collins explained that he was the young lady's chaperone. Drink orders were taken as well wishers came by to thank me for the show as Laurie did. I was looking at Laurie and Slow Drag was looking at me. Slow Drag saw something in me that he had never seen before. I was focused on Laurie, who had my full attention. Normally after my shows I'd be scoping out the room.

He saw what I felt; I was smitten instantly. It was how she spoke and held herself. Laurie was reserved. We spoke about music, hers and mine. I invited her to see my show again and she asked me to come see hers. Before my week was up we had done that. I was taken equally by her looks, presence and talent. I knew very few Hispanics and never dated one. I sensed initially that she was reticent to discuss anything personal and I did not probe. I learned she lived with her parents in Brooklyn and that she had moved there with them from Puerto Rico and had a brother, Julio, and a sister Aida. After seeing her show I spoke to her about her voice which had an extraordinary range from girlish soprano to a throaty alto. She not only harmonized, but could dance around a note and create tension before landing pitch perfect. I assumed she had some musical training. I was wrong.

She was a couple of years younger than me, but had been in the business longer. She turned professional in 1956 and had appeared with her group at the Apollo more times than I had. We also found out that we had both played the Regal and Uptown Theaters. She had recorded with a number of small independent labels both as part of a group and on her own. She told me she had weeks to go on her contract at the Bamboo. I didn't want to leave town, but I was scheduled to leave Atlantic City for nearby Wildwood, New Jersey to do a week with Patty LaBelle and the Bluebells. By the end of the week Slow Drag knew the Wildwood/Atlantic City route with his eyes closed. I pursued Laurie with an energy that I didn't know I had. I was more intent at winning her than I ever felt about advancing my career.

Curtis always tells a story about seeing me at the Hialeah Club. Curtis had enlisted and was stationed at Fort Dix, New Jersey. He said he was making his bunk one morning when he heard one of my records on the radio. Following the record, there was a promo for my appearance at the Hialeah.

This is how Curtis remembers it: "After the commercial I tell my friends in the bunk that I know Gary U.S. Bonds and that he's my homeboy and we've been friends for more than 15 years. Some of them were not believing me. I challenged them. We had a weekend pass, and I told them we should go see the show and I would prove it. Six of us hired a car to take us the hour or so to Atlantic City and we're wearing our uniforms. We get to the club and as they're about to seat us, I tell the maitre'd that Gary is my buddy, and I think he moved us up a little closer to the stage. I asked the maitre'd if he would tell Mr. Bonds that Curtis from Norfolk was at the show. I'm sure he would have preferred a tip, but we were service guys. About 10 minutes before Gary goes on there is a round of drinks heading our way, 'Complimentary, from Mr. Bonds.' Well I was feeling rich and my service buddies toasted me and my friend Mr. Bonds, but I think one or two may still have had doubts. Gary comes out and he's doing his show and the crowd is really into it. He goes into, 'Copy Cat,' and at the part in the song where he starts calling people copy cats he works my name into the song and gives me a shout-out and a big grin from the stage. I felt great and when he joined us after the show it was like I was the celebrity. The ride home to Fort Dix was a chance for me to do some bragging."

Curtis has told that story at every party we've ever been to since 1962, but I need to finally confess to Curtis about the shout-out. Curtis, I love you and that was a great night, during a great week for me, but when I sang "Curtis," it is actually in the lyric. I sing it on the record and I don't think they had you in mind when they wrote it. If you're still in touch with your Army buddies, maybe you can tell them to skip this part of the book, but I just needed you to know.

I'll let Laurie describe the beginning of our courtship. "They didn't see much of Gary in Wildwood that week other than during his shows. By the end of the week we shared that both our managers had changed our names (Laurie, actually Luz Celeste had recorded as Lucy Rivera) and we both confessed as to what our real names were. I asked Gary about his middle name, Levohn, as I was unfamiliar with it. Gary went on and on about his manager Frank Guida, and his band and in particular, Daddy G. He told me about touring Europe, but he never mentioned that he had done a movie which had not yet come out. At the beginning Slow Drag never left his side, but as Gary's week in Wildwood was ending Slow Drag knew that we needed some private time. Slow Drag carried his money, drove him, handled his laundry and ran errands. The record company managed his money and his agent did his bookings. But he was still living with his mother, and I found that funny because of the sophisticated, worldly image he tried to project. I asked him if he had ever been to Brooklyn and he told me he had. The mother of one of his friends from Norfolk lived in Brooklyn and when Gary was playing the Apollo she insisted that he stay in Brooklyn. Gary told me that he would visit me at home when I finished my work in Atlantic City."

Not long after Laurie finished her shows at the Bamboo I drove to Brooklyn. Williamsburg was not like Norfolk. It had a different kind of diversity. As Laurie explained it to me, Williamsburg was a place where in the '50s and '60s, Puerto Ricans, Italians, African-Americans and Hassidic Jews lived in peace. But it was similar to Norfolk in that there were sections, but the divisions were more ethnic than racial.

I met Laurie's mom and dad, Delia and Isabello. If there was an issue concerning my race it was not apparent to me. Laurie's father was a laborer, but his background in Puerto Rico was agriculture and he was successful both here and there. He was a good provider, with a love for race horses that always seemed to be not fast enough. They lived on Marcy Avenue, in what landlords called a "taxpayer," usually a two or three story building which had a store at the street level and apartments on top. Williamsburg was noisier than Norfolk, with an overhead subway called the "el" and streets which were packed with people, both newly arrived immigrants and families that had lived in the area for two generations. The Italians had arrived first, followed by the Hassidic Jews, many from Hungary and Poland who had escaped the Holocaust. Puerto Ricans were the newest arrivals. There were factory jobs available and affordable housing. A busy shopping area centered around Broadway (Brooklyn), and Marcy Avenue was where families did their everyday marketing. The area was 40 years away from becoming fashionable.

Her family was a traditional one, where customs were maintained and both Spanish and English were spoken. Her mother and father were especially welcoming, and the Cedeños were comfortable being around musicians and singers and had accepted their daughter's vocation and friends. They could not help noticing my flashy car and clothes, but I was soft spoken and polite. There was no translation required for them to understand that I had quickly fallen in love with their daughter. I slept on the sofa and drove back to Norfolk the next day.

Two weeks later I invited Laurie to come to Norfolk. I wanted her to meet my mother and grandmother and friends. We had not discussed marriage, in fact I don't recall saying the "m" word, but Mother never heard me talk about a woman the way I went on about Laurie. Love blinded me to Mom's coolness. Laurie and I were prepared to marry but my mother was not anxious to see that day. Upon meeting her, my mom was not hostile to Laurie, but she couldn't hide the fact that even though I was 23 she was not ready to let go. She was still laying out my clothes and she let Laurie know how she still catered to me. While it was unsaid, I believe mother could never accept our racial differences. She would have preferred that I bring home a proper, light skinned black woman. Laurie said she felt Mom looked at her as a "foreigner."

Frank needed me back in the studio, and the failure of "Copy Cat" was fresh in my mind. We agreed that the Twist was not likely to continue into 1963 when these records would be released. I was also against going back to a Calypso theme; he was not. Frank had a song, a Calypso number he reworked. He said the original went back to the '30s, but he had changed it substantially so he could take a writing credit and publish it. He played for me what I first thought was a demo. It was sung by "Wonder Boy," Jimmy McCleese, known as Jimmy Soul since he scored with the "Matilda" song. It was closer to a Calypso number than my Twist records, and clearly done Norfolk style, but I didn't hear Daddy G on the record. It had a steel band sound from some kind of organ. I didn't care for the lyric. I thought it was outrageous and might be insulting to the mothers of the 16 year old girls who bought and danced to my records. It was not what I wanted to do and I didn't know if he was offering it to me. But I listened a second and third time and the song was catchy and had the same spontaneous, party sound of our earliest records. I saw how hot Frank was on the record. I sensed he wanted to serve it up to Bernie Lowe and Cameo Parkway and dare them to copy it. Frank had called in an outside band to record it and that disturbed me.

They were a band from Newport News that had backed Otis Redding who played the area frequently. Bill Deal played organ and Frank would wind up recording his band some years later. After the dispute over Dion's "Runaround Sue," Guida had no desire to put it out on Legrand, which was distributed by Laurie Records. Jimmy's records were on S.P.Q.R., one of Frank's other labels, and S.P.Q.R. had a deal with London and that gave Guida distribution here and abroad. I passed on "If You Wanna Be Happy," but I told Frank I would have Daddy G come into the studio to do the sax solo. If you listen carefully my voice can also be heard in the background.

I passed on what turned out to be Guida's last big record, a Calypso record, a remake of Roaring Lion's "Ugly Woman." It got the angry frustrated former Calypso singer as close to the microphone as he could get. Jimmy Soul was no threat to Guida, and Guida could take all the credit for this one. Having passed on the big one, I recorded "Do the Limbo with Me."

Photographs

Bound for the "biz" at age 5.

All photos courtesy of Anderson Family Collection except where noted.

Mom, "Miss Irene," my first fan.

Pop, Principal Anderson, he never left school.

Photographs

Bonnie McGeachin at her Plaza Hotel. Mom took me there to meet my idols.

Showing some leg at Virginia Beach.

The Turks, our only surviving photo. Backing me up (l to r) Dee-Dee (Melvin McNair), Frissell, and Moose (Thomas High).
Courtesy Frissell Coleman

Gary Anderson pleasing the crowd.

Photographs

GARY U.S. BONDS

An early headshot.

By U.S. Bonds — That's My Story

An Apollo appearance as "U.S. Bonds," warming the crowd for the Drifters.

Photographs

At the hop with newly-named Jimmy Soul (l).

Deli owner and patriot Elias Codd, responsible for my name.
Collection of Norfolk Public Library

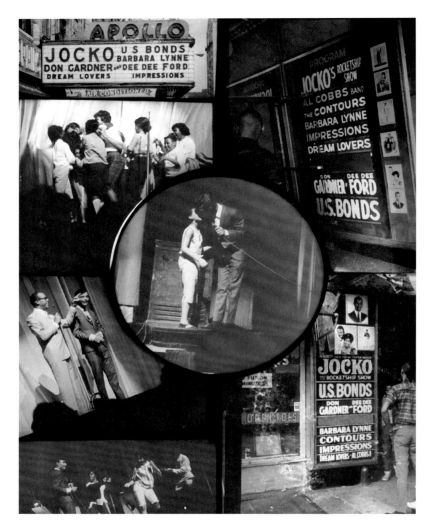

Headlining for Jocko at the Apollo.

Photographs

Singing their hit, "United," the Love Notes.

By U.S. Bonds — That's My Story

A treasured inscription from Big Mama.

My beloved with legendary hit-maker Richard Barrett.

Photographs

Newly married, 1963.

Little Mama's christening. My arm around Jack, Big Mama's nephew.

With Norfolk friends: (l to r) Charles Wallace, Avon Alexander, Bill "Boobie" Foreman, Yvonne Johnson, me, "Little Walter" Johnson.

Photographs

Proud grandparents, my in-laws, (l to r) Isabello and Delia.

Great Grandma Margaret Newkirk, (l to r) Big Mama, holding Little Mama, Mom.

A new look to welcome the British Invasion.

Photographs

Taking to the road, (l to r) Doug Rolle, keyboard, Jean Beauvoir, bass, Tom Lafferty, guitar, Babe Pace, drums.

By U.S. Bonds — That's My Story

GARY U.S. BONDS

Trying to get with that boogie-oogie-oogie.

Photographs

A lot of hair and attitude, with my band Taxi. (l to r) Steve Musso, Pat Adkins, me, Bobby Kibbler, Frank Apollo.

By U.S. Bonds — That's My Story

A recognition from BMI, (l to r) Frank Guida, me, BMI rep and Gene "Daddy G" Barge.

Little Mama with Johnny Paycheck. He took my song "Friend Don't Take Her" to the CMAs.

Photographs

Little Mama and her friend Bruce Springsteen
waiting for the school bus.

By U.S. Bonds — That's My Story

Singing with a guy from Jersey.

Photographs

Looking out from the back of the tour truck with
band member Babe Pace.

Telling the "Big Man" (Clarence Clemons) where I got my hat.
Courtesy Mark Weiss

Congratulating a newly-signed artist. I hold my smallest fan, Brandy.
Courtesy of Mark Weiss

Friend, musician, actor, composer, producer – multi-talented Steven Van Zandt.

Photographs

Must be Easter. Little Mama has her bonnet.

Back on American Bandstand, "Dedication."
Courtesy Dick Clark Productions

From US Magazine photo shoot for *Dedication* tour.
Courtesy of Mark Weiss

Cameo Parkway had Chubby Checker record a vocal version of The Champs' instrumental, "Limbo Rock," written by West Coast guitarist and session player Billy Strange. Strange was a member of the "Wrecking Crew," that group of West Coast session players who backed everyone from the Beach Boys to Sinatra, both Frank and Nancy. Strange's song gave The Champs another instrumental, a follow up to "Tequila." By adding lyrics, Cameo Parkway took the same formula that worked for the Dovells when they did a vocal version of Phil Upchurch's instrumental "You Can't Sit Down." Chubby scored with his vocal about a dance tradition that started in Trinidad. Although the traditional dance was performed at wakes, "Limbo Rock," was yet another successful upbeat dance record for Chubby. It was one of the rare ones that climbs the charts, settles and then ascends again, this time all the way to #2 and it was still on the charts as we went into 1963. My record, "Do the Limbo with Me," was not played and the "B" side "Where Did That Naughty Little Girl Go" was a throw back to our earliest records. Jimmy Soul's record, "If You Wanna Be Happy," did not chart in 1962 when it was released, but it wound up charting in March of 1963, dropped off the list and then roared back with two weeks at #1 in May of 1963.

When I bought the house in Green Hill Farms there was no reason for me to believe that it wasn't going to be temporary, an interim step before something bigger and grander. I didn't know exactly how much I was making from recordings because Frank was taking care of that, but I had gotten some additional checks and my income from personal appearances was ratcheting up with every hit record. Mom deserved something better. I was gone most of the time and I wanted her to be in the best possible neighborhood. Green Hill Farms was a better area.

When I bought the place Frank gave me an advance for the required down payment. In early 1962 the hits were coming effortlessly and I had no fear of affording it. It was a substantial house on a block of newer homes with mostly professional people and business owners. Then the block was mostly white, while it is two thirds black now. Blame it on me. I was aware that I would be in the minority, but

I was not that concerned. Mom and Mimms moved into the house, but Grandma and Newkirk bought a larger old house near where Norfolk State University is today, and they started taking in boarders.

Laurie recalled March of 1963, "I remember the proposal. Gary called me and said, 'Why don't we do that thing?' It was vague, but I knew what he meant. He could command the attention of a thousand strangers and touch their emotions with a song, but in proposing there was nothing that hinted at romance or a love that could last 50 years and counting. I told him I would move to Norfolk because I knew he would not leave. He had bought a house, his mom and grandmother lived there and that's where he recorded. Frank Guida was there and so were his musicians. I told my mom and dad that Gary had proposed and we were going to get married. I told them I wanted to go to Norfolk. Gary and Slow Drag arrived in Brooklyn the next day. I took my dad and one small suitcase and we headed back to Norfolk."

With my bride beside me, my best friend at the wheel, and my future father-in-law in front, our plan was to get to Norfolk by nightfall. It's a full day's drive, but we couldn't make it nonstop and needed at least one meal to hold us. Unfortunately, on the trip home we would encounter as a couple our first instance of racial discrimination. In 1963 in the South, you could still find signs at water fountains and restaurants indicating where blacks and whites were welcome. We stopped at a small roadside restaurant that lacked signage, but the counter man made it clear that our party was not going to be served. Slow Drag and I had experienced this before. It was the first time for Laurie and her dad. I apologized to them for the stupidity.

Hungry and tired, as a couple we entered the house on Sedgefield Drive for the first time. Big Mama reminded me, "There was a little party going on. Westbrook, Jelly and Frissell, Ba-Bee and some girls and us. Gary said, 'C'mon let's go.' He had called a justice of the peace and we left with my dad. The justice of the peace was there with his wife and she was also a witness. Gary presented me with a ring his mother had helped him pick out. No rice, no flowers, no wedding gown, but an embrace that's held us together all these years."

We got back from the justice of the peace and rejoined the party at what was now our house. Some of our guests knew where we had gone and others did not. I held a glass up high and told the guests that Laurie had a new name and it was mine. There was a whoop of joy, handshakes, backslaps and high fives and the celebration was shared with Mom and Mimms, Isabello and all of my friends from Norfolk, the friends we have to this day. I told Laurie we would drive back to Brooklyn the next day to pack up her belongings, and then return to Norfolk. We were anxious to start a life of our own.

Laurie liked the house. It was a split-level of reddish brick, with two bedrooms on the first floor and an upstairs den. The house was impressive, well-manicured with a rolling lawn in front and an attached garage and carport just big enough for my newest Cadillac. The backyard was spacious and the widest part of the pie-shaped lot. When I bought the house I looked forward to doing some of the gardening and maintenance. I enjoy working with tools and I've taught myself how to do basic plumbing and electrical work. I promised myself and Laurie that I would try to do some performing locally and enjoy our home, but in this business it is impossible to predict or control where you work.

One thing that required no adjustment was Laurie's cooking. She told me that she enjoyed cooking both American and Spanish dishes and I immediately started gaining weight. Laurie accommodated my preference for foods that were highly spiced and in Norfolk the seafood, my favorite, was plentiful. Laurie took pride in her cooking and we have never had a houseguest leave disappointed or hungry. What we did discover was that Laurie needed to learn how to drive. "No problem, I'll teach you," and I committed to showing her how.

I called Frank to let him know that I had gotten married and he knew it was the young lady I met during the week in Atlantic City. He offered congratulations and we scheduled a time when we all could meet. He let us know that we were going back into the studio. I tried to keep it upbeat so I didn't bring up the last few records which bombed. I was praying that we could get back our creativity and I put it on my list to call Daddy G. Privately, Frank let me know that they were working on another European tour for the fall. I wasn't anxious to tell Laurie, and it was not definite.

I let Laurie know that I had anxiety about the upcoming sessions. She understood completely how tough it is to make and sell a record, and we needed hit records to support my live performance income. Laurie had some bad luck with her own solo career. Back in 1957 she sang on a regional hit which appeared on the R&B charts with her group the Love Notes. The strength of their song, "United," got them regular work, not only at the Apollo, but at the same theaters that I worked. After doing some touring the Love Notes broke up. However, 18-year-old Laurie Cedeño was noticed and she was signed by End Records producer Richard Barrett. He was best known for his great success with Frankie Lymon, the Chantels and Little Anthony. The label gave her one song which she recorded as Lucy Rivera, but they also gave the song to the Chantels. They did not push her record. The last time she recorded was 1961 with an answer song to the Miracles' "Shop Around" called "Don'cha Shop Around," which was written by Barrett. Motown liked their lawyers as much as Guida liked his. The Motown lawyers prevailed and the record was pulled.

I headed back to work and Laurie did her best to build a relationship with my mother and Mimms. Her efforts would be unsuccessful.

Eight

"CITY JAIL, CITY FARM"

I TAUGHT LAURIE TO DRIVE, BUT ANY man who has tried it knows that it can put a strain on a marriage, especially when it is new, but Laurie learned quickly. But there were two things that continued to be unsettling: the neighbors and Mom. The two problems had some common roots. Green Hill Farms was predominantly white, but after Mom and I moved there we started to see some changes which both of us felt good about. We started to see a few houses turning over, with middle income black families buying homes from older white families, many of whom were original residents going back to when the area was developed.

Laurie did not find the old or new neighbors too accepting of her. She found her neighborly efforts were rejected, and coming from a place where Puerto Ricans, Italians, African Americans and Hassidic Jews figured out how to get along, this was troubling to her. The neighbors didn't quite have a handle on what she "was." Her coloration could lead you to believe she was "different," but it was only on close inspection that you might see some features which suggested

Hispanic. There were few Hispanics in Norfolk, and I was not aware of any Puerto Ricans. Her looks proved bothersome to just about everyone. It was compounded by the fact that her new husband was black, a celebrity and presumably affluent.

This was magnified by Mom's coolness towards Laurie, which would escalate to hostility when I was out on the road. The hostility was amplified when Mom would drink, and the drinking would start when I would leave for a job. Laurie explained to me that her "otherness" wasn't the only thing which troubled Mom. When Mom's inhibitions were down, she let Laurie know that she never stopped loving Pop, and if not for the iron will of Grandma, they might still be together. Mom clung to me, her only connection to the man she loved with whom I shared a name. She lost him, and was not going to lose me. Laurie intruded into Mom's life which was dominated by her mother for whom she hid a deeply concealed resentment. Drink would set that resentment free and Laurie became the target of her anger. This was made more difficult by my being away so often. It was not unusual for me to return home from the road to find Laurie in tears and Mom in her room. I knew why.

Laurie also felt that when she went out of the house, local law enforcement was always nearby, not harassing or menacing, but lurking. It made her uncomfortable, especially when she was driving. Some days she felt that she was getting a police escort for her 10 minute drive to the supermarket.

This discomfort could be contrasted with the warmth and support she was getting from my friends. To say that Laurie was adopted by my friends would be an understatement. She was embraced, and her greatest advocates were my gay friends. She was given the high honor of being named one of the "Children of the Round Table," a select group which would meet in "Little Walter's" kitchen. They admired her looks and fashion sense, and when we would go out and Laurie would be all dressed up, I could've stayed home. They were sympathetic to her feelings and tried to get Mom to understand how much I loved Laurie and that I didn't now love Mom any less. There was little they could do about the neighbors. My friends did not live in Green Hill Farms, but they were from Norfolk where generations have had to deal with the racial divide. My friends probably felt uncomfortable when they came to Sedgefield Drive, but they would never say anything. A mixed couple in a white Norfolk neighborhood in transition could be the target of outrage.

The outrage boiled over and was reported in the *New Journal and Guide* on March 9, 1963:

"The youthful recording artist became entangled in the tolls of the law some days ago when his car struck a dog belonging to a neighbor in the Green Hill Farms section. Bonds' neighbors in the community which is now in transition racially are White and the fact that a high powered, ultra modern costly automobile driven by an Ivy League clad colored person whose repute reaches beyond the confines of the neighborhood, city and state had struck a white dog was apparently a bitter pill to swallow. Charges were immediately forthcoming."

With Earl Swanson in the front passenger seat, I was making a left turn off of Sedgefield Drive. I heard the voice of a woman who was chasing my car on foot. I couldn't make out what she was saying so I stopped the car. The woman said I needed to go to her house so she could call the police because she claimed I ran over her dog. She was not interested in Earl. When I got into her house I met her husband, who anticipating my arrival, had located his shotgun. He said it would discourage me from running off. This was odd because he recognized me and knew I lived on the block. The police arrived. The woman explained to them that I had run over her dog. She didn't say the dog was white, as the paper would report. Her husband put down the shotgun as the police dismissed Earl and invited me to join them with a, "N----r, shut up and get in the car."

They asked me for my license, but I did not have it with me. I rarely carried a wallet, and I rarely drove myself. It's a bad habit, and I was caught once before in Norfolk for driving without a license. I protested. I had no idea what the woman was talking about, as I never saw her dog and didn't hit anything. I was taken downtown to the police precinct and put into a holding pen. They said the judge would be down in a few hours. I was allowed to call Frank and I told him to tell Laurie that I would be home soon. The judge showed up in an hour and said I would need to stay overnight. A hearing would be held the next day.

I loved the City of Norfolk despite its ugliest parts, and some of the backward, bigoted people. I considered my being held as a way for my neighbors to let me know that they didn't like where I lived or the person I married. I told Frank I would stay the night and he got me a lawyer. My friends showed up the next day for the hearing. Lucille was there and she reminded me, "That Judge Hitchings was no fan. Never heard of you, and said he didn't care if you were Gary U.S. Bonds and the only U.S. Bonds in Norfolk was Elias Codd." Judge Hitchings was an admirer of Mr. Codd who indirectly gave me my name. The judge was aware that our government recognized Codd's efforts to sell War Bonds. When my lawyer said that I was given a citation at a bond rally in Harrisburg the year before, Judge Hitchings was not moved. My lawyer then asked my neighbor about her dog and where it was. When she could not describe it, or explain its current condition, Hitchings lost patience with both of us. He dismissed the charge of wreckless driving, but said my prior arrest for driving without a license warranted a ten day stay in the city work farm.

Judge Hitchings ordered me released after six days of the 10 day sentence. Six days for running over an imaginary dog! I met some interesting people at the work farm. A lot of them were music fans and some of them could sing. There were also some who felt the same way about me as our neighbors in Green Hill Farms. My fans at the work farm took care of me. I made the best of it, and Frank Guida saw an opportunity. Whether he thought it was a way to send a message to the City of Norfolk, or a way to sell some records, he hastily put a song together with Joe Royster called "City Jail, City Farm," and gave it to a group called Francois and the Anglos, who recorded for his Romulus Records. It did not sell inside or outside of the City Farm.

At the Farm I had a lot of time to think and I was deeply troubled, but publicly, after my release, I treated the incident lightly. Frank said it was purely a local matter and the publicity might even help my career. I was more concerned about Laurie. She knew this was as much about her as me. She wanted to take matters into her own hands and make a call to some friends from Brooklyn who had their own way of dealing with the justice system. What happened to me could have happened to her and I regretted making light of her complaining about being watched. Norfolk may have changed some, but not enough to allow me to peacefully live where I wanted to and enjoy the benefits of my hard work.

If there was any hard work, it was my club work. I only cut four records in 1963, with just one showing some imagination, "Perdido," a jazz standard originally done as an instrumental by the Ellington Band. It had also been recorded by Sarah Vaughan and Ella Fitzgerald. It was a song that would work in a supper club and possibly take me in another direction. "Perdido" and the other three failed to sell and it didn't seem to bother Frank. I also noticed that I needed to ask him about the checks that were getting smaller every week. My records were not selling, and he didn't have time for me in this, the most successful year of his career. Not only did "Wonder Boy," Jimmy Soul's, "If You Wanna Be Happy," become Frank's biggest hit, he also reaped the benefits of a song that I wrote, "Not Me." My version looked promising two years back, and it sold, but not nearly the amount it would have done if the radio stations hadn't been convinced that it was either too violent or too suggestive.

In two years musical tastes must have changed. "Not Me," bubbled under for Cameo Parkway's "Orlons" on June 8, at which time "If You Wanna Be Happy," had already charted for seven weeks. "Not Me," climbed to #12 and went on to spend 14 weeks on the charts. Jimmy Soul would have two weeks at #1. It might as well have been Frank's last record. Just three years after I stepped into a recording studio for the first time, Frank would never have another hit.

Guida would be celebrated by his peers for his accomplishments in 1963. Publicly and graciously at an industry gala he would accept the toasts of Sam Phillips, Jerry Wexler, Ahmet Ertegun, Syd Nathan, Bernie Lowe, Kal Mann, and the Chess Brothers. Privately, Frank said the whole bunch should have been ashamed of their thievery, and they were too cowardly to admit that it all started in Norfolk.

Frank would no longer need me or Jimmy Soul. When Frank held the microphone he failed, but when he gave it to us, against all odds, we succeeded. It was his Calypso, his number one, and with the admiration of his peers he could now leave the schoolyard a victor. He could stay in Norfolk, build a fence around his studio and be secure in his legacy. He knew how to eat for 20 years off of one hit record, and now he had a bunch, and he would eat well. He could slice and dice and repackage all that we did those three years and it would always be new to someone and it would sell. He would try something new, but none of it was. If the high school song worked, he'd try a song about beaches. If New Orleans scored, why not try Los Angeles. He'd try a song about an ugly woman, a good woman, a bad woman and even "Rufus the Little Black Elf." He was copying those who had copied us and he was doing it poorly. After 1963 there would be no more opportunities for Frank Guida, and few for me for a very long time.

Amidst the gloom there was sunshine and joy and news that would take our minds off recent hard times. We forgot about Norfolk and the tension in the Anderson household. Laurie announced she was expecting. She told me she was due in May. I needed to start earning.

I agreed to three weeks in Europe with two of those weeks in England. I would be working for England's most aggressive promoter, Don Arden (actually Harry Levy) who was managing Gene Vincent at the time. Don's daughter, Sharon Levy, is known these days as Sharon Osbourne, ever since she married her father's former client. Don put me in a multi-act show which included Gene Vincent, Duane Eddy, the Shirelles and Mickie Most who later produced the Animals and Herman's Hermits. The Shirelles backed me up vocally. While the crowds were enthusiastic, things were about to change forever. The Beatles had dominated the English charts since early 1963. "She Loves You" had sold one million singles and "I Want to Hold Your Hand" had pre-orders of almost the same amount.

I returned to Norfolk. We recorded and released Legrand #1032, Gary U.S. Bonds singing "The Music Goes Round and Round," a hit for Tommy Dorsey in 1936, but not for me. "I Want to Hold Your Hand," entered the charts at #45 in mid January, rose to #3 a week later, and then #1. The Beatles would hold the #1 spot for 14 weeks. They would give up that spot only for the Animals, Manfred Mann, the Supremes and the Beach Boys, but they would take it back and keep it for a long, long, time.

I told Big Mama I was done with recording. I never discussed leaving Frank, but these records we were making were dismal. Frank might have sensed that I was displeased with Legrand and he frequently reminded me that we had a contract. Laurie continued to encourage me, and remained optimistic with the hope that next year might be as successful as the two previous years. She would tell me, "Gary I believe in your talent, but it is more important that I believe in you. I know you will figure this all out."

Daddy G packed his horn and moved to Chicago to join Chess Records as a producer. Joe Royster was selling Florsheim shoes when he dropped his shoe horn, packed his guitar and headed south, then west, and then where we just don't know. Great and talented men, they were no longer needed. One survived and thrived and the other we think not. Guida needed them no more. The work he offered, they did not want to do, and the sound they helped create was not theirs. Jimmy Soul was not happy for the rest of his short life, and it was not the fault of a pretty woman.

Daddy G left, his talent too great to waste on "The Music Goes Round and Round." He left his classroom and Legrand to record Howlin' Wolf and Muddy Waters. When Chess was sold he spent some time at Stax and then became a horn for hire. Mick Jagger had met him when the Rolling Stones recorded at Chess Studios and they invited him to join the band for their 1982 European tour. Barge stayed in Chicago where he lives and plays today and still records. He's done some movies, produced for Natalie Cole and if you're in Chicago you can probably catch one of his bands playing loud and fast.

Joe Royster could write a great country song and some day I'll do "New Orleans" the way he wrote it. Joe wasn't getting paid either. He was just 30 when he left Norfolk and he had plenty of songs left in him, but he had a weakness for some bad habits. I'd hear from him sporadically. He had a tough marriage to Lu Faye and they divorced in 1970, leaving behind his two boys, Tim and Joe. Tim was 10 when his parents divorced. Tim told me he saw his father for the last time in July of 1970. His dad was moving some furniture from the house. When he finished he went to the car and got a baseball and mitt and gave them both to Tim. He told his son he loved him and walked away. Joe Royster headed for Florida where he lived for a year and then he spent some time in Las Vegas. His mother was contacted when he passed a bad check there and his family never heard from him again.

I got a call from Joe. He was in Nashville. It was about 1974. I hadn't heard from him in a while, and didn't know he was missing. I knew he had issues and I wanted to help. I told him to come to our house in Long Island and stay for a while. From his voice I could tell he was not well. He said he would come and called with the time he'd get into the bus station in Melville. I went there to meet him. When the bus pulled in the driver got out and opened the lower panel of the Greyhound where they stow luggage. He pulled out a couple of bags including one with Joe's name on it. It was plaid, red and black. I waited for Joe to get off the bus and figured I would have no trouble recognizing him, even though it had been 10 years. I didn't see him so I went inside the small terminal thinking I may have missed him. There were no passengers there from Nashville. I went back out to the bus and saw the driver pick up Joe's suitcase and load it back on the bus. Fifteen minutes later the bus pulled out. The number I had for him in Nashville wasn't his.

Tim told me his grandmother continued to get royalty checks, which she said she put away for him and his brother. "Sometimes Nana would say, 'Do you mind if I use some of it?' We never said no. This went on from 1973 to 1997 and then she died. The money was all gone. BMI was holding a bunch of Dad's money after that. Guida would also send Nana $1,200 a year. He said it was royalties, but we never knew what for. Occasionally we would get a lead, someone saying that they spotted him, but it always turned out to be nothing. As much as you'd like to think he was gonna come back, you reach the point where you know it's not happening and all you want is some closure."

Tim and his brother moved in that direction in 2002 when their attorneys were successful in obtaining a death certificate for their dad who had not been heard from in almost 30 years. The money that BMI was holding they split, but Frank Guida's checks stopped coming when their grandmother died.

The boys got closure and I pray some peace. Elmwood Cemetery in Granville County, North Carolina has been the final resting place for Roysters since 1893. At Section M56 there is an empty grave, with a fine and well-deserved memorial to a good and talented man who gave me a song. I'll never know if he ever made it to New Orleans.

My records failed and Frank Guida became more distant. The money that was held for me was not spoken about and the checks were smaller and less frequent. He would release singles which were unfit for release years ago. I continued to work and the rooms became smaller and the offers were shrinking. Frank tried to convince us that the money he was holding was all gone. It was spent on me, bad records, promotion and the cost of making those sounds that changed the world.

Our daughter we would name Laurie, but we'd call her "Little Mama." I'd been calling her mom, "Moma" for some time, and this way people could tell whom I was speaking about. She was born at Norfolk General Hospital on May 6, healthy and beautiful. We prepared a room for her at the house on Sedgefield, but as proud as we were bringing her home, we knew we could not continue to afford the house. As money got tighter the tension between Laurie and Mom escalated. There were fewer places where people wanted to listen to my music.

Just a year or so since my last charting record and less than three years since my biggest hits, I was playing for the "door." That meant the club owner provided no guarantee. I would bring my band and if people showed up we got paid. On way too many nights I needed to borrow gas money from my guys. British bands were in short supply, so American kids would grow long hair, learn three chords and try to do a Cockney accent. They got work.

Black music became centered around Detroit, and Motown got rid of the grit and funk and tapped into the white teen market that had treated me so well. The Beach Boys and Four Seasons survived and with Roy Orbison they did their best to keep American music on the charts. My records survived on John Lennon's personal jukebox, but they were records from '60 and '61.

We called a local real estate agent and told them we couldn't handle the expense of the house on Sedgefield Drive. We sent them the keys, packed, and told them to get whatever they could. I would have called Guida, but I was just as happy to let it go. We found some subsidized housing in Portsmouth. I hesitate to call it a "project," and it did not look like one, but it was. We moved into an apartment. This area was not in transition. The only transition was for the Andersons. We went from a comfortable but hostile middle class mixed neighborhood, to a poor black one. We were as poor as the others. We just had different jobs, and I did a movie and had a #1 record not too long ago. It didn't matter. It was in a development called Bonnevilla Apartments, and for the first time in my life I was not living with my mother. Mom and Mimms went to live with Grandma.

Laurie remembered these hard times, "Some things stayed the same and Gary and I didn't stop trying to take care of everyone else's problems. Slow Drag and the boys still hung on to Gary. They didn't ask for anything, but Gary would sometimes forget that it wasn't 1961. We lived next door to a family that was also scraping to get by. We didn't see the husband too often. He worked at the shipyard in Norfolk and preferred the women there. His wife would go with me to the supermarket. I would have just enough to buy a pack of hot dogs and we would boil them up and I'd share them with her. I had an extra one when Gary was on the road."

I would spend days on the phone begging agents and searching out friends who had given me work. The calls were not returned or when they were, I'd hear a tale of woe that was sadder than my own. Guys I'd see on the road would call. I'd hear about showbands that had four jobs a week that were now down to one.

I was thrilled to get a call about a job at a place called The Barn on 79th Street in Miami. My records did well in Miami, and in-season owners liked to book acts that were familiar to their customers who were visiting from New York and New Jersey. Whenever I played South Florida, there was no shortage of familiar faces from up north. The Barn was better than most clubs, not quite up to the Diplomat or Newport hotel showrooms, but a hipper room with some younger faces, the type I would see at the Castaways in Sunny Isles, in North Miami Beach. We were booked for a week and the engagement started on a Tuesday and ran through Sunday, with three sets every night.

I took five players and two girl singers and arrived on Monday for the run through. My own songs would be played between current hits with "Quarter to Three" saved for the end. We did the whole Motown songbook, some Twist music and my take on Percy Sledge's "When a Man Loves a Woman." The engagement was not memorable until my second set on Friday night when we were almost at capacity. I saw someone in the crowd by the bar who was causing a stir. Although the spotlights made it difficult to see details, I saw the back of what appeared to be a guy in a jumpsuit with at least a foot and a half of platinum pompadour.

As I started the second set and my horn player was doing a solo, he made his way towards the stage and asked if he could come up and do a number with me. I had no idea who he was, but there was a buzz in the room and I figured everyone was as impressed as I was with his hair. He came up on stage, and in what seemed like a very hoarse, deep, southern accent said, "Can't Turn You Loose." We knew the Otis Redding number and I called the song out to my musical director. My new partner grabbed the mike and waited for the bass to kick off the song. His voice wasn't big, but he could dance and scream and with the jumpsuit and platinum hair, all eyes were on him.

We stretched the song and the crowd did not want him to leave, and I didn't mind. I asked him his name and the crowd was fully standing as he left the stage. His performance impressed me and I wanted to talk to that guy with the hair, but when I finished my set he was gone.

Saturday it was nearly the same thing. This time, before the last set of the evening, someone came backstage and told me Wayne Cochran wanted to come up again and that he had one of his guys with him. I didn't mind, I figured this time I would let him do a song by himself, and enjoy the break. I get on stage and Wayne comes up with a jeweled satin cape that got more applause than my previous two sets combined. He brought up his guy who grabbed a guitar and I introduced, "My good buddy Wayne Cochran." Next thing I know, five more of his guys take to the stage and they're all wearing matching jumpsuits. They borrowed our instruments and Wayne counts off "Can't Turn You Loose." He's shrieking and spinning and dancing on his "good foot" and I learned why the "White Knight of Soul" was starting to be known as the "White James Brown."

Wayne did three songs. My stage had been seized by musical pirates and the crowd was happy about the ambush. He was kind enough to turn the mike back to me but my "Quarter to Three," lacked steam that night. We were cancelled the next day, and Wayne Cochran took over for a three week run. It was the start of his taking South Florida by storm and once Jackie Gleason gave him a slot on national television, the "White Knight" and his "C.C. Riders" were the hottest showband in all major markets despite their lacking a hit record. Wayne had a great run and I loved his act, and his success at The Barn led to his owning the place. But Wayne never did return the favor and I never saw the stage at The Barn again.

Laurie was unshaken by my dismissal from Miami, and never complained about running out of diapers or struggling to make dinner. I'd go to Grandma's. She bought chickens in bulk for her boarding house and supplied us with a chicken a week. I blamed myself for not watching the money or asking questions. On the street corner I said that all I wanted to do was sing and I had done that. I didn't realize that singing came with responsibility once it was your livelihood. I never felt I had leverage, and when I got it everything had changed. Dick Clark had to scramble to get into the British band business, and Cameo Parkway stayed afloat by leasing a couple of British records. Great singers were driving cabs and groups broke up to take straight jobs. I knew guys doing construction and others who went into civil service. Guys succumbed to the bottle and needle and others just checked out.

Unable to find regular work, I was helpless and desperate. I had started driving the interstates where I'd park my Cadillac on the shoulder of the road so I could get out and pick up empties that had been tossed from passing cars. I'd take them to the supermarket and collect the deposit money and bring home some groceries. Sometimes the bottle money would be short and I'd sneak out of the market with food hidden under my shirt. I remember walking into the house one afternoon and startling Laurie when she thought that I was bleeding around the chest. I had taken a large steak from the market and the "blood" from the meat had penetrated the wrapping and my shirt. We hadn't had too many steaks lately, but we discovered that stolen meat is hard to digest.

It was difficult for me not to think about our financial problems. But when I did get a job, I would do the gig and forget about money as soon as I hit the stage. I would play for five or 50 people and let them know how happy I was that they turned out. It was the same show I did for Don Arden, and the same show I did for Dick Clark just months ago. Guida coped. He convinced himself that it was his music they were bringing back from Liverpool. And he could prove it.

We were not the only struggling music family on the block. Our neighbor Jerry was in the business. Jerry Williams had recorded a couple of times, once for LOMA Records a label that started in 1964 when Warner Brothers tried to get into the soul music business, and a few records for Calla Records owned by Nate McCalla, an associate and one-time employee of Roulette Records owner, Morris "Moishe" Levy. Jerry not only saw himself as a singer/songwriter, but also as a budding producer and record exec. He would wind up doing all of that, but first he wanted to move his family to New York City.

Big Mama lent him the $20 he was short to buy a bus ticket. As security, Jerry left his wedding ring.

While I threatened to look for "straight work," it wound up never happening, but Laurie felt we had no choice, she needed to go back on the road. Laurie hooked up with Bernard Purdie who put together a group called the New Century Platters. The group played mainly in Canada. We needed the money and wanted to get out of Norfolk. We found someone to watch Little Mama while we were both on the road and Big Mama stayed with the group for years. The additional income helped us out greatly. Big Mama had a hard time leaving our little girl and I felt bad about Big Mama having to go back to work, but I was grateful. We were committed to keeping our heads above water and leaving Norfolk.

Little Mama was growing bigger and more beautiful every day. As much as we loved her, we were fearful. We wanted nice things for her and a safe environment. She would be starting school before we knew it. Big Mama said, "I can't do this. We're making no progress here at all. I can't do this to our kid." She moved to Norfolk because it was what I wanted and she made the best of it. She worked her way through the hostility, both Mom's and the neighbor's, and visited me at a work farm. She went back out on the road singing to help us and never suggested that I do anything except my act. I could not disagree. It was time to move.

Nine

THAT'S ALL I GOT

FRANK RELEASED MY LAST LEGRAND record in 1968, a song I wrote called, "What a Crazy World." We had done it the year before and it was an appropriate name for my last Legrand record. In five years I went from being an often-copied hit-maker to a roadside scavenger, fleeing my hometown, and questioning the future of my career. In the same time I found my life's love and we started a family. I'd make that trade again.

Big Mama and I both kept working and we grew stronger as a couple, but we were barely making enough between us to handle the rent and food for three. It was time to pack the Cadillac and head for New York, to Brooklyn. All of this had happened before either of us had reached 30, but we agreed it was time for a new start. Big Mama had missed the best parts of my career, but she promised me that better days were coming as long as we kept trying.

I had kept in touch with our neighbor Jerry Williams since he left Portsmouth. He and his wife had rented an attached house in Queens near Laguardia Airport. Jerry could sound like whatever guy he heard singing last. He played keyboards and could do Wilson Pickett, Solomon Burke, or Joe Tex and sing a country ballad. We talked about working together, writing some songs and producing some records on which I would sing. Jerry could have become the next Berry Gordy or the other Berry Gordy. He could sing, develop talent and hustle. His one weakness was sharing. Whether you were in his band, a co-writer, a record label or a distributor, Jerry wanted it all and worked all the angles never letting fairness get in the way. He entered the business before me, both as a performer and producer. He was great at selling himself and his songs, but I had not yet discovered his greed. When we left for Brooklyn he still owed us the $20 Laurie gave him for his bus ticket.

We headed for Williamsburg. Laurie's family looked around and found us an apartment we could afford on Bedford Avenue, but what we really wanted to do was rent the other apartment in the building where her parents lived on Marcy Avenue. After living with my mother you'd think we might have learned something about living with parents that would have kept us from considering it again. But I was working and Laurie was going to continue singing with her group, so it would be a help with the babysitting to be near her family. I felt it would work because my acceptance by her family was genuine, and I could not anticipate them interfering in our relationship.

Although we left for Brooklyn with hope for a fresh start, I did not enjoy the trip. Despite Laurie's encouragement I felt defeated, and if Laurie shared my feelings she never showed it. I felt down about some of the jobs I needed to take, at places and prices that I would not have considered a few years back, and the phone was not ringing with offers. Norfolk had not been kind to Laurie, but she understood that it was my home and we stayed as long as we could. As far as leaving my friends, I think she was going to miss them more than me. Mom and Grandma were another story. They probably blamed our leaving Norfolk on Laurie.

I needed to find an agent who could devote some time to me. Frank Barsalona, who was my agent at General Artists, had gone into business for himself and founded Premier Talent Associates. With

Frank not only handling the Beatles early on, but also the Rolling Stones and Yardbirds, it was impossible for me to compete for his attention, but he did what he could. With Brooklyn as our new base, I was eking out a living at small clubs in Bay Ridge and Bensonhurst, the Jersey Shore and resorts upstate and in the Poconos.

If I wasn't using a house-band I'd pick up a drummer and sax player and hope that the job allowed me to pay them. My hits were more than five years old, but people thought of them as being older than that. The songs sounded as if they were from a different era, too old to be fresh and not old enough to be nostalgic, or so I thought. I also noticed that the crowds I was drawing were older. I didn't see 20-year-olds and high school kids at my appearances. We were doing our hits and they would request older songs from the '50s and we worked them into our act. When I would do multi-act shows, I didn't have to go beyond my hits. Doing two hours in a club meant I needed to do more, and since I was now a "black act" it was assumed that I could do the latest from Motown, James Brown and all the music coming out of Stax in Memphis.

I was learning to entertain and I hooked up with a group called Taxi. The guys told me that they originally called themselves Newspaper Taxi, which they borrowed from the opening line of a verse from the Beatles' "Lucy in the Sky with Diamonds." We became a showband, and our repertoire was heavy on numbers that were danceable. Taxi consisted of Steve Muso on guitar, Frank Apollo on keyboard, Lenny Suma on bass, and Pat Atkins on drums. We worked up some routines which included comedy bits which helped us stretch the musical content to fit the two hour sets we did at some clubs. Laurie continued to spend weeks in Montreal and Toronto and her group benefited from increased interest in Doo-Wop and group harmony.

Five years after the British Invasion the original British bands continued to appear at the top of the charts, but they did not dominate. In 1963, with the Beatles leading, British bands held the number one spot for nearly half the year. In 1968, besides "Hey Jude" which kept the number one spot for nine weeks, there were no other British bands at the top of the charts. Otis Redding, the Rascals, and Simon and Garfunkel ascended with productions that were increasingly complex, personal and political. British bands had moved beyond reworking the songs of their American blues idols. The Rolling Stones had gone from "Time is on My Side," to "Jumpin' Jack Flash." My old competitor Dion reinvented himself with "Abraham, Martin and John," a new sound that Guida could not claim as his own. All these new sounds provoked a rebellious desire by some to go back to the music of the '50s and early '60s.

A trainee at Frank Barsalona's Premier Talent Associates turned visionary. He capitalized on that rebellion and created a new industry. Richard Nader joined Frank as a trainee in 1966 and he sent me some work during which time Frank was busy launching the Beau Brummels and Herman's Hermits. Premier was still known for classic rock acts, but no one came up with an approach as to how to keep these acts working consistently. The problem was more serious for the acts that came into the business five years before me. While I had charting records in the previous five years, there were acts who had not recorded anything new in 10. Former headlining acts had not figured out how to stay relevant and make their hits last for that mythic 20 years. Nader figured it out, or at least he thought he did at the time, and he told Barsalona he was leaving Premier.

Barsalona was a generous man and took pleasure from all the successes that came out of Premier. When Nader told him he was leaving the agency to become a promoter, Barsalona wished him well and told him to take his Rolodex. Nader's idea was to find some of the "authentic" older acts, dust them off, and present them in bunches, lovingly, with good backing bands in a theatrical setting. Nader knew which acts could still reproduce their original sound and avoided those which might prove embarrassing to him and themselves. The only thing that Nader lacked was money.

It took him six months to find a backer, a non-music person, reportedly a manufacturer of office partitions. Nader was equally successful finding some of the old acts, and he chased down a few that had left the business. By this time, Speedo Carroll was working as a school custodian and Darlene Love was cleaning homes. You could find members of top groups working as mailmen, teachers, cab drivers and truckers. They were willing to perform, but skeptical that a show was going to happen. As far as getting paid, if you were in the business in the '50s, you knew that was always a risk.

I got a call from Richard about a show which was supposed to take place at Madison Square Garden, not the arena, but the smaller forty five hundred seat Felt Forum. Nader reached me in Brooklyn and I told him I would let him know. The money was no more than what I was getting to play a club, but I didn't need a band. I wanted to know what other acts were going to appear. He told me Bill Haley was committed to a first time U.S. performance in 10 years, along with Chuck Berry, the Shirelles, the Coasters and the Platters, with other acts considering invitations. As if there were not enough authentic acts, Nader added Sha Na Na to the bill, which was a strategic move. While they were "revivalists" and not of the era, they proved their credibility with a contemporary audience at Woodstock and might help draw patrons whose first exposure to early rock and roll was at that festival. I was impressed by the acts that were promised, but I took this to be little more than Nader's wish list. Similar to my career, all these acts had been off the charts for five or more years, and Sha Na Na aside, all were unsigned to labels at the time. With the exception of members of the Shirelles, and the college kids who comprised Sha Na Na, the balance were older and part of rock and roll's first graduating class. The show was scheduled for October 18, 1969.

I spoke to Laurie about the offer. I had a hard time coming to a decision. I had to get over the hump that I might now be a nostalgia act. I was just 30! Bill Haley was in his mid-40s as was Chuck Berry, and in rock and roll years that's a big difference. I held out hope that I would become a signed artist again. In fact, I saw myself moving in the direction of the singer-songwriters. I had just released my first records with Jerry and they were soul records with contemporary themes. I didn't see how becoming part of a nostalgia show would help beyond it being a night's pay. I was confused and sensed that things were changing. I knew that Sha Na Na had played Woodstock (in front of Jimi Hendrix) and that a festival in Toronto successfully mixed Little

Richard, Chuck Berry, Jerry Lee Lewis and Bo Diddley with special guests John Lennon, Junior Walker and Chicago, but I didn't think I fit squarely into that mix. My fear was that once I was tagged as being a nostalgia act, I would not be marketable as a solo, contemporary signed artist. Big Mama, ever at my side, agreed and I told Nader that I wouldn't do it. Richard was disappointed. I think he felt that if I was part of the lineup for the first show I would attract a slightly younger audience. I did tell him I would keep an open mind.

The show, or *The Rock and Roll Revival: Volume 1* as it was called, was successful, with a second show added for that night and *Volume 2* quickly scheduled for November 29. The first night grossed around $100,000 for the novice promoter doing his first show at the tender age of 30. The reviews were positive, and Nader was right, these acts were certainly viable in a small arena and there were sufficient numbers of balding, pot bellied "rebels" who would turn out to see performers that were not currently recording. The talent was paid, treated well, and if you believed Nader they would benefit from a new business model for classic rock acts. Richard called me for *Volume 2* and I could not mount a good argument against appearing.

Volume 2 sold out, and again the line up was headed by Bill Haley. Other features were the Mello Kings, the Capris, the Five Satins, Shep and the Limelights and the Spaniels. The night needs to be remembered if only for my co-feature, the Capris, whose #3 from 1961, "There's a Moon Out Tonight," opened the show. New to the Capris at the show was their bass, John Apostol, who must have carefully watched what Nader was doing and saw the financial potential of the classic acts. John would continue on with the Capris, whose fortunes improved after their appearance, but he would then leave in 1972 to join Banner Talent Associates and then start his own agency and management company, Apostol Enterprises. He would pick up where Barsalona and Nader left off and wind up representing and managing the groups which were the mainstays of what became the "oldies" circuit. He would become my manager as well.

It was great playing the Garden for the first time, even if it was not the main room, and we were treated well. The work was not difficult.

We had a sound check and brief run through in the afternoon, and then a comfortable wait backstage. I was scheduled to be the lead-in to Haley who would close. It was a bittersweet night. I had worked with all of these groups, but the closest we came to a night like this was years before when we rode the bus for Dick Clark when my hits were just starting to chart. I suspect we all saw this as a turning point in our careers. For some of the acts there was hope that they could give up their day jobs. Others saw these multi-unit shows as a much needed supplement to club work which was getting harder to find. I wasn't sure if my appearance meant I was giving up on the idea of ever being a contemporary act again. I still feared being considered an "oldies" act, but working is better than not working and there were no current prospects as far as a label that might want to record me. I would take these jobs as we had no choice, but I would continue writing, performing and trying to cut some records with Jerry Williams.

Jerry is a few years younger than I am, and if you look back at all the songs, partnerships, labels and reinventions he's been through he must have been 10 when he started in the business. He started out as "Little Jerry Williams." With rock and roll having an excess of "Little" acts he dropped "Little"and since the early 1970s he's been known as "Swamp Dogg." Jerry, aka "Dogg," should be more widely known as an eccentric genius. He's remained active in the business for 50 years, but he is not driven by sounds or themes which are mainstream or easily promoted. Jerry remains overlooked, and he might tell you he prefers it that way.

We did some conventional southern soul and funk. Jerry was thinking Joe Tex when we did "Funky Lies" for a 1969 release on the now defunct Botanic label. In partnership with Jerry my records moved squarely into the "soul shouter" category. However our songwriting for others was more commercial and Jerry had no trouble selling our songs which found their way on to the LP's of leading vocalists of the time. Jerry had been a writer and producer at Atlantic while still living in Portsmouth, and through his connections our co-writes were recorded by Dee Dee Warwick, Lulu, and Wilson Pickett. Jerry had been scouting talent for the West Coast label Canyon Records where he placed some of our songs with Doris Duke.

Instead of spending my afternoons waiting for agents to call, I was hanging out with Jerry, writing songs at his home in Queens. In the six years of our partnership we placed over 60 of our songs, and somewhere there must be hundreds we didn't sell. While Jerry released some of his own material on Phil Walden's (manager of Otis Redding) Capricorn Records, and later Elektra, much of our output was on Canyon Records which was started by former Heartbeat, ("A Thousand Miles Away") Wally Roker. We also sold songs to Mankind Records which was a label created for Jerry by Nashboro Records which was looking to expand beyond its core gospel offerings.

Doing the Nader show did not prevent us from getting a record released by Sue, which was owned by Juggy Murray who had great success with early songs by Ike and Tina Turner. Juggy was partners with Bobby Robinson, owner of Fire and Fury Records and a trend setting music producer and Harlem music retailer for six decades. "One Broken Heart" was not listened to as was "The Star" which followed in 1971 on Atco. Both were produced by Jerry and the Atco flop would be the last recording we did as partners.

When Jerry formed his joint venture with Nashboro, he did his recording at Quin Ivy's Quinvy Studios in Sheffield, Alabama. Quin is responsible for bringing Percy Sledge to national attention and many of Jerry's records make that same emotional connection to listeners found in, Sledge's perennial "When a Man Loves a Woman." Along with Doris Duke, other singers that Jerry worked with were, Z.Z. Hill and Sandra Phillips. Freddie North was the first to record "Friend Don't Take Her (She's All I Got)," and it turned out to be my most successful copyright since "Quarter to Three," with multiple high-charting versions in several formats. It is the perfect example of why many consider deep southern soul and country music to be first cousins.

For Jerry, the song was a way to thank Freddie for blessing the deal which made the Mankind label a reality. At the time Jerry was shopping for a partner for his label. He met North who had recorded for numerous labels as far back as 1958 and showed promise when his single "OK, So What," got him on to *American Bandstand*. But it shows that even Dick Clark had some misses as the record did not chart. He stopped recording and became a part-time deejay in Nashville for WLAC and full-time promotion man for Nashboro, where he okayed the Mankind deal. North had recorded a few more records for a Nashboro subsidiary and when Jerry joined he asked him if he could help restart his career. It restarted a bunch of careers.

"Friend Don't Take Her (She's All I Got)," written in Queens and recorded by Freddie North in Alabama went to #10 R&B and crossed over to the Hot 100 where it got as high as #39 and stayed on the charts for three months. This was Bonds and Williams at their commercial best, but just a prelude to a quick and very successful cover by Johnny Paycheck. Paycheck's cover would go to #2 Country and be the second biggest record of his career next to "Take This Job and Shove It."

These songs paid some bills, and our partnership was flourishing, but when it came to business my sophistication and diligence had not improved at all since my days with Frank Guida. Most successful partnerships have a clear division of responsibility and I was content to write and let Jerry handle the legal end due to remaining uncertainty over the status of my relationship with Legrand. When "Don't Take Her" was nominated for a Country Music Association Song of the Year award, and Johnny Paycheck was nominated for Male Vocalist of the Year, Jerry and I decided we would take our wives to Nashville for this prestigious honor. We were the unlikeliest authors of a country weeper, and Charlie Pride aside, we were instantly recognizable in a crowd that thought we had a reasonable chance of winning. It was a night of very mixed feelings. While I was proud of our work together, it became clear that I was again a very limited partner in what we had created. When Jerry and his wife told us about their new suburban home, furs and jewels, we could not accept the fact that this windfall was all attributable to his "other projects." It would move us to the end of our collaboration, with the Andersons and Big Mama finally collecting the $20 we were owed.

I had gradually overcome my fear of nostalgia shows. I found I was able to balance my appearances as a solo act, with Nader's multi-unit presentations. Nader found I was dependable, low maintenance, and that my up-tempo hard rockers provided good balance for some of the sweet harmonies of the early Doo-Woppers.

Richard gradually moved me up on the bill and increased my fees accordingly. He had expanded beyond the Felt Forum shows and in June of 1971 he brought the show to the Forum in Los Angeles with regulars Chuck Berry and Bo Diddley, the Shirelles, the Drifters and Freddy Cannon with Jerry Lee Lewis on top. It was also fun to see my friend Duane Eddy, my co-bill from a UK tour during the time my Twist records were charting.

Nader proved himself to be adept at managing the often difficult Chuck Berry, but one issue he did not face with Chuck was song selection. This was not the case with Jerry Lee. Jerry Lee had risen to the top of the country charts with a number of ballads with themes ranging from drinking to cheating and sometimes both. These were songs that would not necessarily be the choice of a Nader revival crowd. The other issue was who would close the show. The two remained competitive at this time, and by convincing Chuck to let Jerry Lee close, Richard knew that Jerry Lee would play the much anticipated crowd pleasing early singles in an effort to best his duck-walking rival. Nader operated with the finesse of Kissinger when it came to maneuvering the prickly rock and roll legends and the Forum date was successful. The *Rock and Roll Revival* was a bicoastal smash. Nader was just as successful when the revival show returned to New York's Madison Square Garden for *Volume 7*, and this time he would double-up financially and commit to the 20,000 seat arena.

I was invited to the "Garden Party" that Richard Nader threw on October 15, 1971, with fellow guests Chuck Berry, Bobby Rydell, the Coasters, the Shirelles and special attraction, Rick Nelson. There would be fewer acts than customary, with longer time slots promised to each of the performers. I was backstage waiting for the finale when Rick Nelson unexpectedly encountered the indignity that inspired his highest charting record in years. It could not have been predicted and it's become part of rock folklore. Rick covered most of it in his song. The evening was a lesson for every performer of classic rock and roll. Do not fool yourself, your audience has turned out to hear your old songs the way you sang them way back when.

For those who missed it, Richard Nader's *Volume 7*, was scheduled with the usual cast from previous volumes, and a new addition. This night would be different, but it was not known to us who were performing. It was a pretty standard bill, and other than Rick Nelson, we had all known one another for years. Some of us had ridden the bus for Dick Clark, or at the very least performed on the same shows. The audience would be different for this one. Nader had sell-outs or near sell outs for all his previous New York shows. Taking a measured risk, he stepped up to the arena, with four times the number of seats as the Felt Forum. Now, for a single show he would need to sell twice the number of tickets as two shows in the Felt Forum. As Nelson would tell us months later in his ode to the evening, the crowd included Bob Dylan, George Harrison, Mick Jagger and the cream of the music press.

Billed as special guests were Rick Nelson and the Stone Canyon Band, which included future founding member of the Eagles, Randy Meisner. This made for an interesting addition in that the crowd for a nostalgia show would probably be looking for Ricky Nelson. Ricky Nelson ceased to exist ever since Ozzie's younger son dropped the 'y' in Ricky just in time for his twenty-first birthday. This corresponded with his double sided hit, "Travelin' Man," which was coupled with "Hello Mary Lou." By the time the album with these two sides was released, unlike the singles, the artist would be "Rick" Nelson. Ricky Nelson sold a lot of records, with "Be Bop Baby," "Poor Little Fool," and his cover of Fats Domino's "I'm Walkin'," qualifying him for an invite to a Nader show.

Nader would not have wished to offend his audience nor Rick Nelson, and it probably took some lobbying on Richard's part to book Rick who had worked exclusively with his band as a solo or feature. One obvious concession was the show's title. While it was, *Volume 7*, it was not billed as a *Rock and Roll Revival*, rather a *Rock and Roll*

Spectacular. This was at Nelson's insistence, but with the Coasters and the Shirelles on the bill, it would have been foolish for Nelson to think that this was not a nostalgia show. Nader knew what his audience was expecting. What Nader could not have envisioned was the impact of the visual combined with the song selection. The Nader audience wanted matching dinner jackets, short hair and duck walking guitar players. The Nader crowd no longer smoked Camels or wore their hair in a "D.A.," but they wanted you to know that at one time they did.

To me, *Volume 7* was just another Nader show, so I was stunned by the audience's reaction, and the hostility which built in intensity as Nelson went from his old numbers to a Rolling Stones inspired number. I enjoyed his set, and respected his transition. I even liked his purple shirt, and I wasn't offended by his long hair. I was in the minority. If the songs and look were unexpected, I just did not anticipate the response which might be compared to what greeted Dylan's going electric at Newport in 1965. I also failed to understand why Rick did not change his set once it became clear that he had misjudged the crowd.

"Garden Party" would be Rick (not Ricky) Nelson's last hit. In "Garden Party" Nelson sings that he would rather drive a truck than just sing his old songs. The relationship that older performers have with their signature songs is an interesting one. I know performers who dread the prospect of singing their big hit, particularly when it is 40 or more years old and there have been no comparable hits since. In some cases I have seen crowds go home feeling cheated when a performer refuses to sing those hits, because he or she is selling a new album.

Sometimes it's worse. Particularly when the song is performed sloppily, or when the performer tries something new, forgetting that the original is etched into the audience's memory. Some performers find they just can't do the song, as it has taken on a life of its own. Others view their signature songs as the reason that there has been no acceptance of their more recent efforts.

I checked in with Ben E. King who should be an authority on the subject. "Arrogance," he says, "It's arrogance."

"Stand By Me," is one of the most recorded songs of all time, and the bass line is one of the most recognizable. I have appeared with Ben E. hundreds of times and I hear people humming it as they enter the building. I love the song; I sing it myself along with his follow-up, "Don't Play that Song," which is also a crowd favorite. When Ben E. and I have performed together, I have even heard people humming the song between numbers while I'm performing. Like "Quarter to Three," which charted at the same time as "Stand By Me," Ben has sung his song for 50 years, and it makes it into every show, sometimes more than once.

Ben E. said, "Never in my wildest dreams do I dread it. Once you open your mouth and people are singing along and enjoying it, that's the best reward. You're looking to complete their evening. How can you be so arrogant? You didn't start last week. You started when that record started. It's easy to give people what they want, and to reacquaint myself with my past is a pleasure. Only do my current recordings? That's offensive. It's a luxury to stand up there, say one word, and then the people take over. That's a great accomplishment."

I'm with Ben E., and for me "Quarter to Three," is a new song every night. It bought me my first house and the underwear I'm wearing right now. When I told my Mom I wanted to sing I entered into a contract with every blessed soul who's ever scraped together a couple of bucks to hear me do the only thing I know how to do. Give them what they came to hear.

Rick and Ricky, rest knowing that your legacy is secure. You gave generations a lot of pleasure with all your songs, and my heart was with you that night as I watched. In the end it got you another hit record, and another chance to see people enjoying your talent. I hope you made peace with all those songs. It beats driving a truck.

Ten

TIME TO RE-TIRE

THE NOSTALGIA SHOWS GAVE ME some work on top of my club appearances with Taxi. Big Mama would take her gowns north for weeks at a time to do her shows and the phone activity was picking up. The bass singer from the Capris, John Apostol, was working for me at Banner while he was also managing Johnny Maestro, Tommy James, and Chubby Checker. Life in Brooklyn was peaceful, with little interference from the in-laws who had managed to get us the apartment on top of theirs on Marcy Avenue. We enrolled Little Mama in parochial school at Our Lady of Anunciation, and the tuition was fair. They asked everyone to pay what they could afford and we did. We had considered public schools, but at that time, even in the younger grades, there was little education going on in this rugged inner-city school district. Big Mama had brought up the subject first. Maybe we could once again have a home of our own. Big Mama grew up in the streets of Brooklyn and didn't want that for our daughter. I was brought up in a comfortable home with trees and a yard and we wanted that for our baby.

We had been living carefully and taking every job that came our way. Big Mama's dad would make sure there was always an extra chicken leg or two for us and we were saving a little bit each week. Seven thousand dollars might as well have been a million and it was all we had. It was all from our appearance work. The royalty checks I received for some writing credits were tiny, and it had been a long time since I got a dime from Legrand. With a $7000 bankroll, we headed east in our aging Cadillac with a plan to stop and look at homes near Jones Beach, which we never found. We were open minded and would consider any place where seven grand might get us some trees a yard and a good school for Little Mama.

We found an area in the Town of Babyon, in Suffolk County, in a section which was predominantly African American. It became that way when it was subdivided following the completion of a branch of the Long Island Railroad, when a smart builder offered "non-racial" housing. That meant blacks were welcome, and they came. While Levittown and most North Shore towns were red-lined, as real estate agents engaged in racial-steering, we found a comfortable place that was favored by middle-income blacks, of which many were professionals. We needed a place where an African American, and a Hispanic, both entertainers, were likely not to encounter any imaginary dogs. During one of our weekly outings we found a neighborhood which had the added advantage of being in the Half Hollow Hills School District. These schools were known for their academic excellence and students leaving the district often gained acceptance to the more prestigious universities.

We cruised the streets and saw people of every shade. We saw a "For Sale" sign and contacted the seller directly. We were interested in a modern ranch house with a brick facade and some old trees in back. The rear yard was spacious and level and I imagined grilling burgers and sipping beers on a deck and maybe someday we would have a swimming pool. The house also had a full basement, which may be the key to a long and successful marriage. It wasn't Jones Beach, but we could afford it and it would leave us with a few dollars for sprucing up. The negotiations were successful and we were warmly welcomed to the block by the Thomases, Schexnayders, Richardsons, Stewarts and Hubbards.

With no desire to ever lose this house, I wanted to take every job I could, but I found that some jobs would not work financially. With the band and some horns added, or an occasional back up singer, the cost of getting and staying at some jobs made them money losers. I thought back to the Dick Clark tours and I figured we could take more distant jobs if we had a tour bus, something fitted out for long drives and comfortable enough to sleep in. Most of the jobs were on the weekends, so distance was not a problem. If we could arrange weekend jobs within driving distance of one another we could easily manage the cost of a vehicle. I did some research and found that the cost of buying or renting a real tour bus was prohibitive. We would all be working to support the bus. With pencil and paper I figured out that if we could make a box truck livable we could do shows from coast to coast. Box trucks come in a number of sizes and they are the trucks that "U-Haul" rents to non-truck drivers for household moving. They drive like cars and are stingy on gas. I took some of the leftover house money and put a down payment on a Ford box truck. It was a 14-footer with two wheels in front and four in the back. I bought it new and heading back from the dealer I stopped at the lumber yard and filled up the cargo compartment.

The guys from my band were adequate musicians and Tom Lafferty and Babe Pace were also handy with power tools. It took us the better part of three weeks to finish our conversion. We bought high quality household windows and mounted them on either side of the truck. We used half inch plywood throughout and built a bedroom in the back and banquettes for seating. We hung a television, put in a great sound system and used the engine to heat the box. One of the guys reminded me that engine exhaust could be a problem for those in back, so we bought some extra long flexible hose, the kind you use to vent a clothes dryer, and we directed the exhaust to the roof. Shag carpeting covered all the hard surfaces. We debated whether to put the band's name on the side, but we decided that would not be cool.

We had our own unique tour bus. We took a booking in Reno and we were anxious to get our custom coach out on the road.

I enjoyed the driving. The sound system was cranked, the band was buckled in, and we had a three day trip with 2000 miles of open road in front of us. I noticed that the acceleration was not what I had expected from a new truck and the gas mileage was about half of what I planned. On day two, somewhere in Ohio, we pulled in for our fourth fill. The attendant pointed to our front tires which were badly worn and we saw that the rear ones were nearly smooth. It might have been my imagination but the remaining treads smelled like they were burning. This rig could not have burned rubber. With five musicians, luggage, a P.A. system and a mixing board there was hardly any acceleration. I couldn't believe they gave us defective tires on a factory new truck. Six new tires took some of the profit out of our Reno job, and while our new tires got us to Reno, it took another set to get us back to New York. Ten miles to a gallon of gas and less than 2000 miles on a set of tires and this truck barely made it to 50 miles per hour. Impossible.

Back in Long Island I headed to the dealer. I complained loudly about having to change tires, not once, but twice in 5000 miles. The dealer looked at the truck. He had never seen a fourteen footer tricked out to carry a band. As we walked around the truck, I could see the dealer smiling. He said it looked like we were one of those "low riders" but he never saw a low riding box truck. He climbed inside and it did smell kind of funky having been home for a bunch of musicians for a week. He explained to me that the truck was not meant for the type of conversion we did and with all the lumber and building materials the truck was way over its maximum loaded weight. That was why the tires were wearing out so quickly. I figured I would just have to raise my fee.

Some days I would go to New York City and hang out with the agents at John Apostol's new office. They all knew my work and most had booked me before, but by being there and talking them up I figured I had a better chance of getting the better paying gigs. I was waiting to see Apostol in the outer office when he walked into the reception area with a gentleman who appeared to be his client. "Gary, say hello to Mike Peter," and I extended my hand to the athletically built prospect who looked more like a school boy than a promoter.

Mike Peter had traveled to New York to meet with John. He was the newly appointed General Manager of a private golf club in Orlando, Florida. It was called Dubsdread Golf Course. The club had been around since the 1920s and had fallen on hard times. The club seemed to be heading for failure when it took a chance with Mike Peter. He was an inexperienced honor student from Cornell University's School of Hotel Administration. Mike found a career path following a few years of undistinguished academic work at Syracuse University where he majored in hosting frat parties. Mike was from upstate New York, a small town called Aurora that will become an important place for my family in later years. Mike was the grandson of a farmer and the son of man whose extraordinary achievements on the Cornell faculty started when he left the Air Force as an electrician.

Mike attended American University briefly, but he moved back to New York and completed his degree about an hour from his Aurora home. Graduating from Syracuse with a business degree, Mike credits a series of campus uprisings and a relaxing of graduation standards as the only reason he was given a diploma. Recognizing he was ill-qualified to do anything, he thought he would make the best of his party-making skills. As a Cornell legacy, he entered the hospitality school and graduated with honors. While he could not grasp statistics as an undergraduate, he found statistics applied to projected alcohol consumption and the yield from a well-butchered side of beef to be rather easy.

A professor with foresight sent him as a campus rep to a career conference for hospitality managers and he returned to Cornell with dozens of contacts and opportunities not only for himself, but for other Cornell graduates. He wanted to try his hand at club management.

Mike wanted, "... a situation I could turn around. Some place that was dying where I would be noticed if I did well. I wanted a job where the clientele would see me not just once at a meal, but continually, so that I could build relationships and find an "angel" to help me start my own business. Dubsdread was it, a family run enterprise which was down and almost out, in an area of older, established families who were witnessing the tidal change which was a result of Disney's entering the area. I got to Orlando and there were maybe eighty club members. We let the public in to use the course and we had a restaurant and a banquet facility, the Sand Trap Lounge. I improved the dining room and hired better looking female servers. I also convinced the ownership that we needed live music in our banquet facility. At great expense I hired Frankie Valli and the Four Seasons. There was no way we could make the show profitable, but with two guaranteed sellouts we would certainly have the opportunity to get people to see the club. Frankie Valli sold out a week in advance, but on the Wednesday before the Friday and Saturday night shows I started getting calls with cancellations.

Frankie Valli had done a show in Palm Beach, Florida and it was reported that he headed back to New York, and due to a medical issue he would be skipping the rest of his Florida dates. After cursing Frankie and his handlers, I hastily got the Coasters and the Dovells and offered them as a two for one. It was a valiant try, and I wound up with a half empty house and a very tough show for the two acts. I appreciated the fact that Apostol bailed me out so I went to New York to see him."

I found out that Mike came to New York to book Tommy James. Though it was a few years since his biggest hits, Mike heard that Tommy did a very solid hour and drew good crowds. At that time Apostol even had Big Mama working with Tommy as one of his Shondells. Apostol tried to sell Mike on booking me. Mike recalled saying, "I don't want Gary Bonds and the Playboys, and I don't even know what this Gary Bonds sings. I've got an older crowd and they want upbeat stuff they heard of."

Mike said that Apostol was relentless in pushing me and that he practically guaranteed that I would fill the place. He never told Mike, but Apostol knew that Tommy James was not available for the dates he wanted. Score one for Apostol. I helped by charming my future friend. The guarantee was fair and since I was playing in Tennessee the previous weekend, I might be able to do the drive without buying new tires.

"Picture this," Mike continued, "Gary drives up to the club in a red and white El D'Oro Cadillac convertible. First out of the car is a wall of muscle, Moe, Gary's driver, all around assistant and bodyguard. Gary gets out next wearing some sort of fluorescent suit from a car that looked like the one Superfly used only on the holidays. I leave my office to greet him and I find out that the band is following in Gary's truck. They weren't due for two days, and the exact time was based on whether or not they could find six tires for their coach. I show Gary the lounge and tell him that he can have a room at the club and use the facilities. The next morning I see Gary at the first tee with a single golf club. Clustered around him are six of the regulars, all gamblers who appear to be enjoying their new friend, 'the entertainer.' They see that Gary has a very eccentric golf swing. Three golf carts follow Gary, and I watched with great fear as the 'seven-some' headed for the first hole. Gary hit an errant drive off the first tee. "

By the time we finished 18, I had six new friends who were all at least a hundred lighter. I had a full set of clubs in the D'Oro, and I hadn't done the 8 iron bit in twenty years, but it worked, and they didn't care that they were hustled. They loved losing to "the singer." Most played hearts for hundreds every day. I was a novelty. This was the very, very Deep South and the only blacks there were washing dishes in the kitchen. Some knew my music, but most didn't care. Before Friday I had more money in my pocket than I expected to make on the weekend singing.

"I expected a lynch mob and not two sold out shows," Mike recalled. "Every member he hustled was there along with friends they brought with them to meet their new golf buddy. Gary worked his ass off and when the two o'clock curfew arrived he said, 'Lock the doors, I'm still playing.' He continued for another hour and most of them returned on Saturday night and ate and drank in quantities that the club had never achieved before. Gary stayed for three weeks and he showed the owners that they had made a very smart decision when they hired me. We gave Gary a week off and he and the band stayed at the club. We brought in the Drifters, but by this time Gary had a following both on the golf course and on the stage. He stayed around for three or four months and the business grew. We would soon find out that it grew too quickly. As a result of Gary's shows our membership picked up and we were the 'hot club' in Orlando."

Dubsdread was located within an area of private homes, and word on the street was that the club was now attracting a "fast" crowd. The club could not handle all the business it was getting. It was attracting customers from hours away and the membership had increased four-fold. There was a shortage of parking and the crowds decided that the front lawns of the adjacent homes were perfect places to leave their cars. The town elders prevailed and managed to have the club's liquor license pulled. Mike responded by moving my show to a nearby Holiday Inn which was owned by one of the club members. My new golf buddies followed me there.

The country club owners were not pleased. With no liquor license, Dubsdread became a very quiet place. When we left the Holiday Inn after a month's engagement, and the attractive female servers from the country club took off with the members of my band, it put further stress on Dubsdread and my truck's suspension. Mike had a contract with the club that paid him a percentage of sales and he did very well. Word of my success traveled throughout the Holiday Inn circuit and small hotel showrooms and lounges became most of my business.

I was now commuting regularly between New York and Orlando. Mike left Dubsdread with a nice nest-egg and started his own business. He took some of his money and bought a five bedroom house and with the balance he found a building which he would turn into Orlando's first disco which was inspired by his former Syracuse classmate, Steve Rubell, whose Studio 54 in New York City was home to the glitterati. He borrowed the club's name from a famous New York newspaper. MJ's New York Times was both a disco and live showroom.

It was appropriate for me to return to New York City when *New York Magazine* reported that a new room was opening that was going to bring back, "great names that have been away from New York too long." A valiant attempt was made in the mid '70s to bring affordable live entertainment to the southeast corner of the Empire State Building lobby, where numerous operators had tried to make a go of the Riverboat. I was booked into the room which featured some overly ripe "ghost" bands that remained true to the big-band era and somewhat younger but still classic acts like Gary Lewis and Mary Wells. I mention it and remember it only because during the Riverboat booking I learned of my mother's passing. I was unable to finish the week.

I was a "mama's boy," my Mama's boy until her last breath. I was indulged and catered to, dressed and groomed, fed and supported never knowing when times were good or bad. She didn't need me to sing or be famous, she just wanted me to be happy. Since Ivory Joe and Bullmoose opened my eyes, she made sure that none of my idols left town without meeting me. My friends were hers, and our home was open to all. I regretted the tension between Mom and Big Mama, but I knew where it came from, and that made it a little easier to bear. I told the band I needed to cancel and I packed to leave the Riverboat. I thought it was ironic that they had a big mural of a paddle-wheeler there, just like the one Mom heard me sing about that morning when "Daddy" Jack played my record about going down the Mississippi to New Orleans.

I went back to Orlando. Mike told me to be realistic about my career. He wanted me to move to Orlando, and he had even bought a house I could use. Mike said, "I can guarantee you 250 nights a year in the area. You're not going to do it again and you've built something in Orlando. Forget selling records, do what you love doing, and that's working and you've got that here."

Mike gave me some tough love and all indications were that he was right. I did two singles in 1974, one on Sky Disc and another on Prodigal, which was a start up run by Barney Ales who was formerly at Motown. "Grandma's Washboard Band," my interpretation of the popular "Joy to the World," earned me a quick five grand and if it ever sold it would surely have gotten me a lawsuit from Hoyt Axton who wrote "Joy."

The box truck took us from Holiday Inn to Holiday Inn from New York to Florida. The tires wore out and so did the band and they went their own way without the waitresses from the Sand Trap Lounge. Mike did well in Orlando and parlayed his good fortune into a club and adult entertainment empire.

Mike was a loyal friend and always kept his offer to relocate me to Orlando. He returned to Aurora with the idea of starting a chain of clubs on the order of New York's Maxwell's Plum. It was about this time that Mike bought a ticket to see Bruce Springsteen who was playing in nearby Geneva, New York. Bruce had just started touring in support of *Born to Run*.

Mike remembers, "I watched Springsteen do two and a half hours. He comes out for his encore and he's singing, 'Quarter to Three.' I get it. I replayed his set-list in my mind and I hear bits of Gary in a lot of the numbers. I called Apostol and I told him he needed to get Gary together with this guy. Apostol laughed."

Eleven

A GUY FROM JERSEY

It is now 36 years since I met Bruce Springsteen and neither I, nor John Apostol, nor Mike Peter had anything to do with the meeting. Bruce Springsteen needed no inspiration that fall evening other than my 15 year-old songs. While I have tried, I may never be able to convey my gratitude to him for venturing out that night.

The meeting took place in Hazlet, New Jersey at a club called The Hanger, which had a plane on its roof and sat on a piece of land on Route 35 which was once Walling Airport. I was booked for two nights and the club-owners borrowed from Richard Nader in calling the show a *Rock and Roll Revival*. I had no expectation that this would be anything more than a typical "Jersey" gig and I had never played at the club nor had I heard of it. Bruce showed up for the second set of our Friday opening about 20 minutes into the show. He was not alone, but I do not recall those who came with him; they were not members of his band.

The club may have held three or four hundred standing, yet I have met untold thousands of loyal fans who were witnesses to that night.

The number grows each year, and those who claim to have been there, along with the rock press, give the year of that meeting as anywhere from 1975 through 1980. We met on October 22, 1976, more than a year after *Born To Run* was released. I was familiar with the album which became a staple of FM radio and rightfully elevated Bruce to some new level of rock and roll mega-stardom.

While I must have been familiar with the songs, nothing came to mind when the club owner approached me during a number and whispered that Bruce Springsteen was in the house and wanted to join me on stage. It has also been reported that I welcomed Bruce to the stage and took off for the bar or the restroom. Not true. I read the crowd and figured that this was something that I wanted to hang around for. I introduced him and I would like to buy back my intro. Dead serious, I brought him up by asking the crowd to welcome "a local talent," as if he had just won a high school singing competition. My band members knew who he was as did the crowd, and except for me, he did not need an introduction. I was also unaware that Bruce had been doing "Quarter to Three," during many of his encores. We found him a guitar and we shared a microphone and did 40 minutes of my biggest hits. He was familiar with them all.

It is a misconception that Bruce offered me a song after that meeting and whisked me into a recording studio to launch Act Two of my career. Three and a half years passed between the time we met and the time we started recording what would become *Dedication*. But it was just one week later that I reciprocated, when he invited me to join him onstage at the much larger Palladium in New York City where we sang "Quarter to Three." By this point we had gotten to know one another, exchanged numbers and started keeping in touch.

I was flattered that he knew my songs. I learned that I was amongst a small group that influenced what he did. Big Mama's recollection of some years later is Bruce talking about doing my music as some form of "payback," but unlike some, I initially did not hear that influence except when he was actually doing my songs. If my style is the "Party Sound," he could do that too, but as he showed in *Born to Run* he would not be confined to one sound. Even his straight up rock numbers have a complexity of lyric and orchestration which goes way beyond whatever "genius" lurks within my crude early Guida/Royster records. The same is true when he does covers of my songs or others. He sings "Twist and Shout," but it's Bruce doing the song, not doing the Isley Brothers singing the song. It's the same when he does the Dovells' "You Can't Sit Down," or my "Quarter to Three." When we've performed songs together that I originally recorded, we always kid about whether we're going to do it my way or his way. I let him win those arguments. We always do it his way.

We became friends and stayed in touch, and for me there was no expectation of anything but friendship. I would certainly know him the next time he unexpectedly showed up, and I restarted my subscriptions to both *Time* and *Newsweek* so I could stay current with the latest and greatest in the business. With no inkling there would ever be another Springsteen gig, we packed the box truck and played every club and Holiday Inn that would have us.

Apostol called about a tour that would keep the folks at Goodyear working overtime. End to end it would be the longest road trip of my career and I was excited when he described it. The Air Force was interested in having us take to the road and play almost 100 bases where there were large numbers of enlisted men and non-commissioned officers. They had done some research and checked some references and found my act suitable. They were confident that our show, which was geared to hotel lounges, would be well received by a broad range of ages in any part of the country. My reputation was that I showed up, worked hard and could manage all types of audiences. They liked the fact that we were self-contained, brought our own sound equipment, and were open to playing indoors or outdoors both day and night. They put together a route of drivable dates which would keep us on the road for five months. The money was not great, but it certainly beat sitting home and waiting for the phone to ring. I also liked playing the types of audiences they offered us. Whenever we were booked near military bases, particularly when we had crowds of newly-enlisted men, they were typically young, enthusiastic and appreciative, especially when you played something that reminded them of being home.

I needed some players who would commit to the entire tour and life on the truck. There was no way I could turn down five months of steady work, but I had mixed feeling about leaving my girls for so long. Big Mama had cut down on her performing so she could stay close to Little Mama who was really flourishing at middle school, but the schedule and a tight budget would make it difficult for me to sneak back home, especially with the number of dates out west. The tour would carry us over the summer months, so we agreed that the girls would meet up with us when school finished, and stay with us until Little Mama returned to school in September. Big Mama insisted on bringing Pepe, her pet chihuahua and new best friend.

I put together a band that proved to be durable, a talented group of road warriors. The band included Tom Lafferty on guitar, Babe Pace on drums, Greg Woods on keyboards, and John Clemente on bass. We would sometimes substitute Steve Nassau who would take over for Babe and Steve Ameche eventually replaced Greg.

We filled up the truck with gear and gas and changed the tires for the first of many times. Typically we would play in a gym or a training center, and the base would put out tables, folding chairs or portable bleachers. We played on athletic fields and in warehouses, in chapels and mess halls for crowds that ran upwards of 1000 at the larger bases. It was an event when the on-base entertainment was professional, and if I was still known 15 years after my last record, it was unusual to have an appearance by a known, national recording star. There was great enthusiasm upon our arrival, particularly when we met men who were from Norfolk or New York who were anxious to let us know they were our homeboys. They loved Big Mama and until they met Little Mama we wouldn't tell them that we were husband and wife. On some of the shows we had two vocalists. Big Mama would have one of the guys hook up an extra microphone and pass it to Little Mama who sang from backstage. Little Mama was genetically inclined to sing and this marked the start of her performing career. The NCOs in charge were great hosts. We ate with the men and the few women who were there and they made sure the girls had everything they needed. I shared the driving with the band and we all saw parts of the country for the first time.

The shows were great, but the work was grueling. The box truck was not ideally suited for crossing the desert and the tour took us west through Montana, north to Alaska and then south through Nevada and then Texas near some Mexico border towns. Moving the sound equipment was wearying and sometimes we needed a referee in the back of the truck. Some of the guys had played most of their careers in the Northeast, so it gave them a chance to see some sights and get really good at reading maps. As we left one base they would call ahead to our next stop and let us know who would be our contact person at the next job. And if the show went over well, there was usually an enthusiastic review which helped build momentum for when we arrived at our next show. If they wanted dance music, we did it. If they wanted blues or ballads we covered that. We could do country, '50s, Motown, all we did was play to please. Towards the last third of the tour we were being re-routed to officer's clubs. These were much smaller shows for audiences that were older and not very appreciative. It was also not in our contract. The shows were starting at irregular times and making our traveling difficult. The band was not happy. I was getting tired and testy, and in San Antonio at Lakland Air Force base, things came to a boil.

I need to thank my keyboard player Steve Ameche for refreshing my memory about our experience at Lakland. Steve is a talented musician and I have learned he is equally talented as an attorney specializing in entertainment law. It was recommended that I contact Steve and I auditioned him over the phone when I decided that Greg Woods was not going to be a road warrior for the Gary U.S. Bonds Show. Steve joined us in Denver and he was a welcome addition to the band. We got on like the Osmonds, just one big family, and Steve reminded me about our occasional stops. When the heat was oppressive in the back of the truck, we'd stop when we saw a roadside motel with a very inviting swimming pool. We would stop the truck just long enough so the boys could strip down to their shorts and quickly refresh themselves with profuse apologies to the paying guests who witnessed the band's invasion. No harm, and boys will be boys. After the first few times, we had it down and could be back to our driving in minutes.

Big Mama and I felt like camp counselors shepherding a truckload of teenagers on a cross country tour. When they were not taking dips in motel pools, this ragtag group of young musicians busied themselves playing practical jokes or accusing one another of being the cause of the unbearable aroma in the back of the truck. We could handle all of this, but what was more difficult was when one of our "campers" would lose his credentials. Entering Air Force bases is not easy, especially for a group like us driving a vehicle that was part-truck, part-bus, overweight and clearly homemade. We all had special government identification, passes for each base, proof of citizenship and our personal drivers' licenses. After two or three instances where we needed to head back to retrieve someone's credentials from a motel or restaurant, Big Mama and I decided that we would collect all our important papers and hold them in a tote bag along with our schedules and contact information. We also collected our bills for the trip, because we were going to be reimbursed for some of them. This gave birth to the "bullshit bag" and I don't know who gets credit for the name, but "throw it into the bullshit bag" was repeatedly heard.

Over the course of a couple of months the bag was gaining weight, but when it was your turn to safeguard the bag you guarded it with your life. The downside of the concept was that if the bag was missing, we'd all be without identification. We took our turns hauling the bag and on someone's watch it was lost, with no clue as to where it was and no time to head back and look for it. It happened en route to Lakland Air Force Base near San Antonio, Texas on August 17.

We arrived at Lakland and made it past the entry gates with an escort to the reception center where two of the guys went in and tried to establish our identity and our reason for visiting the base. They carried their instruments to validate their claim of being the musicians who were booked to play the base. The MPs were not sympathetic and Steve recalled that they might have also demonstrated some attitude which was more attuned to the tough streets of New York than rural Texas. I went back to the truck and started searching every possible spot for the bag. I was in the truck for no more than five minutes when someone came running out of the building. He was hysterically shouting, "Big Mama's having a fight, Big Mama's got the MP." I tore into the building to see Lafferty, and Clemente wrestling three male MPs and Big Mama choking a female MP. Lafferty then battered another MP with a metal trash can. There was blood on the floor and I grabbed another MP who came flying in and I knocked him to the ground. I could hear Little Mama crying. Frightened and stunned, she appeared to be choking. The MPs had maced my band-members and a female MP tried to mace Little Mama. Big Mama responded with a choke-hold although being at a hundred pound disadvantage.

The melee stopped and we were all escorted to another building where there were two cells. Big Mama was holding Little Mama and Little Mama was holding Pepe. Big Mama was cursing in at least three languages and you didn't need a translator to know how pissed she was. The band was pretty banged up, but they appeared to have gotten the best of our hosts. The United States Government charged Laurie Cedeño Anderson with assault and disorderly conduct, and the entire posse was charged with various offenses, me included. The cell they put us in was beyond capacity and we were not model prisoners, especially Pepe. They told us that three of the MPs were hospitalized. It took some time for Big Mama to calm down. She explained to me that it all started when Little Mama heard a female MP speak to her in a tone that was not polite.

"You don't speak to my mom that way," Little Mama told the MP.

"I'll talk to your mom anyway I want," the MP answered with a threatening finger, according to Big Mama, too close to Little Mama's face.

That did not rest well with Big Mama, and all hell broke lose.

Now I had to deal with my second prison stretch, though this one turned out to be much shorter. The Air Force was not set up to hold an irate showband and the settlement was a dropping of charges followed by the cancellation of the balance of the tour.

Bruised but satisfied that we prevailed against the U.S. Air Force, we filled the truck and headed back to New York. Steve Ameche neglected to put his license into the "bullshit bag" and he did a lot of the drive home.

With my growing rap sheet, we headed back to a steady schedule of hotel dates. They ranged from the customary Holiday Inn lounges to one memorable date in the Catskill Mountains where I was part of a bill which contained both Smokin' Joe Frazier and Tiny Tim.

If it was theme night I think they would have called it, "*A Night with Three Guys Who've Seen Better Days.*" Frazier was trying to become an attraction and had released a few records with his group, The Knockouts, following his failed comeback attempt against George Foreman. It was 10 years since Tiny's brush with stardom and for me, I had become a journeyman with 15 years since my last hit record. Despite the questionable credentials of the three of us, pride did get in the way and there was considerable disagreement as to who would close the show. Not one of us had a persuasive argument as to why he deserved to close. I had the greatest number of chart records. Tiny was a global phenomena 10 years earlier, but he only had one song. Joe Frazier was a sweetheart who found out recently that there was one thing he could no longer do and another thing he couldn't do, and that was sing. Anyway, Joe found singing safer than boxing at this stage of his life and he had put together an act which was entertaining. Joe argued that he should close but he was hard to understand and the reason he gave was that he was Joe Frazier. I thought it was smart not to argue with Smokin' Joe, but Tiny was fearless. The tough guy won. I opened and Tiny closed the show. I gave Joe some of my time and a good introduction to bring him on. When I hung around to hear Joe bring on Tiny, I was happy I went on first.

We found another untapped market and we made the best of it. We became Gary Bonds and the Mallers. We played at mall openings. They would set up a small bandstand somewhere in a high traffic area usually near the food court and we would do 20-minute sets with breaks in between. We would do these mall tours similar to the way we did the Air Force Tour, but there was less traveling and little need to extend ourselves. It was also day work, and when we could find a nearby hotel lounge job, it was like finding money. But Little Mama saw that better times were ahead:

"I had few problems in high school, with either the academics or the social challenges. I had a small circle of girlfriends and most of the kids in school knew what Daddy did for a living. My neighbors and closest friends knew that I had started to write songs with Daddy and that sometimes I would work with my parents and I was starting to think seriously about the music business. That got me some special attention, but it was nothing compared to what happened when word spread that Bruce Springsteen was standing with me in the driveway of our house when the school bus passed by. My circle of friends quickly expanded."

Bruce found it convenient to travel back to Long Island with me after some long days at The Power Station. The Power Station is now called Avatar Studios and at the time it was owned by the man who designed it, Tony Bongiovi, cousin of Jon Bon Jovi. It is on West 53rd Street and was once a Con Edison power plant. It was considered the finest environment for recording, and it was the studio of choice for top acts like The Rolling Stones, Bob Dylan and Cher. For months, Bruce and the E Street Band had been working on his double album, *The River,* and his call to me about a song came just as he was wrapping up that project at the end of July 1980. The song was considered for *The River*, but he said that as he sang the song, it reminded him of my early records. Even though I have written about the difficulty I have hearing my influence in his work, he was right about "Dedication." To me it sounded like "Quarter to Three."

I showed up at The Power Station by myself, with no warning to my manager John Apostol. I had mentioned to John and my musicians on several occasions that Bruce had talked to me about doing a record, but after two or more years even I was starting to doubt that it would ever happen. Apostol would not have been of any use in a studio with Bruce and Steven Van Zandt and the balance of the E Street Band. Without talk of money or contracts, or who owned what, and where the record was going to go, I sat and listened as Bruce strummed. I heard "Dedication" for the first time and it fit like a glove. He did it on the keyboard as well and showed me where he thought the key change should go. There was no better way to start the second act of my career than with a none-too-serious song about persevering, kicked off with an Old Testament metaphor. "Dedication" was his, but the dedication I was singing about was mine, and after two or three takes the vocal was almost done. Bruce worked deliberately, building the sound and I was especially intrigued with the care he took in getting the precise snare drum sound he wanted.

It may have been the second night at my home when he woke me at some ungodly hour with a rapping on our bedroom door. "Bondsy, Bondsy," I heard him call, and I left Laurie in a deep sleep while I shuffled into the den. He asked me to sit with him while he played our upright. "Bondsy, listen to this." The opening minor chord echoed as he introduced his newly-written chorus and verse.

"This Little Girl," was born on my upright and just days later we heard it complete with Clarence Clemons' great solo. We had two great cuts and no plan as to what to do with them. My thinking was if we stopped here, I now had a complete single that would generate real interest from any label. These weren't just songs, they were Springsteen songs, and they were great! The 15-year drought was about to end, but for the moment we plugged away at the lounges, clubs and mall openings.

Fifteen years earlier I was a charting recording artist. That was interrupted when I took some time out to collect empties, write a top country hit, become an oldies act, play every Holiday Inn in America, scrap with the United States Air Force, open for a washed-up heavyweight and prove myself unequaled when it came to opening shopping centers. Now I had a new best friend, our daughter was the envy of almost every kid at Half Hollow Hills High, and I had two gratis records from the world's most prolific and influential singer-songwriter whose double album would go platinum five times.

Why? He thought he owed me something because 20 years ago I did this song for the failed Calypso guy.

Twelve

"ONE MORE TIME, MR. GARY U.S. BONDS"

I F HE DID OWE ME ANYTHING, "THIS Little Girl," written in our den, paid me back with interest. We cut an additional track which Bruce had performed but never recorded called, "Action in the Streets," which is now buried in the vaults of EMI America. As I recall, it was as much a "Gary U.S. Bonds" sound as "Dedication," and might have given me another hit single. Featuring Bruce and Steven's guitar work, these three were done without any of my musicians or input from my management which first became aware of the sessions as they neared completion.

I was privileged to have made these first recordings with Clarence Clemons (saxophone) and Danny Federici (accordion and keyboards) who are no longer with us, and current E Street Band members Max Weinberg (drums), Garry Tallent (bass), and Roy Bittan (keyboards). In addition to the E Street Band, for some of the cuts Bruce brought in the Miami Horns on leave from Southside Johnny.

I had three songs on a cassette which I was sure would keep me from having to play any more mall openings. It was handed to me at

The Power Station without instructions. I let John Apostol know that the songs were finished, but I told him I wanted to shop it. Piece of cake. Two new Springsteen songs, the E Street Band, even with Gary U.S. Bonds on lead vocals I expected to have choices when it came to selling the single.

I remember sitting at the kitchen table with Big Mama, a copy of the Sunday newspaper in front of me. I had no interest in the news, my mind was thinking about where I should send the tape. I was only thinking majors, Columbia/Epic, WEA (Warner/Elektra/Atlantic), Polygram. These may have been the first three names that I scribbled on the newspaper. Dupes of the cassette went to each that Monday morning and I planned to follow up with my contacts. I kept the newspaper, as I knew I would want this first souvenir of my next assault on the charts. Three more tapes went out the next week, and I am sure that Universal and Arista got copies. My calls to label heads were going unanswered. EMI America never did get a copy, but all the majors and some larger independents did. All I had to show for the effort was a bunch of rejections and an old Sunday newspaper with the names of labels uninterested in a Springsteen/Van Zandt/ Bonds project. I wasn't so sure that I had seen my last mall opening.

Gary Gersh was at EMI America at the time. Today he guides the careers of John Legend, Soundgarden and Chris Cornell at his company, TAO (The Artist's Organization). I didn't know him then and had no idea as to how he heard about the tapes I sent out. He was the only label exec to respond and I could care less about how he found out. He called and said he heard I had something, but he had no interest in a single. If it was produced by Springsteen, he needed an album. He viewed this as a Springsteen project which would likely interest Springsteen fans, and Bruce sold albums with singles geared to FM airplay. I understood his reasoning and trusted his instincts. EMI America was building a number of new acts, and it was part of the company that owned Capitol. If they were inclined, they could invest in this album and my career. I left it to Apostol to put together a deal with EMI America, but the deal would be dependent upon Bruce agreeing to complete the project. I was sure I could seal the deal with Bruce. He and Steven were enthusiastic about what we had done so far and they would be inclined to complete the project.

Bruce, though surprised that we had difficulty finding a home for our collaboration, was all-in for doing an EMI America album. Scheduling would be the next hurdle. Bruce's work on *The River* was complete and there was a tour already planned for the fall. There was just enough time to complete our album which we did in early September. We quickly knocked out both "Jole Blon" and "Your Love." Bruce's band was familiar with both, and I picked up that they may have given some thought to putting "Jole Blon" on *The River*. "Jole Blon," has since become my opening number and it always energizes my audiences and draws them into my performance when I ask them to sing with me on the refrain. Traditionally played in waltz-time by mandolin, fiddle and accordion, Bruce turned it into a guitar and horn-led, mid-tempo rocker where we trade verses and join for the chorus. With a nod to the song's origins, the late Danny Federici added traditional flourishes with his accordion, making it a perfect, if not unique, Norfolk-inspired, Jersey Sound interpretation of a traditional Cajun waltz.

When Bruce strummed the melody and sang "Your Love," I was taken by its soulfulness, a stark ballad about lost love and wrong love, loneliness and despair. I suggested to Bruce and Steven that we get in Ben E. King and Chuck Jackson to do some baritone soul licks as a contrast to my higher strained tones. I laughed when Bruce asked me if I could find them. The song talks about being let down by love, but not by your buddies and they showed up the next day. Bruce and Steven had Ben E. and Chuck add some impressive vocals. I felt great about involving my closest friends in something which would give their careers a boost, and as for Bruce and Steven, I knew that once they heard them, they would want to do more with my friends.

Some months before I got the call from Bruce to join him at The Power Station, I convinced Apostol that we should invest some money and get back into the studio. While this meant limiting myself to jobs near New York City, he relented, and I reserved time at Sound Mixers Studio on 43rd Street to record a song which came to me via Little

Mama's godfather. George Bruno was a friend of Big Mama's from Brooklyn. He was a kindly older gentleman who together with his wife took their roles as Little Mama's godfather and godmother very seriously. They remained in touch throughout our stay in Norfolk, and George was always a big fan of Big Mama's singing. Some might have thought it unusual that George enjoyed writing poetry, as when he was not writing he ran a successful insurance business. Big Mama thought that George was gifted, and he would occasionally share his writing with her. She was familiar with one of his poems, "Way Back When." The theme was nostalgic and philosophical, a plea for simplicity in these complicated times, but musically I wanted something which was not a throwback.

Our work on "Way Back When," started in my den on the same piano that Bruce would use, except I was sitting at the keyboard. My band at that time consisted of John Clemente (bass), a veteran of the Air Force Tour, Mike Micara (drums), Joey Stann (saxophone), Rusty Cloud (keyboard) and Louie Conte (guitar). Joey and Mike had been part of the touring band for a group called Bullet which had one hit and was managed by John Apostol. Joey was also in process of leaving Southside Johnny and the Asbury Jukes, where Rusty Cloud would wind up after leaving me.

When we got into Sound Mixers we invited Rob Parisi of Wild Cherry to play guitar (he wrote and sang "Play That Funky Music White Boy") and an all-star chorus of Ula Hedwig, borrowed from Bette Midler, and Ellie Greenwich, former writing partner of Jeff Barry and co-writer of dozens of girl group sounds including "Da Doo Run Run" and "Leader of the Pack." I supplemented George Bruno's poetry with some power chords and I remember the other band members helping out on the chorus. Once we completed "Way Back When," we did another song. "Too Good For Each Other," written by Lanny Lambert, a guitarist and songwriter who was also an alum of Bullet, but now working with Apostol. He helped us out on "Way Back When." When it was time to go back to The Power Station to rejoin Bruce and complete the album for EMI America, I thought I would ask him to consider adding this track we had done on our own.

Dedication was nearing completion, but that didn't mean we could stop working. While Bruce was paying for the studio time and his musicians, we wouldn't see any money from EMI America until we delivered a finished album. That meant I was still doing the mall openings, club dates and oldies shows and making these appearances fit within our recording schedule. I don't think any of the people in the food court knew we were up the previous night recording an album with Bruce Springsteen, and I don't think they or the mall owners cared, but we all had rent to pay and we had no guarantee that the album was going to be successful. But the buzz was positive within the studio and my name was again being heard within the industry. I didn't mind that some were talking about the soon-to-be released *Dedication* being the "missing Springsteen album" and after a 17-year absence from the charts I felt we were dangerously close to getting ourselves out of the mall opening business.

To complete the album, Steven Van Zandt brought in a dramatic ballad that remains my favorite to this day. With a great orchestration and mournful opening solo by Clarence Clemons, "Daddy's Come Home," may be Steven's finest work and most poignant lyric. When I read the lyric, I couldn't help but think that Steven wrote it with me and my family in mind. He was most proud of it, and I saw he was surprised by my vocal range. Steven thought I would have no difficulty handling some covers of contemporary works. He pitched Jackson Browne's "The Pretender," and I did a reasonable job of interpreting it with some great vocal backing by Brenda Hilliard. Steven made some selections from the Dylan and Beatles' songbooks and Bruce thought both would work. What was in question was whether "Way Back When," would fit both from the standpoint of sonic quality and style. Bruce approved and was comfortable adding it. We had a finished product with three distinct groups of musicians who performed independently and collectively, my band, the Miami Horns and the E Street Band. The album had a total of 10 tracks: three Springsteen compositions, one by Steven, some covers and a song I wrote with Little Mama's poet godfather.

We left the studio and shortly I had the master ready for delivery to Gary Gersh at EMI America. It was an expensive work and a selfless gift from a friend. This gift could not be bought, and if we did not sell a single copy I would not have been any less grateful. Bruce was a friend of little more than three years who came to see my show, play some guitar and sing some songs that brought him back to a time and place.

There was some unfinished business that needed my attention before promotion of *Dedication* would start. John Apostol owned a much abused but iconic '57 Chevy, all red and white with bright chrome tail fins. I bought the car from Apostol and turned it over to a friend from Long Island who restored classic cars. I told him to work his magic. My instructions were to restore the car to a level that would not have prevented an owner from actually using it. I asked him to make it look like it rolled off the set of *American Graffiti*. I had an idea as to who might enjoy it once I had "Dedication" painted on the front passenger-side fender. Bruce didn't have one, though he could have bought a dozen in every color. This was a gift in which there was more pleasure in the giving than the receiving. I watched him perform at the nearby Nassau Coliseum. Following his show, I walked him over to the car and gave him the keys.

I was a signed artist again, but this time at a global major and just months away from a label-supported tour of mid-size venues. We were going to do the United States, Canada, Europe, and Scandinavia. I was working with publicity people from EMI America and they set up a full schedule of interviews and appearances coinciding with our album release. We were working with agents at the William Morris Agency and John Apostol's office was more focused on management than on bookings. The label suggested that we start with some seated shows with a focus on college markets and then some state fairs to give me exposure to a broad demographic range. They wanted me doing larger rock clubs that attracted a younger crowd. They were treating me as a new artist and an extension of the "Springsteen stable." Print advertisements for both the music trade and fans kept it no secret that *Dedication* was a Springsteen/Van Zandt collaboration. While they did not demand that I omit my '60s songs from shows, they absolutely did not want the focus to be my older material. They were not looking to tap into the nostalgia market and they were clear that my look needed to be fresh and contemporary.

All of this was new to me except what I would be doing on stage. The business had changed since the days of my hit records at Legrand. At Legrand, Guida did it all, not always effectively, but it was all him. Now, I had a bunch of people, each working on just one part of the effort to make *Dedication* a charting album.

One thing that did not change was the influence of *American Bandstand* and my friend from the bus tours, Dick Clark. Dick was still able to break a record nationally, but since I was unsigned for years, and didn't have records suitable for national release, 20 years had passed since I had done his TV show. One change within Dick's organization was Larry Klein, who joined Dick in the mid '70s fresh out of college. Larry made his mark producing the *American Music Awards*, and then took over *Bandstand* for which he won a Daytime Emmy. *Dedication* was released in mid March. Soon after, it appeared on the pop album charts and EMI America released "This Little Girl" as the first single. I spoke to Larry Klein who told me that Dick was thrilled that I would be back on the show and the gap of 20 years between appearances may have been a record for any returning artist.

Larry let me to do two songs, and I recommended two Springsteen numbers. We opened with "This Little Girl" and followed with "Dedication." When Dick interviewed me before our second number, the challenge was to stay focused in the present. He delicately asked me about the long pause between appearances without leaving any doubt that I had been alive, well, and making a living in the years between Guida and Springsteen. When he did the introduction to "Dedication," he faced the audience and said, "One more time, Mr. Gary U.S. Bonds," and that really did sum up that miraculous moment.

The band appearing to play behind me on *Bandstand* included Joey Stann, Rusty Cloud and Mike Micara who appeared on the album, but John Clemente was replaced with George Ruiz on bass, and Louie Conte had left and I replaced him with Billy Derby who played lead guitar. New addition Joe Martin played rhythm guitar.

Doing *American Bandstand* on my 42nd birthday, 20 years after my last appearance, gave Dick and I an excuse to open a special bottle and toast to my going from oldie to "newie." We rehashed a hundred stories from the tours and I got to know Larry Klein.

EMI America had not yet released "Jole Blon" as a single when Bruce introduced it to his fans at Wembley Stadium at the end of the European leg of his tour in support of *The River*. I can call his debut a "cover" with absolute confidence, but it would be ballsy to call it a cover of my record which he produced, arranged and sang on. On *Dedication,* Bruce generously credited Moon Mullican, a practitioner of "Texas Swing" from the '40s to the '60s, who did his version, "New Jole Blon," in 1947. From the name alone we know that Mullican's version was also a cover, and his English language variant followed more than two dozen English, Cajun and French versions, some predating his recording by as much as 20 years. Alone, Bruce did "Jole Blon" one more time before we would do it as a duo for the first time.

I stayed on the West Coast following my *American Bandstand* appearance. Bruce finished his last European show in Birmingham, England, where he did "Jole Blon," and headed back to California for the fourth annual "No Nukes" concert at the Hollywood Bowl on June 14. Bruce would be appearing with Jackson Browne, Bonnie Raitt, and Graham Nash. He invited me, and I joined him for one of his five numbers. We performed "Jole Blon" as we had recorded it for *Dedication*. The song was well received and that might have contributed to the decision to release it as a single after "This Little Girl."

Bruce remained on the West Coast and hinted that he might join me unannounced in San Francisco where I was scheduled to perform at the Old Waldorf club the day after the "No Nukes" show. The Old Waldorf was owned by Bill Graham who had years earlier closed both Winterland and the Fillmore West which he had operated since the late '60s. Bruce repeated his entrance from the Hanger, ascending to the stage after paying his way in and milling about unnoticed in the back of the club. But this time I was prepared, I recognized him. Bruce did about 30 minutes with "Quarter to Three," "School is Out," and "New Orleans," getting a bigger response than "Jole Blon" and "This Little Girl." Bruce was clearly enjoying himself. Reborn, I was re-living the dream. More precisely I was living it; it was hardly like this the first time. Before leaving San Francisco he asked me whether I would join him back in New Jersey where he was doing six shows and opening the just-completed Brendan Byrne Arena, now called the Izod Center, a 20,000 seat stadium which was to be the home of the New Jersey Nets and Devils in the Meadowlands sports, entertainment and retail complex.

I was not there for the opener because I had another commitment, but Bruce introduced "Jole Blon" midway through his opening show, making it Bruce's first solo performance of the song in the U.S. I was able to appear at the second show during which we performed "This Little Girl" for the first time at one of his concerts. I was also in attendance at the closing show, which, like the others, was sold out and we repeated our previous performance.

I was starting to feel like I had equity in the "E Streeters," that I was some kind of irregularly appearing member of the "E Street Auxillary," but I was careful to keep that fantasy to myself. *Dedication* was living and breathing and the frequency of "Springsteen-Bonds" sightings gave me coverage in the music press at a level I could not have anticipated nor obtained on my own. My fee for appearances was rising, and club-owners were not shy about fabricating rumors concerning the possibility of a special guest dropping in, even when Bruce was on the other side of the country. When I would deny knowledge of any planned or unplanned "Bruce-appearance," it was always with a wink and a grin from whomever was promoting the show, their defense being that a vow of secrecy was required for such matters. But our shows were entertaining even when I was on my own, and as more of the *Dedication* album became familiar, younger fans started listening to my older material.

All of this was not unnoticed in Norfolk where friends were calling and telling me that they were starting to hear me on the radio again. An old friend, Melvin Marshall, called to let me know that he was starting to see my records displayed prominently in the retail stores. While Frankie's Got It, formerly known as Frankie's Bircland, never stopped offering the full line of my Legrand Records, Guida now had all the old records and albums on cassette. He was even stocking the EMI America product with both the album and singles available. But Guida had not lost his touch when it came to recognizing opportunity. He remastered and reissued all the old material. He also did new compilations of the old material to capitalize on my discovery by a new audience. Fans could chose from the new material, new versions of the old records or the old records.

I would surely not participate in any of this new revenue earned by Legrand, but I took satisfaction in the fact that Guida would not benefit directly from my rediscovery, though many years later this would prove not to be true.

Our live performances were at the direction of EMI America and the agents at William Morris, and in retrospect their decisions turned out not be in the best interest of my ongoing career. EMI America had a number of emerging acts at that time, though none similar to me in the sense that they were making a second pass. EMI America was trying to advance my career along with that of Kim Carnes and the Jay Geils Band. Kim had the monster "Betty Davis Eyes" which was the second biggest song of 1981, and the Jay Geils Band had "Centerfold," which went to #1 in the beginning of 1982. EMI America was devoting the balance of their resources to David Bowie who was higher up on the ladder. With EMI financing the tour, and in control, they thought a pair of emerging acts could sustain itself in multi-thousand capacity theaters. With the paired acts both having recent high charting records, the combined drawing power of both fan bases was anticipated. This was not always the case.

If EMI America was truly concerned with the long term success of their newer artists, they would have been better off having each open for larger stadium acts that didn't need to re-establish themselves each year. If I would've opened for an established headliner and settled for less money, over an extended time I could have built a loyal fan base that would turn out to see me, rather than turn out only when I had a charting record. When Kim and I were both slotted to do an hour, I sensed that her fans were not there to hear "Twist, Twist Señora," and were probably just born at the time that "New Orleans" was selling. Doing a shorter opening set for a headliner I would have limited myself to the newer material. I will know better for the next time!

The William Morris people put together an ambitious tour. In a four month period we would do 70 shows. For most of the larger U.S. concerts in which we were paired with Kim Carnes, we switched off at the top of the bill depending upon the city. William Morris did the "routing." Routing refers to the sequencing of appearances from a geographic standpoint. Logistics is a challenge. Travel is expensive and we were moving a crew of 15. We used a luxury tour bus and air travel, with the goal of satisfying EMI America's financial objectives without having the talent wilt from exhaustion. Better and larger dates would be on Fridays and Saturdays with smaller venues occupying mid-week slots along the route.

In advance of the tour our publicist arranged for features in both *People* and *US* magazines. The *People* issue was available on newsstands at the start of August. The article ran for over a page, and while I did not get my picture on the cover, there was a nice teaser below the masthead which read, "Springsteen Sells Gary U.S. Bonds." Written by Sally Rayl, the article invoked the Bob Seger, "Rock and Roll Never Forgets," theme to a pretty standard story about my early career, absence from the public eye and recent rediscovery by Springsteen. There was a wonderful picture of me and Bruce at the "No Nukes" concert. Asking me about my "rediscovery" I told Sally Rayl that there was still a place for me in rock, and the picture accompanying the story captured that feeling clearly. In the photo Bruce is looking up at me while we both clutch our microphones, smiles on our faces. I know why I was smiling, I was singing with my friend and "This Little Girl" had made it to the top 15. With Bruce's help, I reclaimed my place in the music business.

The tour commenced in my back yard, Garden City, and was followed by an appearance with Tom Snyder on the *Tomorrow Show* which aired late nights on NBC and followed *The Tonight Show* with Johnny Carson. We stayed in the northeast for the first month playing in New England with some dates as far south as Baltimore before finishing September by heading to western Canada and then south for a swing through California. We came back east and did a great show in Starkville, Mississippi at a blues festival before playing throughout Florida. On our way to Florida we got a call that they wanted us to duck into a studio to do a quick take on a song that was going into a National Lampoon movie, *Class Reunion*, written by John Hughes. We motored on looking forward to our trip overseas.

Joey Stann, my talented horn player, who paid his dues riding buses with Southside Johnny, recalled two of his favorite bus drivers on the tour and both are well known in rock band circles. "My favorite driver was 'Earl the Curl.' Earl trained for driving rock bands by serving his country in Vietnam. In 'Nam' he distinguished himself by jumping out of helicopters and strangling enemy forces with piano wire. Earl shared stories about his war experiences and the miles would fly by. But the interstates can get tedious, and we would all doze off eventually, even Earl. Our guitar player, it could have been Joe Martin, comes towards the back of the bus where I'm spread out over two seats, deep into a dream. He tells me that the driver is out cold, sleeping. I don't know about most people, but I can't sleep on a bus when the driver is sleeping. I jump up and run to the front and wake up Earl who is not happy to see me. He explains to me that he knows Interstate 80. No turns, no traffic, and he had done it a hundred times. He could sleep with his knee holding the wheel and he knew instinctively when to wake up, usually refreshed. He showed me, but I couldn't sleep, and I didn't want to take the chance that he still had that piano wire. I never told Gary, who had a private area on the back of the bus. Earl would get us where we needed to be on time, but not 'U-Turn Bob.' Bob was a poor map reader in the days before GPS systems. 'U-Turn Bob,' had no sense of direction and he earned his nickname on every stop of every tour."

After Earl got us to our two shows in the Chicago area, we flew to Los Angeles for one last show before we left for London. William Morris offered us the opportunity of doing either NBC's *Saturday Night Live* or a show called *Friday's* on ABC which had been on for less than a year. *Saturday Night Live's* popularity had been in decline since the departure of many of the original cast members, and *Friday's* audience was building along with its reputation for showcasing more edgy musical talent. They left it to me and I chose *Friday's* and we did "Jole Blon" and "Way Back When." It was not the right pick, with *Saturday Night Live* episodes in heavy syndication and *Friday's* now forgotten except in discussions about the early careers of Larry David and Michael Richards who were both cast members.

I've had a friend and fan for 30 years, Mike Lancaster, a true Brit with whom I consult whenever I'm at a loss about some bit of obscure information on my career. Mike writes about music and his reviews have appeared in *New Musical Express* and *Now Dig This*, two leading UK pop music journals. Mike saw me perform for the very first time at our show in London and in an e-mail he shared his recollections:

"I recalled Gary U.S. Bonds as one of the early rockers, but had never seen him. He had not been seen or heard of in the UK for some years and I assumed he was trudging round the oldies circuit. I picked up a London newspaper and was pleasantly shocked to see prominent coverage on his new album, *Dedication*. The press article played heavily on the link with Bruce Springsteen who was more than hot at the time. It has to be said that the EMI label and their PR people did a great job making us aware of the second coming of Gary.

I decided that I should attend the London show to promote the album if for no other reason than to tick Gary off the list of rockers I had seen. A majority of the audience were 'Boss' fans eager for any link with their hero. This did not phase Mr. Bonds who absolutely tore through the album and even reprised favourite numbers. I am not sure I have encountered such an atmosphere since. I do recall a little fat guy in front of me who placed his shirt on the floor and proceeded to do the Mexican Hat Dance round it for the whole of the show! The rest of us just contented ourselves with being exhausted. Music writer Dave

Marsh called *Dedication*, 'one of the most successful comeback albums in rock and roll history.' I do not want to take issue with Dave Marsh (a Springsteen biographer) but *Dedication*, was one of the best rock and roll albums, ever, without any caveats."

Nice words, and Mike has summed up my love affair with British fans since my first trip with Johnny Burnette and Gene McDaniel 20 years earlier. I have been back many times since.

EMI America was pleased. They released three singles from the album. While "Jole Blon" and "Your Love," did not sell at the level of "This Little Girl," EMI felt their investment was paying off and they needed more product and they let us know before we returned to the states. Looking to expand his "friends of Springsteen" franchise, Gary Gersh decided to add Steven Van Zandt to the EMI America roster and he bought Steven's first solo effort, "Men Without Women." Our deal called for an additional album at their option, and they asked for it. I did not need convincing, and as it turned out, neither did Bruce Springsteen or my new label-mate Steven Van Zandt.

Thirteen

ON THE LINE

THE TOUR WAS A MONEY MAKER FOR all the promoters, and EMI America had a reasonably successful entry into the Gary U.S. Bonds business. I provided them with the next best thing to a Springsteen album, and as a veteran performer, grateful to be new again at 42, I took direction willingly. The tour finished in Paris and we felt triumphant. I remember how great I felt about the hundreds of older fans who let me know that they saw me the first time I played their city, in some cases at the very same theaters. They loved the new sounds, and when we played the old songs they got a huge reception. We did television spots in Hamburg and London and I was shocked to find audiences in Norway and Sweden familiar with my music. Big Mama and Little Mama joined me for the end of the tour, a chance for us all to see some great European cities together.

I was on a high, but a very sad incident happened as we were ready to leave. I was the target of racism at a Paris club where we were booked to play our last show before heading home. It was especially shocking because it was 1981 and we were in a city known for tolerance, a city that decades earlier became a haven for many African American performers seeking greater personal and artistic freedom. It was the day before our show and I entered the club with one of my musicians, Joe Martin. We wanted to see where we would be performing and have a drink. We both ordered, and the waitress told me that she "would not serve a n----r." Joe demanded that the manager fire our server immediately. Joe was outraged and I was stunned. The waitress was terminated on the spot but it did not make me feel any better. This was Paris in the '80s and I encountered a type of ignorance that was more typical of the Deep South of the early '60s. I was ready to return home and do another record.

Like *Dedication*, *On the Line*, was recorded at the Power Station. We started recording in February a few weeks after Steven completed his EMI America album and just after Bruce completed at his home studio the sparse tracks which would become *Nebraska*. As we finished *On the Line*, Bruce and Steven commenced work on *Born in the U.S.A.*

According to Steven Van Zandt, "Coming off the tour for *The River*, Bruce says we should do another Bonds album because the first one was great. He [Bruce] wrote the whole thing and most of the record was written for Gary."

Many critics feel *On the Line* is the better of the two albums, with stronger songs and vocals that critics have called "impassioned." I wrote two of the songs, Steven did one ("Last Time") and Bruce contributed seven. There was one cover, the Wayne Carson song, "Soul Deep," which in 1968 was the third of three smashes he wrote for the Box Tops. "Cry Like a Baby" and "The Letter" were earlier. Steven and Bruce brought back Chuck Jackson to join me on Bruce's "Club Soul City," and Jersey Shore vocalist J.T. Bowen did the harmony on "Out of Work," the only charting single from the album.

"Out of Work," was a lament on the difficult economic times we were all facing and it referenced former President Ford's "Whip Inflation Now," campaign. Some say elements of the song can be found in "Hungry Heart," Bruce's first #1 single which preceded it, and that my song would have done better (it reached #21) if the theme were more positive and encouraging. It was "boy meets girl, boy loses job, boy loses girl, help me Mr. President."

To promote *On the Line*, EMI America repeated what worked for the previous album, but added to my contract a consent that I would appear in a promotional video. This was new. MTV had been launched the previous August and music videos were just emerging as promotional vehicles and an entertainment form. Videos ranged from simple one camera recordings of a performance, to highly stylized three-minute dramas in which a songs' performers did not even appear. The idea was not entirely new, and the industry generally credits Richard Lester, who directed me in *It's Trad Dad,* as the creator of music videos which he used in the Beatles' *A Hard Day's Night*.

Bookings were again handled by the William Morris Agency, and I continued to be managed by John Apostol. There was a very lucrative addition. I now had a major corporate sponsor, Miller Beer. Miller was looking to increase its market share in a hipper and younger urban contemporary market. I tested well. With two careers 20 years apart, they thought that I would be able to reach people as young as 20 and as old as 50. Miller Beer became the sponsor for most of the U.S. tour dates. I recorded some jingles for them which were in the style of "This Little Girl," and we did a series of radio promos in which I swore my allegiance to the product after the jingle played. Miller's ad agency produced and distributed a costly souvenir program that was given away at all of our shows.

All sources considered, the money they paid me and the money they invested was very significant. John Apostol let me know that we were approaching a very significant financial milestone which we would likely achieve during the next tour. The label and our sponsor were betting large on *On the Line*. With Apostol managing the tour and our personal finances, my cares were limited to what happened on stage.

The tour route would be a variation on 1981, with a U.S. tour first and then a return to Europe and Scandinavia. I took the same band except Rusty Cloud would no longer be on keyboards. His replacement was Nick Bariluk.

The initial U.S. dates did not draw as well as they did the previous year. EMI America had concerns about the failure of "Out of Work," and they decided to release "Club Soul City," as a single in the U.S. It was released before we left for Europe and it did not appear to be bound for the Top 20. EMI America was also starting to complain about the cost of the tour support and word got to me through one of my musicians that John Apostol was not responding to the label's request for records and accounts of some of the advances they were providing for things like transportation and local promotion. When I questioned John he became defensive, and dismissed my concerns explaining that delays were due to the expanding size of our business and growing pains at his office. I believed him.

Before we left for Europe, I participated in the two largest events of my career, one in New York City and the other in Pasadena, California. I had met Jackson Browne the previous summer when I joined Bruce at the "No Nukes" concert at the Hollywood Bowl for our first public performance of "Jole Blon." While I enjoyed the concert and participated at Bruce's invitation, I learned about the need for nuclear disarmament and I was pleased to lend my name and support to the cause. In successive weeks in June 1982, the Committee for Nuclear Disarmament had planned two events. The first one was on my birthday, June 6, "Peace Sunday," at the Rose Bowl with 100,000 attending to hear Jackson Browne and friends, Bonnie Raitt, Linda Ronstadt, Joan Baez, Bob Dylan, Donovan, Stevie Nicks, Bette Midler and Stevie Wonder. While I remember Jesse Jackson's remarks and a finale of "Give Peace a Chance," nothing could top Bruce and Jackson Browne leading the crowd in a rousing "Happy Birthday."

The following Saturday I participated in what was considered the largest public protest ever assembled in New York City, with anywhere from a half to one and a half million people participating. Events included a demonstration which started with a walk from the United

Nations to Central Park's Sheep Meadow where the concert took place. Bruce Springsteen performed as did James Taylor and Linda Ronstadt. It made sense for me to join Jackson Browne for "The Pretender," and we did a version that paid respect to his original. The song's message was not wasted on this crowd and I have always considered his suggestion that we do the song as an indication that he was comfortable with my cover.

We left for the UK and Mike Lancaster was at our largest show, the 4,000 seat Hammersmith Odeon, now known as the Apollo. He remembers the show vividly:

"With *On the Line* issued, a European tour was scheduled. I believe that some of the dates were shuffled around and deferred as the hype at this time was nowhere near the level accorded *Dedication*. I vowed to attend the Hammersmith Odeon show which was the prime UK date. It seemed like everyone who saw the 1981 show wanted a repeat performance as the theater was sold out. All I could do was get three tickets standing at the rear. I felt I had let down my two friends, so I arrived very early hoping to get seats. The theater had nothing, so I did a deal with a ticket shark [scalper] who gave me three seated tickets in exchange for mine plus some cash.

I tell you this as I really should not have bothered. Gary came out and stormed straight into 'Jole Blon.' Not many rockers would have opened with such a strong number and built from there. The result was that during the first few bars the whole theater was on its feet and remained there with the building rocking for the duration. I need not have worried about the seats was the moral."

The British did not let me down, but I can't tell you that all the promoters were pleased. Some of the UK dates only did 50 percent of capacity and I knew it was the failure of any single off the album to create the same type of stir as in 1981. I can hardly blame Bruce, but it was a quiet year for him with no touring, and no arena shows. He spent the year recording, and as far as live gigs, he mostly sat in with Jersey Shore friends at Clarence Clemon's club, Big Man's West, or with the house band at the Stone Pony in Asbury Park, Cats on a Smooth Surface.

We limped back from Europe disappointed more in the failure of any single from the album to break out than our mediocre box office receipts. Multiple attempts were made after "Out of Work" stalled at #21. In different markets EMI America released "Rendezvous," "Soul Deep," and "Turn the Music Down." Including the original two releases, "Out of Work," and "Club Soul City," almost half the album was released as a single. In some markets, the "B" side was taken from *Dedication*, with "Way Back When," paired both with "Rendezvous," and "Turn the Music Down."

We needed to regroup and see where we stood with our label. But I was not prepared for what I encountered when I returned home. Big Mama looked grim when I walked into the house. After a long hug I needed to know what was on her mind. She told me she had a visitor to the house the day before, the County Marshal. We were served with a notice of eviction, as our bank had foreclosed on our house for non-payment of the mortgage. Since I was away Big Mama called John Apostol who was handling our money and she could not reach him. Big Mama was aware that the Apostols had just acquired a new home at a time the Marshal was looking to remove us from ours. Big Mama also knew that I had told John that he could use some of our money towards his down payment. I told her I would speak to John in the morning. It didn't make sense, we were so close to a major financial milestone.

John Apostol said that while I was completing the tour he was negotiating with EMI America. So far they were unwilling to meet "our" requirements for a third album. And as far as reaching that financial milestone, we had a setback and about the foreclosure on my house, he was sorry, but the office must have screwed up on those mortgage payments. I hadn't learned much since my days in Norfolk. I was an "A" student in loyalty, but I was still failing financial responsibility.

According to Apostol, EMI America said that *Dedication* was marginally profitable, and that the advance for *On the Line* and expenses from the two tours had put the entire project into the red. John dismissed my questions about whether they were upset about his record-keeping for tour expenses. He said that we should leave EMI America. We were no longer dealing with Gary Gersh who had been our supporter. Apostol felt that there was no way they lost money on my records, and I agreed with him. *Dedication* had a number of charting singles, including a #11, and the album did well on the pop charts. As for *On the Line,* he said it was respectable, getting as high as #54. But unlike *Dedication,* EMI America paid significantly more for the second album than the Springsteen-financed first album, and they provided a larger advance.

I was hearing from friends in the industry that EMI America was dumping us, but Apostol spun the story. He told me and others that the label had not properly reported our album sales, and that they did in fact want a third album, but at a much lower price. EMI America also figured it was unlikely that Bruce Springsteen and Steven Van Zandt would sign-on for a third go-round. While they were in the Gary U.S. Bonds business, it was never a secret that their interest was in leveraging my relationship with Bruce. Apostol said "we" would form our own label and put EMI America on notice. They did not flinch.

Apostol picked the right name for our label. The "phoenix" is a mythological bird that rises out of the ashes of its predecessor. No doubt I was his inspiration, and Apostol in choosing the name was saying that the old bird had flown and it was newly toasted. It was time for the next one.

Although we were no longer signed to a label, and there was little income from the second album, Apostol did not seem to be suffering. Upon my return home from touring I could not avoid noticing that he had acquired, for me of course, a new limousine. He had also significantly upgraded "our" office in the mid '60s on Manhattan's East Side. He had also furnished his new and larger home in Long Island. For his personal use he had acquired a fur coat. My guess was EMI America had somehow paid for it.

Apostol was focused on buying a studio and becoming a label head, but what we really needed was work. I had been away for a while and promoters no longer viewed me as an oldies act or leader of a show-band. We had been a signed international touring act for over two years, but without a hit record, and with the disappointing sales of *On the Line,* we were not in demand in any market and the price we offered promoters was no longer realistic.

Despite the slow sales of *On the Line* I still got a call from legendary producer Phil Ramone. By 1983 Ramone, a principal of A and R Studios, had worked with a score of multi-platinum selling acts and his call concerned work he was doing for a Universal Pictures movie, *D.C. Cab*. Phil said he was doing two songs at his studio, one with his wife Karen Kamon, and the other he wanted me to do. I had never worked with Phil Ramone, and unlike *Class Reunion*, there would be a soundtrack album released with 10 or 12 different singers. The song, "Once Around the Block Ophelia," was also a possibility for release as a single by Polygram. Phil said it was no more than a day or two at most and that he would send me the demo in advance so I could learn the song.

Phil Ramone has a warehouse full of Grammys, but not one for "Once Around the Block Ophelia," but I got paid for doing the record in more ways than one. It was at A and R Studios that I met Yank Barry. Yank's working on his own book, and when it comes out they will sell it as a business book and a "how-to," as a book of inspiration, politics, true-crime, fantasy, wonder, tragedy, and a lot of rock and roll. No one could have dreamed or invented Yank Barry except my friend Gerald Barry Falovitch.

When I met him, the Montreal native was in his mid-30s, and he told me he had been in the music business for half his life. He said he had some formal training in music theory, played a few instruments, and had a hand in a number of big records from acts like Tom Jones, Loggins and Messina, and Englebert Humperdinck. He had written jingles, but he was most proud of his work as a member of a Kingsmen (of "Louie, Louie" fame) touring band. Yank Barry was at A and R finishing an album. It might have been for Englebert Humperdinck or Julio Iglesias. Yank told me that he did some producing and arranging and that as a teen he had performed and recorded in Canada and Israel, singing in French, Hebrew and English. He rattled off names of acts that he had worked with in various capacities as far back as the late '60s when he was barely out of his teens. I was impressed. When he told me that other than music his passion was golf, I knew I had found a friend. But while Yank spent a lot of time in studios, in the first hour that I met him I sensed his ambition could not be confined to a glass enclosed booth. I told him I was recording with Phil Ramone, but I didn't have to tell him much about what I did. He knew my music, and not just the song names and melodies.

Yank could pull apart a song and tell you why it worked, how a particular sound was achieved, and how he could have done it better. He told me he'd be in touch and wanted me to join him at an upcoming charity golf event. I also told him that I was newly separated from EMI America.

I thought it odd that Neil Sedaka would want to record "New Orleans," and odder that he would want to do it as a duet with me. Neil is a huge talent, and while we had entered the business at about the same time, I never had occasion to work with him. Although I was not the prolific songwriter that Neil was, there were some parallels in our careers. We were both casualties of the British Invasion, and with the sponsorship of some major talent, we both returned. In his case it was Elton John. But even during what he calls his "hungry years" Neil had wisely cultivated huge followings in Australia and Italy. He had successfully regained control of his copyrights and was able to maintain a busy performance schedule. Our "New Orleans" is an interesting cover which showed that Neil could stray far from the sweet orchestral ballads of his later career and the catchy, uptempo songs of teen love that established him. The song became the "B" side of the single "Rhythm of the Rain" on Curb/MCA, but neither side got much play.

Apostol convinced me that our separation from EMI America was actually going to be good for us in the long run. We had two successful albums and I had established myself as a contemporary act. He told me we needed to control our own destiny, in our own studio, with material of our own selection. While he did not say it outright, I interpreted that as meaning that we didn't need the sponsorship of Springsteen and Van Zandt, or the promotion machine of a major label. I would be part of the ownership of Phoenix, and the plan was to look around for other acts we could sign. We would have our own studio as well, although we needed to come up with some additional investors.

We started putting together some material for our first album, and I had a song called "Standing in the Line of Fire," a minor key ballad with a solid hook and a disco-inspired back-beat. Despite Apostol's feeling that we did not need Springsteen or Van Zandt, I sent a demo of the song to Steven for his recommendations. As is his habit, he said he liked it, but it needed work. He agreed to work with us in our new studio, Kingdom Sound, with our additional partner its former owner, Bill Civitelli.

I was happy to give Steven a co-writer credit on the song. The result is a clear departure from what I am known for, but a very strong record that has held up to this day. The reason I am sure of the song's durability is that I performed it at Steven's request, at a banquet of which he was the honoree. In October 2012, at New York's Hammerstein Ballroom, Steven was given the "Big Man of the Year Award," an honor inspired by his departed band-mate, Clarence Clemons. The dinner benefited Little Kid's Rock, a not-for-profit that brings instruments and music instruction to schools in need.

The album had some standouts beside "Standing in the Line of Fire." There was a cover of Ritchie Valen's "Come On Let's Go." Frankie Vinci, a guitarist and future "King of the Toy Jingles," lent four songs including, "I Wish I Could Dance Like Fred Astaire," which he wrote with Rascals' drummer Dino Danelli who helped design the album. Little Mama contributed to three other songs.

One person who is uncredited, but deserving of a mention, is Fred J. Lincoln, the director of the album's accompanying video which we shot in Washington Square Park. Lincoln is an award-winning director of more than 300 films with titles like *Never Quite Enough*, and

Sweet Desires, and the classic, *Thighs Wide Open*. Outside of my rock video, and some horror/ slasher films, his work was mostly limited to adult features, for which he was named to the AVN (Adult Video News) Hall of Fame. Some New Yorkers may also remember him as the one-time proprietor of the social club Plato's Retreat. The video was shown on MTV for a month when I pulled it. I was uncomfortable with it, as some say it shows classic Lincoln style.

Although Apostol had failed at getting any meaningful distribution, it was time for me to do what I could to prevent this album from being stillborn. I contacted Larry Klein at *American Bandstand* and I sent him the album. Larry and Dick Clark remained supportive of my career. My last appearance on *American Bandstand* was on September 22, 1984, on which I sang "Standing in the Line of Fire," and "Sneakin' Away." If anyone liked what they heard they probably had difficulty finding these songs in stores. Our domestic distributor went bankrupt without paying us for the records we shipped. The album was issued later in Canada on the Attic label, and in the UK it was found on both Surf and Making Waves.

The album did not improve my bookings. I couldn't keep my band busy enough and I knew that Joey Stann would have to leave when he had the opportunity to rejoin Southside Johnny and the Asbury Jukes. For the album I put together a new backing band which we called the American Men. Apostol thought that the American Men might be able to work without me at smaller venues, and that I could take other musicians when I was doing oldies shows.

Joey Stann reminded me about one of our drummers who was really into astrology. He did a chart for me and it showed really good success for two years and then things would fall apart. He was not a great drummer, but sadly the chart was dead-on.

Fourteen

PERPETUITY IS A VERY LONG TIME

Apostol tried to brush off the failure of "Standing in the Line of Fire." He blamed it on the distributor, a distributor he had selected. We learned that our records were sitting in a warehouse due to the distributor's bankruptcy. We had no income coming in to support the studio and I needed to turn to a friend. Mike Peter joined us as a partner. I had never done that before. Mike and I had some history, working together in Orlando. He had good business sense and a successful track record, but his focus was on expanding his club business, which by now was national. I offered him the opportunity to buy-in, and he agreed, but his real interest was in helping me. With my failing grades in financial responsibility and an "A" in loyalty, I knew that once I asked him to invest there was a good chance he would lose money and I would lose my friend. But I needed help. Apostol's behavior had become erratic, and he had just about given up on trying to find work for me. But one thing I shared with my new partner was confidence in my ability to sing, and the knowledge that all it would take was my next hit record to make us both look smart. We just had to make one. This was no time to take chances with a new sound. It was time to go back to what worked and I called up Daddy G.

I tracked him down. He was at a studio in downtown Chicago and I told him I needed him quickly. Our record label was running out of gas, and I feared I would be back doing shopping center gigs if I didn't come up with a hit. Daddy G could hear my desperation but he really could not understand how fast things had changed. Daddy G still believed that a hit record could keep you working for 20 years, and in his mind I had another 18 to go. He packed his horn, cancelled some jobs, and came to New York. We brought him into the studio along with my band. Little Mama and I hastily put together some songs which combined the '60s sound with the feel of *Dedication*. We ignored the direction we took with *Standing in the Line of Fire*. We were not looking for a creative success. We were under immense pressure to make a record that would be played.

The first record we did was "Summertime Fun" on which I shouted, "Blow Daddy," just as I did in 1961. The flip side was "Dance to the Beat." In all we did about a dozen songs. To conserve funds we sent out demo copies of "Summertime Fun" to deejays with the idea that once we got some airplay we would press records. After *Standing in the Line of Fire* fizzled, it was too soon to ask my friend Larry Klein for another appearance on *Bandstand*. He was loyal, but he had a network to deal with and he could not justify it. While the records were fit for airplay, we had no promotion money and no distribution. We pressed a small quantity of records and if any sold, they sold near Asbury Park, one of the few markets where the record was played. I needed to focus on getting back into clubs.

Big Mama welcomed me back home from the road with a warm hug, but she could not hide her pained expression. It was a look I remembered, the same one that greeted me when I returned from the *On the Line* tour to find that we were facing foreclosure of our house. Big Mama said she didn't want to bother me while I was working, but the bills were not being paid, the mortgage was in arrears, and she couldn't reach John Apostol or anyone at his office. There was no money going into our accounts. Unable to reach John at his office, she tried him at home. Instead, Big Mama reached his wife and their exchange was heated with accusations flying in both directions. With our record company failing I am sure that John's wife was under similar pressure. It was time for change.

We convened a meeting of the Anderson family at our kitchen table, and it would have been so easy for Big Mama to start off with a resounding, "I told you so." She was entitled. In fact, she was entitled to two "I told you sos," one about Apostol's mismanagement, and the other about this disease I had called loyalty. Loyalty is admirable and valuable when it is coupled with sound judgment. In my case I put loyalty first and if I showed any judgment it was poor judgment. I was no better at managing our finances, I was too trusting, and the result was I squandered my talent and once again put my family at risk. But Big Mama saved the lectures. First, we agreed to be honest with ourselves and the prospects for a middle-aged rock and roller. Second, we would separate from John Apostol. We pledged to maintain control of what I did, and never let this happen to us again. I was 45 years old, the age when those who rock and roll go into overtime. But rock and roll overtime rarely pays time and a half, and it is usually followed by a quick fade. I had my two bites at the apple, and very few get the chance to take three. But my audiences were still responding. They were telling me that my talent had not yet betrayed me.

As with all performers, I have had more than a few nights when I have just not connected with my band, or my voice was not where it should have been. It may be the sound system, the crowd, fatigue or the rock and roll gods keeping you humble, but the audience picks up on it immediately. When people are paying $20 to see you, and they have to buy two over-priced beers to hear you sing your song, they will not hesitate to let you know when your talent has left the building. I was not getting complaints, but I needed more work. I was again in a very awkward place. I migrated away from the nostalgia circuit, and with my recent hits I was too new to be an "oldie." As for my being a contemporary act, the new songs were beginning to show age.

Big Mama and I made a pact that night. We would take back what was ours, trust only in ourselves, and not be fooled again. Our family was intact and our marriage was sturdy, but my career was badly bruised. It didn't make me feel any better that my story was not unique. Retelling my story to Southside Johnny one evening I remember his words ringing true as he described his own experiences with a handful of labels and agents, "Everybody owns you, except you. The only money you make is on the road."

I got back on the road and I started where I was known. I trudged up and down the East Coast, from The Stone Pony in Asbury Park, to The Bottom Line and The Lone Star, in New York City, north to hotels in the Catskills and west to the Pocono Mountains. I could always count on deejay and club owner Jerry Blavat to put me into Memories in Margate, New Jersey. I worked for less money than I was paid before the Sprinsteen/Van Zandt albums, but I was happy to get it. My options were limited. Mostly, I found my own bookings. I would do multi-act oldies shows and I was working the same hotel lounges I thought I would never need to play again. I wasn't picky about the size of the places I was playing either. I wasn't looking for empties on the side of the road, but it was a far cry from flying first class to the capitals of Europe. If they offered me a shopping mall job I would have taken it. My financial milestone was a laughable fantasy that would need to be deferred. Having realized the dream of being signed to a label, I'd never pray for that again; the dream turned out to be better than the reality. My goal was keeping food on the table and my family together. Mike never saw anything from his investment, but he let me hold on to what was really valuable, his friendship.

Keeping my family together was threatened with violence. We had left Norfolk to escape ignorance and find a safe and peaceful place to raise our daughter. The peace was shattered with a pipe bomb. The police said it was not the work of an amateur. Two feet of black powder and a tidy fuse showed the bomb-maker to be better than average. It was likely tossed from a moving vehicle, and it landed within a foot of the front of our house where the kitchen is. Big Mama and Little Mama were in front, but luckily, not near the windows.

I was in the basement when it went off, and when I ran up to see a new two foot deep divot in the lawn I knew someone had some seriously bad intentions. Frightened but unharmed, we didn't abandon our home; we had done that once. We had suspicions and no shortage of friends who wished to settle the score on our behalf. Neighbors came to our side and I remember good friend Ronnie Brandenburg standing guard in our driveway, taking turns as a look-out with the neighbors. Ronnie knew I had commitments that I needed to fulfill, and he reassured me that he would be there for the girls.

If there was any question as to how promoters saw me, it was answered in 1986 when I was booked for some UK appearances as part of a promotion called *A 1960's Revival Tour*. True to the title, at several of the shows this mismatched group required reviving. The tour was promoted by Mervyn Conn. Conn not only promoted the Beatles pre-1964, but he would eventually be the largest importer of U.S. country acts to the UK, a business he developed after successfully representing Johnny Cash. I do not know what inspired Conn to think that a show consisting of The Mamas and Papas, Martha Reeves, Lou Christie, and Scott McKenzie would appeal to any kind of audience, even with me added as the second act on the bill.

After receiving my contract for the UK tour, I needed to return to Jacksonville. My father passed at the age of 80 and on April 19th his life was celebrated at Jacksonville's Davis Funeral Home. At the service I realized how far we had grown apart. I didn't recognize any of his friends. People were talking about "Bo-Peep" and I didn't know that Pop was known by that name in Jacksonville. My step-sister Joyce and I spoke and she told me how proud Pop was about what I had accomplished, but I wasn't convinced. It was easier for me to believe Joyce when she told me that Pop was thrilled when he heard that Little Mama would be graduating from college that June. Joyce and her husband, Chaman took the trip north to see Little Mama graduate from New York Institute of Technology and then we all went to the Poconos where they saw me play one of the resorts. It was a joyous trip and I closed my eyes and thanked Pop for bringing us all together.

I left uneasily for the UK to join the tour, with the recent viclence against my family constantly in mind. We were scheduled to do two shows a night, and play 15 theaters over 17 days. It was 20 years since the final hit of the Mamas and Papas, and the group now consisted of original "Papas" John Phillips and Denny Doherty, John's daughter Mackensie, and "Spanky" McFarlane, formerly of Spanky and Our Gang. The group was sometimes billed as "The New Mamas and Papas," but fans who turned out to see them were well aware of the personnel changes. Despite press accounts that Denny Doherty wasn't talking to John Phillips due to John's continued drug abuse, I found them both to be cordial, professional, and committed to a successful tour. We sold out the Hammersmith Odeon in London, the largest theater on the tour, just as I did two years back as a solo, but on other nights we only managed to fill a quarter to a half of the seats.

It was concerning when at the mid-point of the tour at Birmingham, and just before the Hammersmith show, that we had not yet been paid for the completed dates as promised. John represented the Mamas and the Papas and Scott McKenzie, and our failure to be paid did not seem to trouble John as much as the others. Lou was concerned and he turned to me along with Martha Reeves. Martha went "racial," attributing our lack of pay to the color of our skin. I calmed her when I explained that the promoter was not a racist, and that he had not paid the white acts either. Conn sent an assistant to the box office every night to collect the evening's receipts and at Birmingham, John and I collared him and explained that there would be no show at the Hammersmith if he did not pay us in advance of the next performance. Not wanting to put the only sold out show at risk, Conn's assistant returned the next day with a satchel of cash which he handed to me as if I were the paymaster. I asked John to hold the bag and open it while I held the messenger. Opening the bag, John quickly confirmed it appeared to be all there, but to me it looked excessive. I took the bag from John and counted out what everyone was owed. I left the balance in the bag, handed it back to the messenger and told him to return it and thank Mr. Conn. Conn paid us promptly and accurately for the balance of the dates.

After seeing my performance at the Hammersmith, Jim Cullinan reported in *TheNorfolk Echo* (December 1986), "Seeing Gary U.S. Bonds perform is an unforgettable experience. He is not a staid over-the-hill rocker who should have quit years ago. His music grabs you by the throat—it is vital, fresh, exciting and as new as the moment." These are kind words from a long-time fan, the type of encouragement that convinced me that the time for a quick fade had not yet come.

Cullinan was one of two enterprising Englishmen, diehard fans, dedicated to making sure that what we had done in Norfolk was not forgotten. In September 1986, Cullinan and Brian Walsh commenced publishing a newsletter that would meet the pent up desire for information of the global community of fans of the Norfolk Sound. They started a journal which was devoted to the life-work of Frank Guida. *The Norfolk Echo* concerned itself with every record done by Frank, every label, and every artist he recorded. What is fascinating is that the first issue came at a time when Guida's work was at its ebb, and not just because it was 18 years since he had released my last record.

As Frank Guida did, I cooperated with the writing partners, but never really got a sense of how many people read the newsletter outside of Cullinan, Walsh and Guida. I will admit to consulting the *"Echo,"* in writing this book and overdue credit and appreciation goes to Cullinan and Walsh for their efforts. They got most of it right, and the stuff they missed, well they now have a reliable source for corrections.

It was around this time that I started to get some calls from the music press about "Wonder Boy," my former partner from the Azalea Gardens Club who sang about how to be happy for the rest of your life. I hadn't seen James for at least 10 years and the last time I saw him puzzles me to this day, but it was prophetic. I was coming out of a building on Broadway after visiting with some publishers when I saw

Jimmy running towards me as if he was being chased. I knew it was him and I tried to stop him, but he sprinted past me and yelled, "Gary, I'll catch you later." That was it.

He took that one record as far as he could. Guida tried some other things, but Jimmy was a "one and a half hit wonder." I heard indirectly that he was in prison; somebody said Sing Sing. I was told it was for embezzlement, but I have never confirmed it. I have often wondered what would have happened, and if I would have spared Jimmy by recording that song. What would have happened if he continued to sing the Lord's word and what made him put that loincloth on? Jimmy and Royster, young men both gone.

The calls I got from the music press were interesting and I gathered that the old rumor about Jimmy and I being the same person had resurfaced. People were asking me if I was aware of the death of Jimmy Soul, but I think they wanted to know if I was still alive. They finally put that myth to rest and Jimmy as well at Olive Branch Cemetery in Portsmouth, not far from the Azalea.

Jimmy's passing was sad and unexpected. Grandma's passing was anticipated. She was in failing health and had lived with my Aunt Louise since my mother's death. Mother never discussed her age and Grandma probably taught her that age was something that a "lady" never spoke about. At a private service she was interred in Jacksonville. She was a quiet presence, and after Mom, my biggest fan. She had been in business most of her life and she considered herself a professional and conducted herself accordingly. The only ill word that I had ever heard her utter, was when an unflattering word was said concerning me or my mother. Newkirk predeceased her, and according to Aunt Louise she seldom spoke since my mother passed. Aunt Louise let me know that my grandmother left something for me and I was curious. My inheritance was an envelope. It contained her beautician license from the State of Virginia. I did not remember that she displayed it in her shop, but I recalled her telling me that unlike some of the other beauticians, she was "legal." The license had a small photograph. Her pose was serious and business-like, her hair and makeup tasteful, sure signs that she knew her trade. The license had her date of birth. I've kept it to this day, as well as her secret.

Some nights it was as if someone else had those early '80s charting hits. When I would get hired as part of a nostalgia show it was mainly due to a clubowner's familiarity with my earlier songs. In performing for older crowds, when I reached the point in my show where I did material from *Dedication*, I would often get a response like, "That's his song?" When I appeared as part of a multi-act show, where I was limited to 15 minutes, promoters were not interested in the Springsteen/Van Zandt songs. They wanted me to do "New Orleans" and "Quarter to Three," and I obliged. The exception was when I played my favorite clubs along the Jersey Shore. There, the crowds knew the Springsteen association, and were well versed in the influence and crossover between the "Norfolk" and "Jersey" sounds.

My current musical director is a product of the Jersey clubs, a self-taught prodigy that I am honored to have as a co-worker, traveling companion, golf partner and friend. He has brought and maintained consistency, professionalism and stability to my shows. When I take to the stage and see a new player we've picked up for a gig, I'm confident that Mark has told him what is expected. When we provide backing for an opening act or an entire show, I rest knowing that after a run-through and sound check, that every performer will be well-supported. I found Mark Leimbach when he was touring with Eddie and the Cruisers, a band formed to capitalize on the fame of the fictional group depicted in the movie of the same name. He didn't need rehearsing. The Cruisers and I had been playing the same places in the late 1980s and Mark had seen enough of my shows to know what I needed him to do.

Rock and roll is about 20 parts waiting to one part playing, and when you're waiting around, traveling, eating, drinking or just killing time before or after a show, it is so much easier when the person you're doing it with is someone whose company you enjoy. Mark is that person and he has been with me continually since the late '80s. He has also appeared on all of my recordings during the period and he has developed into a talented songwriter. During that time we've acquired some interesting rituals. One ritual involves my response to an evening's performance when it just doesn't measure up to what we're capable of doing. This is how Mark tells it:

"It could be two or three in the morning. We've had a few after the show, and we're in some hotel whose name escapes both of us. If the room number isn't on the key, chances are one of us will forget where we're going. When we finally find our rooms on a night when a show has not been one of our best, I know I can expect a call from Gary. I get into bed, but I know it's no time for sleep. Years ago Gary would call on the house phone, but now it's a cell-phone call. Gary usually starts the conversation.

"Fire those assholes."

"Why?"

"I told you they can't play. Why'd you hire those guys? They screwed up the medley, they don't watch. Did you tell them we repeat the ending? Don't they know what two fingers means? The drummer came in late, and why'd he ride that cymbal all night?'

"I told them everything. I went over all of it. They had the music. You're right. I'll speak to them again in the morning. I promise. Tomorrow will be better. They can play. I've heard them play, now go to sleep.

All is forgotten in the morning and often the next show is better. Sometimes it's just the two of us and we're playing with a house band and they're terrible. Sometimes it's something you never prepare for. We're at the Fox Theater in Detroit for one of those multi-act oldies shows. It's me with the house band and they're actually pretty good. We're scheduled to go on after the intermission. The weather was horrible, there must have been a foot of snow when we arrived and it was still coming down heavy at show time. Gary goes out to a good reception and then the theater goes dark. We've lost power. The emergency lighting goes on and there's barely enough light to see him onstage. The crowd doesn't know whether they should stay or leave. Gary starts singing, by himself, unaccompanied. The sound guy gets a flashlight and shines it on Gary. The audience starts singing along. I had a hollow body electric, so I picked it up and started strumming. He sang the whole show. It was a crazy, moving experience."

While we're doing it 20 years now, I still recall Mark's first show, talk about a baptism by fire. The Cafe Bar in Long Branch is mostly forgotten, it was one of the dozens of pier-side bars that come and go on the Jersey Shore. The place probably held 300, but there must have been twice that number on a Sunday night during a four-day July 4th weekend. Not only is the place packed, but people outside are pressing against the large windows. I know that Mark is too focused on getting the music right to realize what's going on. I hadn't done anything with Bruce since the beginning of '85 when I joined him briefly on stage at the Greensboro Coliseum. He got word to me that he might show up. Mark finally sees that Springsteen is standing in the corner, stage-right. Mark will never forget that night.

"All I'm thinking is don't make any mistakes. It's my first night, I'm trying to impress Gary, and now I've got Gary and Springsteen. We finish the fourth or fifth song and Gary speaks into the mike to Springsteen in a way that only Gary would have the courage to do.

"You coming up, or what?"

"He came up and I handed him my guitar. I gave him my Telecaster and I picked up my hollow-body. Bruce and Gary huddled, and since we had not yet done anything from *Dedication*, or *On the Line*, they decided that's what we'll do before finishing with 'Quarter to Three.' Bruce walks over to me and tells me that he will follow me. I barely knew where I was going. My first Gary gig and Springsteen is following me! I didn't think I was imagining it, but the whole club was bouncing and the four-foot-by-eight-foot windows were starting to flex. Before we ended the set I think they let in another hundred people. It was craziness. I bluffed my way through 'Bony Moronie.' Bruce stayed with us through the finale, and it took the bouncers a while to empty the place. The bartenders were gone by the time we packed, but someone brought us a case of longnecks from the cooler. We averted a crisis. These were not twist-off tops and no one could find an opener. Springsteen showed us how to open a beer on the corner of a speaker cabinet. I can still do it. What a night. I got a lesson from The Boss and I made the band."

While the Springsteen/Van Zandt numbers continued to be part of my live act, the albums had long since stopped selling when the people at Rhino, pioneers in the creative repackaging of vintage music, decided to do a newer type of compilation to ride the Springsteen crest which only escalated at the end of the 1980's. It was their novel idea to put together an album called, "Cover Me," consisting of Springsteen songs which were not all in fact covers. These were primarily songs that Bruce had written, but not recorded, although he had performed them. The compilation included Southside Johnny, Dave Edmunds, the Pointer Sisters, Johnny Cash and The Hollies. On the CD were "This Little Girl," from *Dedication* and "Club Soul City" from *On the Line*.

The Rhino compilation sold, and a promoter decided to do a show at The Beacon Theater in New York City with a few of the acts from the CD and some additional performers doing covers. It was a charity gig, and I agreed to do it. While the Springsteen fans who helped make it a sell-out were pleased to have me on the bill, they fidgeted through a series of acoustic sets and some unaccompanied keyboard players who wailed their way through some of Bruce's more serious numbers. I closed the show with "This Little Girl" and "Club Soul City" from the album and "Quarter to Three," as an encore as Bruce was in the habit of doing.

Mark recalled, "This was one of the best shows we ever did in terms of crowd reaction. The audience sat through two hours of 'mellow' and they were waiting for something to happen. It felt like there were a dozen guys who came out to play solo piano. These were Bruce fans, they were waiting for something loud. After the last acoustic set the stagehands started bringing on guitars and horns and the place started erupting, like it was going to explode and this was for the stagehands! We walked out on stage and they announce, 'Ladies and gentlemen, Gary U.S. Bonds.' It was 'Beatle-esque.' He hits the stage and they're standing and he hasn't sung a note. We did an hour and probably could've played two. We ran out of covers."

Mark made the band and stayed to this day, but I didn't take him to a job I had in Norfolk in the Fall of 1990, a few months after he joined me. I wasn't so sure that I wanted to take the job, or the trip back to Norfolk. I claim to have never left the city, and I would say that is true if a place remains the home of your oldest friends and fondest childhood memories. But when I think back to the cruelty that caused me to leave, in some ways the place betrayed me. I can't blame a place for the stupidity of a few people, or a city for some dumb business decisions that I happened to make there, but I was not happy with the idea of going to Norfolk in September 1990.

The invitation to return came from Norfolk State University. The occasion was an honor. The college had received a gift from the Guida family, artifacts from Legrand, and they wanted to mark the occasion with a weekend celebration of the musical contributions of Frank Guida, Gene Barge and myself. The weekend would start with a jam session at the Mark IV on Friday night, followed on Saturday by a presentation to the three of us at the University before a football game. If I agreed to go, this would not be my first attendance at the school.

I enrolled at the school when it first opened, and the first few weeks I attended I truly enjoyed. If it had not been discovered that I failed to graduate from high school, there was a possibility that I might have been an honoree of my alma mater. That was not the case, but I accepted the invite and the school was kind enough to send tickets for Big Mama and Little Mama as well.

I was inclined not to go because of the ongoing and bitter dispute between me and Frank Guida. How could I share an honor with him for the music we made when he sought to deny me any financial benefit from what we created? The legal issues surrounding my writing, publishing and performing royalties consumed 25 years of my life. Today, I derive no benefit from my work with Frank Guida and Legrand, and those records with which I am most connected were bartered away under duress so I could continue working

Frank Guida, if he were alive today, would say the agreement I willingly entered into was a small price to pay for the benefit I gained from him making me his life's work, and the focus of all his creative energies. He would tell me that his efforts have allowed me to have a career for more than 50 years. He would remind me that I was any one of a dozen kids that he could have taken off the street corners of Norfolk and that I should be thankful. Trusting Frank Guida. who was my label-owner, manager, accountant, and legal advisor, I signed an agreement that prevented me from ever recording the early songs again and compensated him for being my manager during my years at Legrand.

He never took any steps to enforce the agreement until 1979, a low point in my career, when I signed over my rights and a lien was placed on my royalties. These liens were satisfied by earnings from the EMI America albums and singles. I signed the earliest agreements at Frank's advice and without the benefit of a lawyer. I have since learned the meaning of the word "perpetuity." "Perpetuity" earned me another lawsuit when I rerecorded my old hits for a compilation album that was going to be sold on television.

In advance of the celebratory weekend, the local press tried to stir up my decades-old feud with Guida, but I would not participate, and Frank responded similarly. I told Jim Morrison of the *Virginian Pilot* before the weekend's events, "We had our problems, Frank and I. But that's been a long time now. We no longer do any business together so what the hell? Let bygones be bygones."

About the "feud" Frank would only say to the same reporter, "It's part of the story I don't even like to discuss."

We made the trip and did our best to be gracious to our hosts while avoiding contact with the Guida family. When the Norfolk State University marching band struck up "Quarter to Three," and then went into a medley of my hits during half-time of their game against Livingstone College, I reached out for the hand on my left and the one on my right. I held my girls' hands firmly as the crowd thunderously applauded at the end of the number. When the public address announcer asked me to stand, we stood proudly to the crowds' delight. I remembered all those years ago, and Frank saying we were doing something important. I don't think he anticipated this.

Looking back at the weekend's events and press coverage, Frank's daughter, Anne Guida Kent wrote to the *Virginian Pilot,* commenting on an interview I did, "As for the embittered Mr. Bonds, I am reminded of a quote by Mark Twain, 'If you pick up a starving dog and make him prosperous he will not bite you. This is the principal difference between a man and a dog.'" I did not respond.

Fifteen

NO BEEF WITH ALI

At the time we met, Yank had toiled in the music business for almost as long as I had. He started recording as a teen, both in Canada and Israel. When *Animal House* became a box-office hit and re-popularized "Louie, Louie," he hit all the East Coast campuses with a Kingsmen touring group. He did turns as both a solo performer and group member. In 1971, he recorded one of the first "concept" LP's, *The Diary of Mr. Gray*, and when I met him he was helping make hits for others, doing hasty in-studio arrangements for horns and strings during larger sessions. Yank's ambition and imagination were not going to be satisfied with a bunch of gold records, and when you are versatile enough to go from the studio to stage with Tom Jones, you accumulate a bunch. He's put them to good use and they can be found covering the walls at his various offices.

Yank is restless, and dreams on a grander scale than most of us. Many of us have trouble connecting all the pieces of our lives, while Yank is a master at putting together the puzzle. He used his background in music and access to celebrities to help him sign his first professional golfers as clients for his sports management company, and from his work with golfers, he launched his philanthropic efforts.

I sing better than Yank, but he's the best salesman I've ever met. From a distance I've watched him work, win friends and influence people and with an endless supply of behind the scenes showbiz stories, he is a master of the "schmooze." Yank is engaging, up front about his strengths, blunt about his weaknesses, and candid about his past from which he's learned. He was about to sell me.

Yank invited me to a golf tournament at Wild Dunes in Charleston, South Carolina, a celebrity pro-am that preceded a tour event. The event had proceeds going to a drug prevention program and Yank and I found that ironic in that not so many years earlier Yank would have been a poor advocate for the cause. My hustling days long behind me, I was now playing with a full set of clubs and my handicap was hovering around five. While this did not help us much playing with cagey duffers who consistently outplayed their handicaps, it did motivate the professionals we were paired with. Instinctively, the professionals became competitive when they were paired with "country club" players who had some "game." When Yank focused on his game he was a skilled shot-maker, and we would normally contend, if not win. He gained introductions that were more valuable than the golf bags or engraved crystal we took home. This trip to Charleston turned out to be business for both of us.

Yank was animated when I met him in the clubhouse, more so than usual, but not about the prospect of playing a few rounds of golf. He told me he identified an opportunity while playing at a similar event in South Africa. He was introduced to a food chemist who had developed a product which he described the way you might tell someone about a perpetual motion machine, or a way to get an automobile to run on water. Yank never was very good at "subtle" and this idea could not be described in the millions. This invention required the "b" word, and he used it liberally between strokes which were amazingly effective despite his having no interest in golf that day.

He had obtained the North American rights to a patented formula for processing soybeans into a nutritional protein-rich powder and

Yankee fan and a piano man, Billy Joel.

By U.S. Bonds — That's My Story

Bruce Springsteen adding another song to my album.

Dedication goes gold 1981.

Photographs

Yank and Yvette marry at the Nevele. (l to r) Shirley Austin Reeves of the Shirelles, Chuck Jackson, Big Mama, Yank and Yvette Barry, me, Smokin' Joe Frazier, Larry Chance.

Working with the Champ, Muhammad Ali.

Muhammad Ali, helping us feed children.

Photographs

At Master Sound studio with Ben E. King.

With Merv Griffin, a great host and fan at his Resorts International in Atlantic City.

My "homegirl" Ruth Brown at her birthday celebration.

Bo Diddley, a giant talent, a lifelong friend.

Photographs

Ruth Brown and George Clinton on hand to watch me receive a Pioneer Award.

Congratulations from Bruce Springsteen at the Pioneer Awards.

Jerry Blavat, Steven Van Zandt, me and Bruce Springsteen.

Aretha Franklin at the Pioneer Awards.

Photographs

Two men of the blues, with Charlie Musselwhite.

Allman Brothers Band guitarist Dickey Betts.

By U.S. Bonds — That's My Story

Accepting honors for "Comeback Blues Album of the Year" from the Blues Foundation.

Photographs

Tony DeLauro with me and my girls at the Stone Pony in Asbury Park, New Jersey.

Little Richard getting ready to rock.

Stopping by to see Chuck Berry at the Westbury Music Fair.

Helping my "teacher" B.B. King celebrate his birthday with Bo Diddley.

Photographs

At a Light of Day Concert in New Jersey with Bruce Springsteen.

My wingman, "Slow Drag," Walter Johnson.

The Haskins brothers, (l to r) "Fat Rat," me, and "Jelly Belly."

Photographs

Helping me "fool 'em again," my Musical Director Mark Leimbach.
Courtesy of John Cavanaugh

Onstage with the Andersons.
Courtesy of John Cavanaugh

Photographs

My favorite girls.
Courtesy of John Cavanaugh

Jon Bon Jovi joins the Anderson family.

With Bruce Springsteen and Jon Bon Jovi at the Count Basie Theater.
Courtesy of John Cavanaugh

Photographs

Reminiscing with Chubby Checker at the Dick Clark memorial service.

Forgiving Bill Wyman and Spencer Davis for the British Invasion.

Steve Winwood backstage in Brecon, Wales. *Courtesy R. Golinucci*

Photographs

Harmonizing with Ben E. King on the *Great American Soul Book* Tour.   *Courtesy R. Golinucci*

Greeting a special fan, Randy Cooper.

Bill Reid at his office in *The* NorVa urging me to get my story down.
Photo Eric Lusher

My star on the Norfolk Legends of Music Walk of Fame.
Photo Eric Lusher

Photographs

With Duchess (Joyce Moore) and LuLu (Vernon Wilson) at the Mark IV. *Photo Eric Lusher*

Purcell Beale at the Mark IV. *Photo Eric Lusher*

"Ba-Bee" Richard Gault-Page. *Photo Eric Lusher*

By U.S. Bonds — That's My Story

Our house on Middle Street. *Photo Eric Lusher*

A favorite son of Norfolk at Mayor Fraim's office.
Photo Eric Lusher

Photographs

Convincing Paul Shaffer that I was not Jimmy Soul.
Photo Matthew Ziegler

Stopping by The Underground Garage and sharing a laugh with Steven Van Zandt.   *Photo Matthew Ziegler*

Me and Steven. *Photo Matthew Ziegler*

Photographs

Just pronounced man and wife, Mr. and Mrs. Eurel Tobias.
Courtesy Jon Reis

Rocking out with (l to r) Hal B. Selzer, Joey Stann, and Mark Leimbach.
Courtesy John Cavanaugh

Joining Bruce on the Wrecking Ball Tour at Metlife Stadium. *Courtesy of Eason Jordan*

Photographs

Bruce and I please a fan with "Jole Blon." *Courtesy of ron ring*

Thanking the crowd. *Courtesy of Eason Jordan*

Max Weinberg and Jake Clemons join their "Boss" and me. *Courtesy of Eason Jordan*

Photographs

Mark Leimbach with Bobby Bandiera and Lance Hyland Stark keeping time.   *Courtesy of ron ring*

Hope Concert VI, Southside Johnny with Ben E. King.
Courtesy of ron ring

All I wanted to do was sing. *Courtesy of ron ring*

meat substitute. The powder can be reconstituted with drinking water and the resulting paste can be creatively used in place of beef, chicken or pork. It was stable, required no refrigeration, mixed well with spices and flavorings and could be used as an extender of the real thing, or on its own. But, as they say on infomercials, "Wait, there's more!" It costs a fraction of even the cheapest meat products. When I asked Yank the logical question, "Was this unique?" He told me there were others, but he had a way to beat the competition. Leave it to Yank to figure out how to turn an invention into billions. His method defied logic. He was going to give it away, make money, and end world hunger at the same time. How could I doubt my friend, a rock and roll singing Jewish sports agent and recent emigre from Tin Pan Alley by way of the hardscrabble streets of Montreal? Yank was going to make billions by giving the product away. Sure.

He said he wanted me to work with him; he needed introductions to more celebrities, and he explained why. The product was called VitaPro, and he had arranged to have it manufactured in Canada. He saw no reason why his desire to be rich and famous could not further his philanthropic goals and vice versa. From this philosophy emerged his tag line, "Doing well by doing good." He would allocate part of VitaPro's revenues to a foundation which would combat world hunger. But unlike similar efforts which channel dollars into impoverished nations, Yank would manufacture and land this product within the borders of countries that had populations in need.

With my assistance, he would organize celebrity-led missions to attract attention to the need and the product. The goodwill generated by the free distribution, and the attention that the celebs would bring would be the best advertising for the for-profit side of the business. I know little about processing soybeans or food chemistry, and there are few meals I have had to skip in life, but I did not need proof to know that there were places in this world where a nutritious meal is a luxury. When I wasn't selling records, maybe I could feed my family by helping feed others whose problems dwarfed my own.

The entire Anderson family got involved. Big Mama was working with the product in our kitchen, helping Yank put together recipes and demonstrating how versatile the product is. Big Mama confirmed what Yank claimed. With simple ingredients and presentation the product could take on the characteristics of meat and poultry. As Yank boasted, VitaPro could be served as a standalone or as an extender. Little Mama signed on full time with Yank and she took off to live in Montreal near the VitaPro offices and work as Yank's full-time executive assistant. I was doing my part. I went to my closest friends in the business and told them that I had volunteered to be a celebrity spokesperson for the Foundation. I would be leading missions to different impoverished parts of the world where we planned to set up shop, bring the product, and build facilities for preparing it.

Global Village Champions, the foundation, was not a hard sell, and Ben E. King and Chuck Jackson joined me early in the project. While Yank was happy to have this support, he was candid about needing a marquee name, one that would be instantly recognizable globally, and someone whose personal beliefs were consistent with the mission. Yank told me he needed to meet Muhammad Ali. I knew Howard Bingham, the photo-journalist, and one of Ali's oldest friends from Louisville. He was a confidant of Ali's and someone I had met while performing on the charity circuit.

Through Bingham I arranged an introduction and we had the opportunity to serve VitaPro to Ali at his home. It was Yank, Big Mama and me and Yank told the champ, "Muhammad it's not meat."

"It's not beef? Then it's chicken," guessed Ali as he tried another fork-full of Big Mama's recipe.

"It's not chicken, Muhammad," Yank boasted to a disbelieving Ali, visibly fighting a tremor as he haltingly lowered his fork to his plate.

Eyes shining, he looked up at us, hesitated, and softly spoke, "I can sell this. You'll make a lot of money with me, but I want to feed hundreds of millions of kids. Shake up the world." He signed on as the worldwide ambassador of Global Village Champions and with Ali on board Yank had no trouble getting others to follow.

Yank started selling VitaPro to food processors and municipalities, and true to his vision we worked together to organize celebrity missions. Standing with Yank and Ali in remote regions of Liberia and the Ivory Coast, I learned what true celebrity meant and how that power can translate into measurable results. We coordinated with local aid groups, and the presence of Ali gained us cooperation and access to the local government agencies that we needed. Humanitarian, religious and civic groups joined with us to feed children. It took money, mostly Yank's, but we fed children and taught others how to feed children. Yank's product, along with drinking water, cooking implements, and sweat equity accomplished what money alone often fails to do.

There were mishaps along the way, different marketing plans, a blurring of boundaries between the profit and not-for-profit activities, and a decade spent by Yank clearing his name in Texas. He will tell the story better in his book, but he did learn that Texas is not a good place for a Jew and a Muslim to take on the local beef interests. During that time he continued his efforts to promote his product and help end world hunger.

As if ending world hunger was not sufficiently challenging, I never understood why Yank felt that I needed to get back into the studio to record. Yank wanted to record me. He fit the puzzle pieces together and explained. If I was helping him give away his product, then my return to the charts would help bring attention to his humanitarian efforts. In the world according to Yank, everyone benefits, and we were back in the studio. It was 12 years since *Standing in the Line of Fire*.

Before we entered the studio, there was one deal that I needed to help close for Yank. Big Mama and I had come to know Yank's intended better half Yvette, a most beautiful young lady from the Bradenton, Florida area. They met at an art gallery where she worked. Yank and Yvette had traveled north to see me perform at the Nevele, one of the most classic of the "Borscht Belt" hotels in New York's Catskill Mountains. I was part of a show which included Chuck Jackson, the Shirelles, Smokin' Joe Frazier and Larry Chance and the Earls. I told Yank I could bring a justice of the peace to the stage of the Nevele, and we could make this thing legal and the honeymoon suite at the hotel would be theirs. He questioned my determination, but there was no questioning his love for Yvette. Another act was added to the show at the Nevele that night. To the delight of a packed room, not only did they see a wonderful show, but they served as witnesses to the marriage of our good friends.

With my newly-married producer we decided to record in Long Island City, New York at Master Sound, and at Le Studio in Montreal. As with Springsteen before him, it would be at Yank's expense, with no real plan as to where we would take the album once it was complete. Yank talked about starting his own label, part of his for-profit world. If it clicked, we could feed more kids.

Yank recalled, "Gary had never been recorded properly. Whenever he went into a studio, he had to carry everything. I realized as a producer and arranger that he had real chops, like Tom Jones, or Englebert [Humperdinck]. I needed to give him some great string arrangements and I brought in Denny Christianson, a celebrated arranger, to do the horns. We put together a mix of songs. We started with some very big ballads with Gary in front of an orchestra. We did love songs, some French songs that Little Mama did new lyrics for, and something that Gary wrote which he had always wanted to give to Ben E. King, '1950s Kind of Mood,' which was Drifters to the core. We added Pomus and Shuman's 'Youngblood,' which covered the Coasters with Ben E. King doing the bass part."

The opening track gave the CD its name, *Nothing Left to Lose*, and including the two EMI America albums, it was easily the costliest recording I had ever done. Yank knew what he was doing musically, but without a plan to monetize this work, all the studio time we were consuming was troubling me.

We never managed to sell what may have been the best Bonds album to that date. We put out a limited number for friends, family and industry contacts. When Yank and I get together we always talk about somehow getting this great music played, but it has not happened yet. Muhammad was kind enough to lend his best smile for a picture we took for the CD liner, but for the moment, collectors have determined this limited edition Bonds album a widely sought rarity.

I continued to work to prevent hunger on two fronts, the world's problem with widespread famine, and the need to prevent it from entering the Anderson household. The transitions were difficult. I would play on the world stage with Yank and Muhammad, and on the Jersey club stage, or a hotel lounge with Mark and the guys. It was a living, and we weren't missing any meals, and if I had any thought of again being a "contemporary" artist those hopes were dashed by an honor I was named to receive.

As much as I didn't like the ring of being considered a "pioneer" by the Rhythm and Blues Foundation, I was flattered and it came with a nice check. The Rhythm and Blues Foundation was started with a donation by Atlantic Record's founder Ahmet Ertegun, following some very public lawsuits about inequities in royalty payments. In this case the litigation was started by my homegirl and traveling companion Ruth Brown. Reparations had been made to many of the earliest Atlantic artists for inaccurate reporting of royalties, and as part of this effort a number of the major labels contributed to create an endowment for the Foundation. The Foundation not only gives awards for achievement, as with my "Pioneer" award, it also provides grants to in-need artists for things like medical expenses, in memory of songwriter Doc Pomus. Frequently we hear about performers whose brush with fame was all too brief and now with limited resources they've become homeless or ill or both. Their songs are known but their names have been forgotten, and the Foundation has quietly aided scores of needy performers.

I didn't know that a sequel to the 1980 film, *Blues Brothers* was in the works, but it showcased a score of pioneers and legends that I was happy to join. It was almost 18 years after the original movie that *Blues Brothers 2000* was released. It must have been wishful thinking on the part of Universal in that they released the film almost two years before the millennium, but by the year 2000 the film was mostly forgotten except for the musical finale. I would like to believe that with the musical climax of the film happening in the city of New Orleans with a battle of the bands featuring my song, that they had me in mind for the scene. Rather, it was a chance meeting with Paul Shaffer at an airport where he was heading to Canada for filming. For those who saw the first film with John Belushi and Dan Aakroyd in the leads, it is understandable why 18 years transpired between the original and the sequel. I am sure the money interests were concerned that there would be no credible substitute for John, and any effort made to write him out of the script would be viewed as a lame effort to exploit his memory. *2000* was a game effort, but it failed with the critics and at the box-office in its initial release. What cannot be overlooked is the appearance of original Blues Brothers band member Paul Shaffer who did not appear in the original. He also served as the film's musical director.

I had worked with Paul before at a concert for the Foundation for the Love of Rock and Roll. This was an effort by rock and roll artists to do something to help their needy peers. The original sponsors painted a pretty picture. They planned a retirement home for aged and frail performers of modest means. Their plan was to provide housing along with medical care and recreational facilities on a campus to be constructed in southern Florida. The expense would be funded by current performers. It was on the order of what the stage and screen actors' unions had successfully done many years ago. The seed money would come from a series of concerts in which I participated along with Joey Dee (Joey Dee and the Starlighters) and Paul Shaffer. Sadly, the shows turned out to be mostly for the benefit of the promoters, but Paul and I had reconnected at one of the events.

At the airport Paul invited me to appear in a scene as part of a super-blues band led by B.B. King, my former instructor. It was a formidable group, a homecoming for many of us, with three days of reminiscing. On the set we had, Wilson Pickett, Bo Diddley, Sam Moore, Eric Clapton, Eddie Floyd, Issac Hayes, Koko Taylor, Steve Winwood, Clarence Clemons, Billy Preston and Travis Tritt. In recalling those that appeared I am further indebted to Paul for getting this group together, as so many of these giants are no longer with us.

Again, I took off for Norfolk, but this time I took Mark. It was another honor. My friend, promoter Bill Reid, who influenced me to write this book, had convinced the City of Norfolk to establish a Legends of Music Walk of Fame on Granby Street. It is near Bill's club, The NorVa, and I was grateful to Bill and the City for making me part of the first group of legends to have their names embedded in the concrete sidewalks of Granby Street. I had good company. In the first year, inductees joining me were Ruth Brown, Johnny Carson sidekick and *Tonight Show* bandleader Tommy Newsom and Bruce Hornsby. Guitarist Charlie Byrd, soprano Dorothy Maynor, Ella Fitzgerald, and Pearl Bailey, were given posthumous honors. The ceremony was followed by a free concert at the Roper Center for the Performing Arts with all the surviving inductees performing. I had heard that Bill was trying to broker an appearance by Frank Guida, whose witness to my award would have been viewed as a very public "burying of the hatchet." I was curious as to why this would be important to anyone. Bill felt that a public unification of the Norfolk Sound's two major proponents would make for good reading and an increase in goodwill and interest in our sound. I graciously accepted my bronze star on the walk, but there was no sign of the Guida family. Frank would receive his star the following year, and I was not invited. There was a musical tribute to Frank Guida. I do not know what they sang.

As golf enhanced my philanthropic efforts with Yank, it also enabled me to continue recording. Near my home was a course named Half Hollow Hills Country Club, owned by a man named Jeff Denlea. He lives nearby, and he always let me play as his guest. I learned 10 years ago that Jeff was attempting to get into the recording business, and that he had built a studio in one of the buildings on the golf course. Jeff was my idea of rich; he owned a studio and a golf course. Jeff was serious about recording and he bought some decent equipment, but if that was all it took to put out a hit record, everyone would be in the business. He would talk to me about the difficulty he had in getting out a record whenever I went to the course. I'd offer him advice; it was better than paying greens fees. He was working with some local talent, and I learned that Jeff's real talent was as a technician, and that as far as musical chops go, he was a more talented technician. Frustrated and ready to give up, he made me an offer I could not refuse. He offered me the recording equipment, the sound board, monitors, microphones, and all the cables. The offer got better. He offered to truck it over to my house and set it up.

Jeff wanted only one thing in return. If I had a hit, he wanted me to say that he made it possible. I had the space for the equipment and the price was right. Little Mama was back home, on leave from Yank who was still trying to extricate himself from his legal problems in Texas.

The recording business had changed again. As we passed the millennium, the major labels accounted for a smaller share of recorded music sales, and with the advent of the iPod, downloads exceeded the sale of physical CDs. There was much consolidation amongst the major labels and some of the surviving ones were financially impaired. Many of the larger successful touring acts controlled the production, sale and distribution of their music and the larger acts that were still signed were able to command a growing share of revenues. This threatened the entire recorded music industry.

Thinking back to the last meeting of the Anderson family, I remembered that we all agreed to take back control of what was ours. I called for another meeting. I told them about Denlea's offer and that we were about to take delivery of enough equipment to start making music. Big Mama was justified in her skepticism and she asked all the logical questions. Why was someone giving us this equipment, and how would we use it? Denlea's offer had no strings and we agreed to accept the gift. But Little Mama said we needed a computer and software, some training, a little bit of construction and electrical work. Our basement was going to be turned into "GB's Underground," the home office of GLA Records. GLLA just didn't work.

Denlea delivered as promised, and spent a day or two hooking up the components. It was more compact than equipment I had seen at the Power Station and Master Sound, but Jeff explained that pro quality recording equipment had gotten smaller and more sophisticated. With Jeff's gift we could do 90 percent of what they did at the big studios. We would only be limited by our space and budget. The Anderson family approved the purchase of a computer and software and we were in business. All we needed to do was master a 500-page manual and come up with a dozen great songs. I told Little Mama to start reading the book, and I would start thinking about some songs.

I had the easier job. I just had to pick out some songs and sing. Little Mama had to handle the technology, but she had experience with some of the concepts from her college work in audio engineering. What I found fascinating was how the equipment and software would enable us to shape sounds. We could change tempo, pitch and key without re-recording. If we wanted four brass players we could create them and six was just as easy. String players were virtual as well, and the more she read and the more she explained it, the more excited I got about doing our own record. We could also record anywhere. Players could do their parts any place in the world and send them to us digitally. For someone whose first engineer was a clothing salesman working a two-track machine, this was difficult to believe.

For a concept I need to credit Jack Kreisberg. Jack is an independent producer affiliated with a label started by the people from the Blue Note jazz club in New York City. He had done an album of big band music with Ben E. King, and I met him when I went to the Blue Note to see Frank Wilson, my friend from Norfolk who was playing drums with Jimmie Smith. I told Jack I was thinking of doing an album and he started to send me songs, some straight up blues numbers by contemporary artists. I had never done a blues album, but I felt comfortable with Jack's suggestions and it became the theme of our first homegrown album.

I had learned a lot from working with Springsteen. Most importantly, that people will listen to anything he is attached to. I contacted him and thought of others who had expressed interest in working with me over the years. I was realistic. I had not released a studio album in 20 years and I wanted to give this album the best shot I could. Southside Johnny was interested in contributing and as I went through the song selection it made me think of various artists. I had met the Allman Brothers Band guitarist Dickey Betts at a golf tournament. He lives near Tampa, and I called and told him I could use him. He said if I brought my clubs we had a deal. I came back with some of his money and some guitar licks we put on to two tracks.

Springsteen played and sang with me on "Can't Teach an Old Dog New Tricks," and Southside Johnny played harp behind us.

I added Phoebe Snow's vocals to one of the Dickey Betts tracks, "Bitch/DumbAss." The song selection included an original from Mark Leimbach and two from the archives, Otis Redding's "Dreams to Remember," and we went further back for a cover of Buster Brown's "Fannie Mae." The name for the album came from Little Mama, and there was no argument. *Back in 20* said it all.

We gave some thought to making it a total home project, but I was fearful that without any established distribution the record would not get played. Thinking back to *Standing in the Line of Fire*, I didn't want my next try to be *Back in 40*. We did a deal with a small local label, M.C. Records, that specialized in roots music, so it was not shocking that we got a lot of play at blues stations and college radio. We sold some CDs and some downloads and started offering the album on our own website. *Back in 20* got us a nomination and a win from the Memphis-based Blues Foundation, whose W.C. Handy Awards recognize the best in blues each year. Our award for 2005 was in the category of "Best Comeback Blues Album." I told Jeff Denlea that he finally had a hit. I told Big Mama we had another comeback.

Sixteen

FOOLED 'EM AGAIN BRO'

MARK LEIMBACH AND ALL MY current band members have that same disease I have, loyalty, and I'm thankful. It's loyalty when they're playing twice a month with me and they will rearrange their schedules to do one of my shows. It's loyalty when someone asks them what they do and they say they're with Gary Bonds' band. They're billed as the "Roadhouse Rockers," a name we came up with after the blues album. Its got a good ring to it and they can rock. Joining Mark on most nights are Joey Stann, Hal B. Selzer and Lance Hyland Stark. Joey's been with me since *Dedication*, another survivor of John Apostol's management, and Hal and Lance started with me in the late '90s. Hal and Lance are tight, friends onstage and off. Hal plays bass and Lance is on drums. After 50 years, I'm convinced that on any given night they play my music better than any group I've ever appeared with.

When *Back in 20* came out, my artists' representative Tony DeLauro came up with a strategy that drew upon my strengths and maximized the value of the album. He skillfully put me back into all the clubs in Jersey, but not as an "oldies act." He positioned me as a legendary innovator whose Norfolk Sound provided the foundation for the Jersey Sound that followed. We featured the new cuts in our set, played fewer dates at better prices, and avoided the multi-act shows if possible. He was able to move me into all the new casinos, Las Vegas, and as an opener at some large music festivals in support of bigger contemporary acts. He tapped into the market for corporate jobs and private events, something which I had not done before.

These guys were with me for some great jobs we had following the release of *Back in 20*. With Tony negotiating, the jobs were lucrative enough to allow me to take them. We did a bunch of the casinos in the Gulf Coast area, Cancun and some fabulous dates opening for George Thorogood, and Bella Fleck and the Flecktones, including one at a Canadian music festival. Lance remembers it well:

"This festival must have had thirty to forty thousand people. It was a sea of faces; it looked like they were spread out over four or five football fields. Thorogood was enamored with Gary and knew Gary's entire repertoire. What a nice guy. He made me feel like a rock star. After we would finish our set he'd start pointing out things that I did. Damn, I'm just the drummer. He couldn't believe he was closing; he didn't understand how he could top what Gary did. He said he'd been in this position before, especially in the '80s when his albums were really selling. He told me about a night when Stevie Wonder opened and then Little Richard performed. It was a night when Little Richard played with the conviction that made him a legendary live performer in his younger days. George tells me Richard did a blistering set and came off the stage. George goes up to him and says in desperation, 'Why do they make me go on after all you guys?'

Accurately, but not subtly, Little Richard replied, 'Because you're the only stupid motherf----r here.' George and I shared a laugh. I was flattered he put us in that same class.

My kit is on a riser and I'm watching Gary from behind. He signals us to bring the volume down. Mark starts picking that slow intro from, 'Dreams to Remember,' the Otis Redding song off the new album.

It must be ninety under the lights. Gary moves center-stage and thanks his buddy Otis for the song. His voice pierces the dense heat and I'm getting chills. I understand how George felt."

Hal B. Selzer is a touring musician, and does a lot of shows with Bon Jovi guitarist Bobby Bandiera. He gets steady work with Mark and Lance as part of Jimmy and the Parrots, a Jimmy Buffet tribute band. Hal's a performer with a capital "P" and he belongs on the stage. These days he does my shows, "Parrot" gigs, and on Broadway he's part of the band appearing in *Rock of Ages*. But ask him and he'll tell you he's with me.

"I joined Gary, and for one of the first gigs he tells me to 'turn it up.' So I tested it. Now, when I play, I like to turn it up. I also like to jump off the stage, run around, get into the audience and be outlandish, but I wouldn't typically do that with Gary, although he's seen me do it.

We're in England in 2005. I'm playing with a wireless, feeling bold, and I jumped into the audience. He wanted it loud; he wanted to rock out. He got it and he loved it. He doesn't want to be an 'oldies' guy. When we do 'Parrot' gigs he's glad we're working. We were at a show in Long Island. He comes over and does a few songs with us and then invites us all back to his house including Parrots lead Jimmy and his wife. It's two in the morning and Big Mama is up frying chickens. She wraps one up and tells Jimmy to take it home. They're feeding the competition! Bobby Bandiera, who's played with Bruce and Bon Jovi and all the biggest acts told me, 'You should be honored to take the stage with that guy,' and that's Bobby talking about the man as much as the musician."

On that same tour they sent us to Wales, where I've always been puzzled at how well we do. When we checked into the Hotel Talbot I thought our luck had changed. We would be playing the lounge. The hotel had eight rooms and we had four of them. From the drive to the Talbot we could tell that sheep outnumbered residents 100 to 1. We passed seven cemeteries and figured that was why business at the Talbot was kind of slow. We went to the bar and at two in the afternoon and found a bunch of townies already hammered. Between drinks we were cursing the agent who put us into this dive. Mark and I got as hammered as the townies and we went to our rooms to rest before the show. We returned at seven to find 500 people in a room that holds 200 comfortably. The Welsh knew the words to every song. It was the best show of our tour. The local press took notice and this excerpt is from a local review as reported by M.C. Records,

"Gary's energy is boundless, and the range and power of his voice is inspirational. From the above mentioned early hits to great self-penned songs from the new CD like, 'You Can't Teach an Old Dog New Tricks,' via songs from his 1980s Springsteen produced era like, 'This Little Girl,' and inspired covers of Ray Charles, Presley and Chuck Berry standards, the man is nothing less than a human jukebox…standouts were Gary's touching version of Otis's 'Dreams to Remember,' and the breathtakingly moving, 'Daddy's Come Home,' which surely brought a tear or two to many an eye…"

Guida would not benefit from this CD, but that was not why Bill Reid called. He called to let me know that Frank Guida was failing. If we had any contact over the previous two decades it was through our lawyers, and the hatchet was never buried. He had closed his last retail store and retreated to a fenced-in compound from which he managed his copyrights and leased masters of all the old songs. I can't be sure he knew I called, but I did. Had we spoken before his death in May of 2007, I would have told him the very same thing that I told the Virginia papers when they contacted me following his death. Frank would have heard that I was grateful for the start he gave me and proud of what we had accomplished. It would not have taken long. There was no need to tell him that what we did was important; this we both knew.

Mark's loyalty is especially appreciated on the tough nights. The nights when the bartenders and waitstaff outnumber the patrons. The money is lousy, the club owner is pissed, the sound system is awful and you want to go back to the hotel or crawl into a bottle of scotch and just blow through the set. As tempting as that may be, you don't, you can't, and I never will. I won't break the contract I've entered into with every lonesome soul in the room. Mark can make light of the situation, distract me and help me get through the set. And as we're walking back to the car, or the hotel, he'll turn to me and say something which means more than just the few words, and something he tells me on the great nights as well. It has a meaning known to just us two. It's not a son talking to his father, or an employee to his boss. It's two men bound by a respect for what each other does, two men who are so much more than partners in delivering some well worn tunes. It's two men grateful for the privilege of sharing a stage and a big chunk of each other's lives. Mark will turn to me and say, "Fooled 'em again bro'," and I will turn to him and say the same.

Mark was at my side for what has become an annual event, the celebration of my birthday, with family, friends, and fans, all my loved ones, at B.B. King's on 42nd Street in New York City. The first gala was in honor of my 70th. It also marked my 50th year in music. Big Mama and Little Mama worked to make it a special night, and it was one of the personal and professional highlights of my career. I am told that the room was at capacity and most of the well-wishers bought tickets to witness the festivities.

I was gratified by the turn out, and Yank and Yvette were there with some special gifts. First, Yank brought greetings and an award from my fellow Global Village Champions. Second, Yank introduced an elaborately produced video of birthday greetings from long-time friends, Dick Clark, Neil Sedaka, Joan Jett, Jon Bon Jovi and Muhammad Ali. In the room and joining me on stage were Ben E. King, Chuck Jackson, Steven Van Zandt, Southside Johnny, and Darlene Love. At my left on stage were Big Mama, Little Mama and Nicole Powell. My guys were backing me. Vincent Pastore from *The Sopranos* offered birthday wishes.

Before the evening would end we also had an opportunity to premier a few songs from my new CD, *Let Them Talk,* the title track a cover of Little Willie John's 1959 hit which I had first sung when I entered the business. The show was covered in the Huffington Post by Holly Cara Price who reported, "His longtime background singers, his wife and two daughters came onstage to join him." An innocent mistake on the part of the reporter. We can blame Little Mama, as she has often referred to Nicole Powell as her sister ever since they became best friends in high school. When Nicky's mom passed the girls became inseparable. Nicky has a wonderful voice and when she's not on Broadway or doing a workshop she joins us. She is an extraordinarily talented addition to our family.

It was an evening of warmth and great music. We have a video taken for non-commercial use which has some of the best performances I've ever seen from a group of performers I've been watching for most of my professional life. Tony DeLauro was an energetic master of ceremonies who shared with all the celebrants what would turn out to be a very significant career event on several levels.

After the video concluded with a very stirring message from an ailing Muhammad Ali, Tony took to the stage. Tony announced that I was signed to join former Rolling Stones' bassist Bill Wyman and his Rhythm Kings for a 32 show tour of the UK, Scotland and Wales. This would mean six weeks of sold out theaters with one of the world's greatest rock and roll bands. Since 1997 Bill Wyman has been touring Europe with some great players, and I would be taking a coveted spot previously held by other special guests, Gary Brooker (Procol Harum), Eric Clapton, Peter Frampton, George Harrison, Eddie Floyd and Odetta. I was honored by the invitation and Bill Wyman reminded me how it came about:

"I became aware of Gary U.S. Bonds in 1960 when I first heard "New Orleans," which had this unique sound like it had been recorded in a barn full of people— I loved it. Then with the release of "Quarter to Three" the following year I started to collect his records when I could get hold of them which was rare at that time. I managed to find "School is Out," "School is In," and "Twist, Twist, Senora," before his records seemed to fade.

The years passed and on brief occasions while on tour with the Stones in America I would see the odd poster proclaiming that Gary was still doing the business.

Then when I was looking for a special guest to tour the UK with my band, the Rhythm Kings, I chatted to friend Steven Van Zandt who informed me that Gary was on form, and after watching a few video clips on YouTube, I decided to have him as our guest on our 2009 UK tour."

Wyman is a few years my senior, but musically of the same era. His band specializes in roots rock and American soul music, and I had been told that on occasion the Rhythm Kings would do a classic Gary U.S. Bonds number.

While the Rock and Roll Hall of Fame is yet to consider me a worthy addition, the invitation by Wyman told me that British audiences, which have always been welcoming, would consider my addition to Wyman's all-star band well-deserved. Wyman's tours consistently include the best British players, and while the composition of the group did change from tour to tour, there was never a weak outfit. Many of the players had their own solo careers, and the balance were sidemen considered "the best of the best." I learned that I would be performing with Georgie Fame, master of the Hammond B-3, who had a number of U.S. hits in the '60s ("Yeh, Yeh" and "The Ballad of Bonnie and Clyde") and spent many years as Van Morrison's musical director. Also, Albert Lee, thought to be the world's best finger-picker, who tours with his own band as well as Hogan's Heroes, and has played with everyone from Jerry Lee Lewis to the Everly Brothers, Emmylou Harris, Eric Clapton and earlier, Head, Hands and Feet. Longtime core members were Graham Broad (drums), Terry Taylor (guitar), Nick Payn (saxophone), Frank Mead (saxophone) and Mike Sanchez (keyboards). Beverly Skeete handles background vocals and takes a solo turn on most shows.

I was told by Tony DeLauro that Wyman's road manager Tony Panico had assured him that the tour was run "first class" and that they were open to having Little Mama join the tour as my escort. Regrettably, there was no need for me to bring any other musicians. Travel would be by motor coach, as Bill had avoided air travel for quite a long time, accounting for the Rhythm Kings' need to limit their appearances to places that could be reached by bus.

My 70th was a milestone, with much to look back at, but more to look forward to. There were 30 shows with Bill Wyman, a format for an annual birthday show at B.B. King's, and enough bottles of good cheer to last me til next year. Someone presented me a few copies of some Rhythm Kings DVDs. I needed to learn what their shows consisted of and how Bill liked to present his band. We had a few months to prepare and Wyman's office said I'd have a segment in every show and join the band in the finale. Bill wanted me to do the '60s material, but the band was well equipped and not unaccustomed to changes if Bill's reading of the audience warranted a change. The plan was to arrive at a rehearsal studio a few days before our opening at Sheffield. On the flight to London I looked at the tour route and the theater names were familiar, with only a few that I hadn't played over the years, with houses ranging in size, the largest at 2000. These were places Bill's band had visited before and my understanding was the band's loyal following would put tickets in great demand.

Following check-in at a nearby tourist class hotel, we met up with the band at the rehearsal studio. Little Mama and I were taken aback at the lack of response when we entered the studio. Nothing stopped. Although the musicians were familiar to us in name only, as new imports we expected a response, a greeting, or just some acknowledgment of our arrival. They continued to the end of the number after which the tour manager greeted us and offered introductions. Bill was there, and Georgie Fame appeared to be putting the band through a workout. Bill aside, I guessed that I was the eldest player in the group, but I was amongst peers. A few were eligible pensioners, or near eligible, but even the youngest appeared to be comfortably seasoned. They knew one another and at the outset the atmosphere could best be described as professional, efficient, and cordial.

As I observed, there was no "battle of the band members" or attempts at one-upmanship. All were supremely and appropriately confident in their abilities and lacked the need to upstage or impress each other or the American visitors. They saw themselves as hired hands of the highest echelon and most had maintained that stature for two to four decades. I learned quickly that this would not be a "Stones" show, but a well mannered ensemble performance with few words. The spotlight would find each of us at an appointed time and remain with us for an appointed time. This was Bill's band, but I was told to expect him to lay back and play bass. This was one of his many passion projects, with his singular objective to present an authentic, high quality, rock and roll show to a discerning audience that has stuck with the band since its formation. Their aim was to leave every theater with the knowledge that if given another opportunity the patrons would return for another Rhythm Kings show.

We brought some music and some lyric sheets but these could have been discarded after the second show in Hull. I had some concerns about my turns during which I sought audience participation. I was still following Sam Cooke's advice and opening up to the crowd. During my up-tempo numbers the otherwise reserved audiences found it difficult to remain seated. When during my segment I inquired about their readiness to rock and roll, I wondered whether I should have checked with Bill first. As it turned out, they were ready, and Wyman enjoyed the bits as much as the audience did. I became comfortable rocking progressively harder as the tour went on. I think we had inspired Nick Payn and Frank Mead who had great fun with their honking sax duo which was enhanced with some deft choreography. Mark Leimbach will understand when I say my music never sounded better, at least when its been played by Brits.

Apart from the music, Little Mama and I thrived on the personalities we encountered and relationships we formed on the trip. The bus rides were a pleasure. Everyone had a place and took it. The hearts players found each other. Those who chose to read and respond to emails had their quiet spaces. Little Mama and Beverly Skeete got along well and Georgie Fame and I became brothers. Georgie (actually Clive Powell) witnessed and joined in the birth of British rock in the early '60s while still in his teens, but his musical preference has always been his American counterparts. In the '50s he toured with Eddie Cochran and my fellow Virginian, Gene Vincent. Georgie is steeped in American rhythm and blues and classic rock and soul. His jazz infused covers of Billy Stewart and King Pleasure have helped rekindle interest in the originals. He was a fixture at Ronnie Scott's jazz club in London, and his songbook is best heard with drink in hand at the hour when evening meets morning. Seen through a haze of cigarette smoke perched at the Hammond B-3, he is magisterial.

Georgie and I quickly discovered that we shared the custom of a cocktail or two following a show, and if its been a particularly good one, another is often deserved. Georgie shared this ritual with me, and at times we'd relax the limits. While I maintained some discipline, Georgie was oft-challenged. Suffering some throat issues or perhaps the flu, Georgie was tended to by a friend whose gift of some brandy or some other similarly potent remedy was greatly appreciated. But Georgie over-medicated. He required more than coaxing for the scheduled departure the next morning, but all was resolved by showtime. He was the best story teller on the bus. Whether it was tales about his years with Van Morrison, or his well documented early years when he was consistently page three news in the British tabloids, he entertained. Above all, upon taking the stage Georgie was in control. He knew his part and yours, and once seated at his instrument his command made all of us sound better.

According to Bill, my addition to his band did not disappoint, "To say that Gary was a success is an understatement. The crowds loved him singing his hits, but particularly loved his rendering of Otis Redding's 'I've Got Dreams to Remember.' It was a great tour and we all loved him."

Bill was a consummate host and tour guide. An occasional recollection of an early Rolling Stones tour would be shared, but Little Mama and I were just as impressed with his knowledge of architecture and history. As promised, the treatment was first rate and fitting for the caliber of talent. Although most could have made more doing session work, solo work, or one off concerts, it was understandable why they signed on with Bill for these extended runs year after year. For me it was a great birthday present and probably the reason why I was asked to return to the UK about a year later.

I can't take responsibility for the Rhythm Kings' selling out all of their dates, but a promoter did take notice of the great reception I got at every stop on the Wyman tour. His idea was a tour of longer length, with a mix of larger clubs and smaller theaters. This tour would include some of the secondary cities which would not be the first choice of a Wyman tour. The concept the promoter had was a revue, a loosely scripted tribute show paying homage to the great soul singers and groups of the '60s and '70s. It was a departure from what I would normally do, but it reminded me of something I learned from Tony DeLauro. He always says, "It's all about the song. They may love you, but it's all about the song." Tony says this is the reason that multi-act shows thrive and why jukebox musicals have become a staple on Broadway. I questioned whether I could support a revue alone and do two hours. I suggested we make it a duo and offered a couple of names. I approached Ben E. King with the idea. Ben E. King is identified with some of the most recognizable soul anthems, he's always done well in the UK, and as co-headliners we could easily fill two hours with our hits and some soul standards.

The promoter was able to sell the dates and put together about 50 nights, but at guarantees that would make this tour a chore. This was not going to be a well-oiled Bill Wyman production, but instead Ben and me and Little Mama in an SUV with a driver. We were booked into mid-size clubs, smaller halls, family resorts and a mix of performing arts centers. Promotion would be left to the venues with no central ticketing agency handling sales. Little Mama would not only be reading maps, she would be handling background vocals as well. This was going to be rugged. It was budgeted with economy in mind. Limited service motels and long drives would be the rule. I explained it to Ben as I understood it, and he was still up for it. It was still 50 nights of work, but mostly for the love of rock and roll. I started to appreciate Bill Wyman the minute I climbed into the back of what I recall was a Subaru. There would be no card playing between cities, and no narrative on British architecture. A week into the tour the 50 year friendship I shared with Ben was being tested.

I was sick of Indian food, and Little Mama kept us both from pummeling the road manager. The shows were entertaining and most did three quarters to capacity.

Ben and I paced ourselves, we added some humor and had no trouble doing the two hours. At the end of most nights the crowds went home smiling. But our smiles would vanish once we realized there was a four hour drive to the next show. I missed Big Mama, I missed my band, and I missed my bed. This was easier at 37 than at 73 and Ben agreed.

Seventeen

INVITED TO THE BALL

For Little Mama, not only did married life hold the promise of years of happiness with the man she was destined to be with, it also promised a more conventional home life and some separation from the world of rock and roll into which she was born. Laurie and Eurel had known each other for more than 20 years, and while there was a long pause during their courtship, Big Mama and I know that they were meant to be together. As a couple approaching our fiftieth, we speak from experience.

When your only child's courtship has gone on longer than you'd like, and you have postponed that walk down the aisle so many times, you start to think that it may never become a reality. But I kept hope alive, and the call from Laurie and Eurel announcing that joyous day was the best way to start 2011. Big Mama and I were tucked in. We had spent a long evening with friends, had watched the ball drop, and the new year was just hours old when the news reached us. In Nuevo Vallarta, Mexico, where the children were spending New Year's, 2011 was just minutes old when they called to tell us that Little Mama had accepted Eurel's proposal of marriage.

We should have asked our friends to stay, as a long awaited celebration was certainly in order. I would take Little Mama's arm and walk her down the aisle next summer. We had just spoken to our nearest and dearest, but despite the hour it was time to call them back. Big Mama started speed-dialing from her cell phone and I was doing the same. She called up Yank and Yvette Barry, and I called Mike and T.C. Peter. Mike picked up the phone, and while talking to him it finally hit me; my baby was getting married. Two tough guys were both in tears.

Mike wouldn't let me go. He sensed my elation and didn't know what to say except that he and T.C. wanted to host the wedding. "We want to do it Gary. The yacht, the house, whatever they want, whatever works for them, our gift and our pleasure. It's theirs." Mike's offer overwhelmed me. I knew he was sincere, but if it was just an outpouring of emotions or an earnest offer, it didn't matter. I was moved. I told Big Mama what Mike said and she was overcome. We split the list of friends from Norfolk and started to let people know. Big Mama and I needed to call everyone.

When morning came we had slept for maybe an hour. We were thrilled, but also feeling some sadness. That bit about not losing a daughter and gaining a son was going to take some getting used to. The Bowl games could not compete with wedding plans which were already being floated.

I feel confident that Little Mama's marriage will last forever and then some, but as to that part about distancing herself from rock and roll, I may have prevented that promise from becoming a reality even before the honeymoon commenced. Worse still, I almost stopped that honeymoon from happening. I had a problem. I needed Little Mama for about an hour and Big Mama as well. It was for a corporate gig at good money, with an opportunity to get recurring jobs by signing with a growing international marketer of health-care products and supplements. I would be their spokesperson, endorser, and go-to person for entertainment at their global conferences. Bless my friend Yank for setting it up, but it was not without complications and some fatherly guilt. The job was in Hong Kong a week after the wedding.

With a week separating the wedding and the Hong Kong job, at least Laurie and Eurel would have some private time. But as it turned out, if they agreed to go, there would not be much time at all. It takes a day to get to Hong Kong, and the show required preparation and rehearsal. While I was told that my music was known in Hong Kong, the company wanted some additional acts whose songs would be familiar to the predominantly Chinese audience through karaoke. We added B.J. Thomas and Brian Hyland, and while I had worked with both of them (most recently with B.J. at an upstate New York show with the Turtles and Ronnie Spector) we needed to craft a fun hour's entertainment with a new multilingual band. I wouldn't know if they understood English until we got there, and my hope was that they were fluent in American classic rock. While I would be taking Mark to play lead guitar and help pull the show together, and a drummer I knew who worked with B.J., to make the show fit the budget the balance of the musicians would be hired locally. We needed ample musicians to fill the room with sound, and my recommendation was for at least three horns. The venue was the Hong Kong Convention Center which was configured for an invite-only crowd of about 5,000. So much for the newlywed's private time. Doing this gig meant leaving on Thursday for the Monday show. The kids agreed to join me.

The wedding ended Sunday morning at about 4 a.m. Their destination wedding was in Aurora, NY at the lakeside estate of gracious hosts Mike and T.C. Five hours from the New York metro area, and a full 12 hours travel for the contingent from Norfolk, Laurie and Eurel decided that their traveling guests deserved a brunch the next morning. The brunch ran overtime, and by late Sunday afternoon the exhausted couple returned to Mike's estate for some much needed rest, or whatever exhausted newly married couples do. For them, Monday was a day for sleeping late. When they awoke they watched from their bedroom window as the crew took down the tent and stage and turned the lakeside estate back to its pristine pre-wedding condition. At nightfall the couple headed back to Eurel's house in Westchester to start the rest of their lives, unpack, sort through the wedding gifts and pack for a Thursday night departure to Taipei and the connection to

Hong Kong. Private time would be at most 72 hours, but probably less, allowing Little Mama just enough time to follow up on the production of our Christmas CD, speak to Tony about offers, and update our website and social media.

Before we left, I talked to Yank about how bad I felt about Little Mama and Eurel, and as he always does he came through with a solution, both for the kids and my conscience. His wedding gift to the children would be a week alone in Hong Kong following the show, complete with a honeymoon suite at the Intercontinental. Arrangements were made for mindless shopping through Kowloon's open air markets, and the required visit to a custom tailor. Laurie did her homework. The hotel offered harbor-view Cantonese dining, a spa and health club, and a real chance for the Tobiases to retreat to a world of just two. Thanks to Yank they would be alone, eight thousand miles from home, with no need to think about rock and roll. We left that Thursday night for my first ever show in China, barely recovered from the weekend.

We arrived at JFK at about 11 p.m. Thursday for our 1 a.m. Friday EVA Airlines departure. Given the hour and the complimentary cocktails, we were all intent on sleeping on board. We sat in the EVA Airways First Class lounge awaiting our flight. Passing time, I connected my iPad to the Wi-Fi and went through my ritual of checking e-mails, and "googling" my name to see if any ugly rumors about my career were bouncing around cyberspace. That idea about Little Mama distancing herself from the world of rock and roll was looking less and less possible as I read an article from the Finger Lakes Press. It was an article about Laurie's wedding which did not even mention her name. "No Springsteen Sightings, But a Nice Wedding Anyway," was the title, and it spoke about how some Springsteen fans (and the press) aware of the wedding, decided to stake out the location of the rehearsal dinner and the church the next day. One guest leaving the church wanted to know why they heard a bystander yell, "That ain't Patty, she's got red hair." We were warned that there was local interest in the event and we advised some guests accordingly. While we may have disappointed the gawkers, I give them credit for their persistence and thanks for keeping a polite distance. As for the guest list, it will remain confidential, but the jam session was first rate.

China worked. The band was tight, the sponsor was pleased, and five thousand predominantly Cantonese speaking Chinese got to sing along with Brian's "Itsy Bitsy Teeny Weenie (Yellow Polka Dot Bikini)," and B.J.'s "Raindrops." Yank led us all through a finale of "Louie, Louie," which required no translation. It was not only my first appearance in China, but also my first time watching a thousand person "conga-line" form for "Quarter to Three." The show ran over an hour, and when you do a corporate event, you can tell the sponsors are pleased when senior management is up and dancing with the troops. They were pleased.

Eurel and Laurie's private life started to flourish the moment Big Mama and I left for the airport to return to New York a day after the show. It was kisses and hugs and a farewell to our dumpling-filled days. We did not hear from them until they returned home, but when we spoke to them they sounded relaxed despite our intrusion into their first week of married bliss. Finally, the time had come for them to start building the future of Mr. and Mrs. Eurel Tobias. Little Mama was now first and foremost a dedicated spouse, and a corporate wife to boot. I was fully prepared to accept second call on her time and talent. My son-in-law is accomplished, brilliant, a Columbia graduate, a devoted son, and dedicated to his three sisters and brother. He is an executive at a company which might have been known as a printer at one time, but is now better described as a diversified developer and manager of marketing strategies.

When you are building a career, growing a client base, and nurturing important contacts, it helps when you are able to move relationships beyond business to a more social level. It helps when your wife is as attractive as Little Mama. It also helps when you've married into this family and your company grants you the privilege of hosting clients for the opening night of Bruce Springsteen's *Wrecking Ball Tour* at Metlife Stadium. This was just days after their return from Hong Kong and less than two weeks after the wedding.

Eurel has been with his employer for seven years. Some of his coworkers are aware of his wife's family, and that I have known and worked with Bruce Springsteen and various E Streeters for more than 30 years. But they may not know that a still teen-aged Little Mama joined me and Bruce at two of his 1983 Shea Stadium concerts. Or, that some years earlier he stood with her in our driveway as a school busload of her friends passed by while we were in the midst of recording *Dedication*. Who better to add color and dimension to the evening's concert than Little Mama? What better hostess than one who knows "The Boss" up close and personal? It would be Little Mama's first opportunity to put to use her previous life in her current role. Or was it?

Little Mama tells me that the evening was going as planned. There was plenty to eat and drink with two dozen clients and their significant others enjoying a priceless evening. They were able to move freely between the suite, and the private box within the arena. Little Mama made sure she "touched" all the guests and offered up stories and insights to all who inquired. What Little Mama did not reveal to me was that she placed a call to Bruce's assistant before the show, to let her know that she would be attending with Eurel. Nothing more than a courtesy to an old family friend, and maybe an opportunity to wow a client with a once in a lifetime "meet and greet."

The show was acclaimed by critics and Little Mama as well, a balance of classic Bruce and cuts from his new *Wrecking Ball* CD. More than 30 years later, Bruce, the same guy from our driveway, was fearlessly crowd surfing to the delight of 55,000 fans. The weather remained true to the last days of summer. Three hours into the show Laurie's phone rang. It was a quick call and she turned to Eurel. "They want us to come down. It's Bruce's assistant, they invited us to the hospitality. There are passes for us but maybe we should stay with our guests."

"Let's go," Eurel responded. Even though he had met The Boss on numerous occasions, he must have had a feeling that it was important for us to leave.

The walk from the suite was a long one. When they left the suite Bruce had come out for his encore, and by the time Little Mama stepped inside the hospitality Bruce had closed with "Twist and Shout." As they walked in, CNN anchor Brian Williams exited, leaving Laurie and Eurel alone with the bartender. The stadium's din was quieting and Laurie told me she could hear the sound of footsteps departing the arena. The hospitality started to fill with guests. The room was decorated with a Jersey Shore theme. Beach balls, pails and shovels and random sea shells adorned the walls, attempting to obscure the fact that the room also served as the New York Giants locker room.

The newlywed corporate couple wore their coveted all access passes which were gray that night. The flimsy adhesive patch was designed to prevent the unauthorized from glimpsing at The Boss from close range. With a drive ahead of them, they chugged Poland Spring. Laurie suggested to Eurel that they hang around for a little bit.

Little Mama told me what happened. Without prior warning, or the sounding of trumpets, Bruce entered the room with his assistant steps behind. Bruce saw her from across the room and he made his way over, with only brief interruptions to accept the congratulations of the other dozen or so "all access" well-wishers. He greeted her, "Hey you," with a big hug and he extended his hand to Eurel. Yeah, it was Springsteen, but to her it was the same guy she knew from our kitchen, the same guy who stood in our driveway and made her the envy of every kid in high school. To Little Mama he was just Bruce. But to those who were less familiar they could not help notice his look, part dustbowl but mostly south Jersey. The jeans and shirt may have been those worn on stage or ones just like them. They glistened, as did his hair, either with sweat or the result of a hasty shower. He was kind, spoke plain, and the only excess is his modesty. When you are capable of making 55,000 friends from a distance, up close is a cinch.

Little Mama told me that he humbly thanked them for coming and offered his gratitude for their kind words about the show. Laurie told Bruce that they had hosted Eurel's clients at his company's suite.

Spontaneously he said, "Why don't you tell your old man to get his ass down here. We'll get him up to sing a couple of songs." Without hesitation, the corporate wife placed her escape from the music biz on hold and put my career first. She softly and simply replied,

"I'll ask him." He posed with the newlyweds for a few pictures. They separated from The Boss and moved into the night. She called me from the car. "Daddy, Bruce asked if you would sing a couple of songs with him."

"You saw him?" I asked, and she told me about how their meeting came about.

"That's what he said, I think he meant it." My take is that there is little Bruce says that he doesn't mean, and that there is nothing he says without carefully considering the consequences. I am not saying that his invite was planned or calculated or voted on at the last meeting of "Springsteen Inc.," but the man is thoughtful and justifiably careful with his career and each detail of every performance has a purpose. He is instinctively brilliant and protective about his art in the way a grand master is at the chess board. He knows the impact of every move before he commits. But he is generous, and has never stopped being my friend since that evening in 1976.

I don't need to be reminded that we do the same thing, but we do only in the most general sense. I respect the differences, accept them, and marvel at all he has accomplished. I'm not just a friend, I'm a fan, and I value our friendship and wish it to continue. Bruce has made doing that as easy as he can.

We practice the same art, and when we are on stage the differences disappear. In that moment we're back in my living room banging out ideas on my old upright. In that moment we are "Bondsy" and Bruce at the kitchen table sharing Big Mama's gumbo and going over a lyric. I am grateful for those moments and recognize that they have a beginning and an end. But hopefully others will follow, and our friendship will continue.

"Call him, and see what he wants to do," I told Little Mama, and I knew she would follow through. I can't overstate his impact on my career. He helped expose my sound to a new generation, started the next chapter in my career, and continually credits me as an early influence. Nothing causes my phone to ring as much as when he closes a show with "Quarter to Three," as he had already done at tour stops in Hartford, and at the Turning Stone Casino near Utica, New York. I had last appeared with him in 2010 at the Count Basie Theater in Red Bank, New Jersey when he unexpectedly showed up at Bobby Bandiera's annual holiday show. I had not appeared with him in an arena show since 2003 at Shea Stadium. Little Mama told me she would call the next day, Thursday, to see what Bruce had in mind.

I wasn't there, but I knew the invite was sincere. It would help. Standing next to the man increases interest in what I do. Singing with him exposes me to an audience of 55,000, and the global community of "Boss" fans in the tens of millions. They follow, analyze, study and debate the significance and meaning of his every move. We were working on a lot of things, this book, a new CD, and more corporate jobs. Appearing with Bruce would help all of these, and it had been some time since we last did it.

Midday Thursday Little Mama called me. "I haven't heard from them. I'll keep trying." I thanked her and she told me she would call if she heard something.

I told her I was scheduled to be in New York City that Saturday afternoon to do some book interviews, and I told Cousin Brucie I would do his live show from the Feast of San Gennaro. I had booked a room and told her that I would be home Sunday. I had been on Brucie's Sirius XM show a month back when he asked if I would do an appearance with him. Brucie's been good to me. We go back to the middle sixties, about the time he returned to New York AM radio. If I'm in town and available, I'm there.

Little Mama called, "They want you there early for a sound check Daddy. They'll call Friday morning. He wants to do 'Jole Blon' and 'This Little Girl.' I was gratified and thankful for Bruce's invite, but at a loss as to how to thank my little girl. This rock and roll thing won't let go of her. Big Mama and Little Mama and me, we've been in this thing together, and now we have Eurel, that's my organization. Bruce has one and I have one. Mine is smaller and unpaid, but like the name of the song Bruce wrote for me, when it comes to "dedication," mine cannot be beat.

"A run through? We've done that song a thousand times." I was referring to "Jole Blon," and when you're my age you have a license to gripe, even when it's about Springsteen. "It's his song." My complaining was not convincing; we would sound check. Since I started on the book I had been using a driver. Danny was my first call, and the middle row of his Suburban was becoming my office. I told him to be ready for a Friday pick-up and a late night. Little Mama called me about 2 p.m. on Friday and Danny was smart enough to be in my neighborhood so he could steal a few extra minutes of road time. It would be needed, with the early Friday rush into New Jersey from Midtown. I had Laurie picked up about the same time. We planned to meet Eurel at the stadium.

I convinced them both to stay in the city with me and I told the W hotel that we needed another room and that we would be late. Although Danny did his best with the traffic, we missed the run through and sound check, but I had time to sit with Bruce and go over both "Jole Blon" and "This Little Girl." We would do it as we did it on the record. We just needed to remember what we did more than 30 years ago. We would trade verses on "Jole Blon," and I would start "This Little Girl," with Bruce joining in on the chorus. Over the last 30 years I have used "Jole Blon" as the opener of my shows, and it has evolved over that time. There are differences between how I do it with my band and the way Bruce did it in his shows; the song has never appeared on a Springsteen album. He wrote "This Little Girl," but it has never been part of Bruce's show and he has never recorded it. When I do the song I stretch it with a minute or two of audience participation on the chorus and I repeat the closing refrain if the crowd is really into it. These are not complex songs, but meter is important and when I perform them live the tempo is quicker than on the recordings. We talked about it and Bruce and I agreed to pay attention and let it fly. The set-list indicated that I would come on after "This Depression" from his new album, and my two songs would run about 15 minutes.

I need to acknowledge a very special fan of Bruce's, and unfortunately I don't know her name. At the opener on Wednesday, Laurie told me that a female fan standing stage right was holding a sign which stated her request, "Jole Blon." Signs are a regular part of Bruce's shows. Some are song requests, some are romantic invitations for various band members, and I am told at MetLife Stadium there was a plea for a dance with a guitar tech (which was granted). The signs vary from vintage photos with autograph requests, to memorials for loved ones, usually lifelong fans who have passed. Bruce has a history of acknowledging them, and it is not unusual for a "sign waver" to be invited onstage for a dance. The young lady requesting "Jole Blon" must have inspired Bruce because he brought me on by saying something to the effect that he has seen the "Jole Blon" sign for the last ninety four shows and that he was about to make her happy.

He made me happy too when he said, "We imported him from Long Island. Let's get Bonds out here, Gary U.S. Bonds." Bruce counted it off and led with the guitar intro with Soozie Tyrell and Charles Giordano following on the fiddle and accordion which propel the Cajun anthem.

I sang about bells ringing from the mountains to the valleys and my voice filled the infield and the stands. The "sha-la-las" were loud and strong and I looked at Bruce and I am sure he could see my joy as I saw his. I was beside him once more and his invite was sincere. He would continue to be true to that friendship started in Hazlet 36 years ago. Applause rolled over me to the playing fields and up through the stands to the heavens and then back down upon me and then it repeated. I saw Bruce beaming and we hugged and separated waiting for the right moment to start the next song. Unaccompanied, Bruce strummed an F sharp minor and Max Weinberg waited for me to start the vocal that kicks off, "This Little Girl." It lumbered in spots and I looked to Steven and he shrugged, and then mugged for the crowd and they loved it. The bridge appeared and disappeared, the sax solo was misplaced, but by the time I offered the microphone to the crowd for the sing along we had all reconnected and it was glorious. My friend Bruce, my buddies in the band and the 55,000 were one.

I knew when it was time to get off. I waved to the faceless multitude and walked off a few inches taller, my feet not touching the ground. Bruce continued to sing the refrain with the help of the crowd. I slumped into one of the backstage chairs and heard the crowd continue to yell after Max crushed a cymbal after the final, "This little girl is mine." The production manager told me to hang around for the finale and that I should grab a tambourine when I went out. The show was approaching three and a half hours by the time I took my tambourine and joined the band for the finale. I had the privilege of taking a bow with the E-Street Band while Bruce bellowed, "The E Street Band, Gary U.S. Bonds, The E Street Band, Gary U.S. Bonds, we'll be back tomorrow with another Spec-Tac-U-Lar." Without giving this last announcement a final thought I headed for the dressing room and then the hospitality suite which was attached to Bruce's private dressing and wardrobe area. The E Street Band members went to theirs.

I was beaming when I walked in to find Little Mama and Eurel. I still did not know how to thank my little girl, but I did my best, and I saw in her face the joy she feels when she has done something for me. How lucky and blessed I am. This would not have been possible without her. It was time for the evening's first glass of wine and "my organization" toasted to our shared victory. As we toasted and sipped, the evening's statistics were tallied by dozens of Springsteen bloggers. Authorities on The Boss would collect their thoughts to share with the masses.

Bruce arrived, freshly showered and hastily combed and we hugged it out and exchanged thanks. He congratulated me on Laurie's marriage, and asked how Big Mama was. I inquired as to where Patty was. Bruce explained that his daughter was in an equestrian competition and that Patty was with her and wouldn't make the

Saturday show either. Bruce broke away to spread the joy and make sure that everyone in the now crowded locker room had an opportunity to extend greetings and have a photo opportunity. I was elated, proud, and satisfied with the performance and hungry as well. We said our good nights, and said we would be in touch. By morning there would be no shortage of concert video on YouTube, with five or six posts covering my two numbers and the finale.

As we left the hospitality I saw a familiar face. The only thing that would have made me happier was if he would have been on stage next to me. Mark Leimbach lives in southern New Jersey, and he and his wife Laurie (to avoid confusion we call her Laurie) told me they bought a pair of premium priced seats that morning. Mark and I had a laugh. While he was thrilled seeing his boss with "The Boss," he quickly pointed out the differences in the way "they did it" and "we do it." I told him, "You're better," and we exchanged "high fives." We decided that Mark and his wife needed to follow us for an after show meal which we would now have in New Jersey so that Mark's trip home would be no longer than necessary. We had Danny follow Mark to the Tic Toc Diner which is on Route 3 and never closes.

It was packed with revelers who were celebrating their witness to another remarkable Springsteen show. People were waiting to get in, and as we approached, the line parted. People started to applaud as they let us pass. Seated patrons looked to the entrance. One by one they stood and clapped. I never got a standing "O" in a diner before, but I like it, and I'm going to see if I can get booked into more of them. We ordered some combination of breakfast and dinner and they quietly sent out some mildly alcoholic beverages although the bar was closed due to the curfew. I think everyone in the Tic Toc paid their respects and I didn't mind posing for a few pictures.

It was past three by the time we settled our tab and headed back to New York. We recapped the entire evening for Danny who by then must have been glued to the driver's seat as it was 12 hours since he picked me up. The car was quiet and I may have dozed for a few minutes. After a nightcap at Whiskey Blue, Little Mama and Eurel went to their room and I went to mine. Sleep would come easy.

Eighteen

ANOTHER BRUCE

"WE'LL BE BACK FOR ANOTHER, "Spec-Tac-U-Lar." I hadn't given it much thought. I was still reliving the previous evening as I ate a late breakfast near the W hotel. With some time to kill before Danny picked me up for my 8 p.m. appearance with Cousin Brucie, I called Lou Christie to see if he had plans. I knew he would be doing the Brucie show as well and I thought Lou could share a couple of stories I might be able to use in the book. Any time I'm with Lou the conversation always includes reminiscences about the European tour we did in the late 1980s. He told me he was scheduled to do the Brucie show after me, and that we could meet afterwards if I would stay in Little Italy. I told him I was interviewing an editor and that I would pick a spot. Brucie was broadcasting under a sky that was promising rain and the only question was when.

Brucie has a couple of years on me, but he has not slowed a second in the 50 years I've known him. After being a fixture on oldies format WCBS-FM, until 2005 when they changed formats, Brucie has continued to serve his audience on Sirius XM satellite radio Channel 6 where he plays the hits he introduced on AM radio WABC in New York. Brucie and I have remained close and I see how much he is enjoying the freedom which satellite radio allows. He plays what he wants, when he wants and still talks to his "cousins" as if they are joining him for Thanksgiving dinner in his dining room. I've done so many appearances with Brucie, that I recognize his "cousins" and they continue to turn out in numbers wherever he appears.

The weather cooperated for a while and we were able to play a few records and meet some fans and answer their questions before the skies opened. By that time I was tucked into a Little Italy café, waiting on some pasta while our waiter opened some Nero D'Avola that he assured me my "paisan" would surely love. Lou caught some of the downpour before he found me sitting at a back table. I had already poured a glass for him when as anticipated he started to retell the story of our 1986 European tour. Lou told the story, and at the point where I returned the excess payment to the messenger, the downpour got more intense.

Laurie called. She was at MetLife Stadium with Eurel. It was now past nine and the Springsteen show was delayed. She asked if I was coming. I said no, and that I had ordered some dinner. I always enjoy Lou, and I was not coming to watch, and with the miserable weather it would be a very sloppy evening. We drank, ordered dinner, and I reminded Lou that Martha Reeves was with us in England. Lou liked the wine and we finished the bottle. Little Mama was calling again. The show was going to start. The rain had slowed to a light sprinkle.

"How long will it take you to get here?" asked Little Mama.

"Why?" I inquired.

"They have you on the set-list singing 'Jole Blon.'"

"Twenty minutes," I lied.

I apologized to Lou, and told him I had to go see a guy from Jersey. He understood. I called Danny. It was Saturday night, and the weather was threatening. Luckily, I told him to wait. I never saw the pasta, but I paid for it and headed for the car. It was still drizzling in Little

Italy. I called Little Mama and told her I was in the car and that I would call back once the stadium was in sight. She told me Bruce was going to call an "audible" if we were delayed.

My night of "Two Bruces" was starting to unfold. Fans would never know that Holland Tunnel traffic would determine the ultimate set-list for Springsteen's final *Wrecking Ball* show at the Meadowlands. The "EZ Pass" lanes were moving freely as the weather must have changed the minds of a lot of people who stayed in New York. I called Little Mama. "Have them notify security so I can drive up to the building and get to the stage." Springsteen's staff is organized, though if I knew about this earlier….

Danny saved his vehicle permit from Friday, and he remembered where the artists' entrance was. I was met by the production manager who escorted me to the backstage area. We set a new land speed record for the Little Italy to Meadowlands trip on a soggy Saturday night when Springsteen is playing. I was dry, and I had 10 minutes to spare. Enough time to collect my thoughts and fix my hair. We've done the song a thousand times. A thousand and one should be easy.

"Where's Bondsy? Let's get him out here, Gary U.S. Bonds." My friend was calling. There were 55,000 out there and I'm told many were there for all three shows. With Friday's show fresh in our memories this would be easy, and it was. I caught my image on the giant screen in back of us as I headed to the microphone. Man this is fun I thought as I looked left to see Steven. The crowd was wet. They had been standing for two hours waiting out the rain, and they were poised for a rewarding finale of Bruce's three show homestand. They were louder, and we were sharper. I could put 110% into "Jole Blon" because I would just be doing one song. We stretched it and it was party time on the bayou. Specifically, birthday party time and the multitude knew they were invited to the celebration.

"Jole Blon," worked. Perfect tempo, flawless, they loved it, Bruce loved it and I turned to walk a champion's walk to the ramp, the night's work done.

"Do the other one."

Do the other one? He was calling to me. It was a Springsteen audible. He was calling me back. He wanted to do "This Little Girl." I put it all into "Jole Blon," but I had more than enough in reserve. I came back to the mike and waited for Bruce to play that minor chord. Timing is everything here. His chord is unaccompanied, and I wait as it fades. Acapella, I sing, "Here she...," with the band starting as I sing, "comes." We nailed it. It was crisp. It was long. It was as it should be, as he wrote it and the crowd joined in an endless chorus and erupted. I finally did make it down the ramp, but just briefly. The concert dissolved into a raucous affair and Bruce timed it perfectly. More than 50,000 well-wishers, acolytes, fanatics, all celebrants knew there was one reason Bruce dug deep for the Pickett-Cropper "In the Midnight Hour," another audible which would take us to the countdown to the Boss's birthday.

It was a traditional affair, balloons, family and 55,000 friends. Bruce's mother, mother-in-law (with a nod to Ernie K-Doe), and siblings in law were brought to the stage to see the Boss cut the first slice from a giant Fender shaped cake with neon colored icing. The accomplished showman and host generously shared the first slices with a few of the fans in the infield. The music could wait. There was no better place to be, and end to end it would be more than eight hours for many of the faithful. No one complained. I knew Bruce's Mom and I had met his in-laws. All beautiful people, all fans, you'd never guess they were part of America's first family of rock and roll. They would exit the stage before the finale which started past 1 a.m. I played my tambourine, joined in the vocals and partied with everyone onstage. By this time I felt I was no longer "guesting" and not a "drive by." I belonged. It was almost two when I put my tambourine down. I headed for the hospitality.

A few hours ago I was deep into the Nero D'Avola with Lou Christie and now it's time for more birthday cake with the Boss. But the Fender cake was largely ignored, the fluorescent icing starting to melt as the cake sat unattended. This was a family affair. Patty's Mom chatting with the all access group, and Bruce's Mom holding court as she received thanks for what she did 63 years ago.

My bandmate came out in his jeans and chambray and walked toward me, stopping to hug his mom and Patty's mom. He headed for us and extended his right hand to mine, found it, and I brought him to me. We embraced. Bruce and Bondsy. Another moment, another start and another end. Ten years between us, 30 years behind us, and much more in front to look forward to. I had Little Moma and Eurel at my side. I thanked him and he thanked me and said it was great. He moved about the room. I offered greetings to Bruce's Mom and fielded congratulations as if it was my show.

Springsteen is a big man. His voice rose above all the others. "Do you know it is a quarter to three? And there's the man who had the number one hit." Pointing at me he announced it. There was silence. The oracle had spoken amongst his closest. He wanted them to know. He wanted me to know that he knew. It was his birthday, but it felt like mine.

It worked on Friday, so we did it again. I like the Tic Toc, but it was way past three. There were fewer patrons, and those who were there who were at the show were too tired for a standing "O." Danny joined us this time. I never did get that pasta I ordered with Lou, but the steak and eggs were a victory feast that I shared with my organization. I called Big Mama. It had been Sunday for a while, so when I told her I'd see her tomorrow she corrected me. I told her I missed her and about what had happened. I sensed she already knew.

Nineteen

BLOW DADDY

The kerosene heater made the house nice and toasty, but I lit a fire anyway. A well-tended hearth always makes the wine taste better, and recent events had thinned the stocks of better vintages available from the Anderson wine cellar. But there would be no shortage of firewood or kindling in our house for the next couple of years courtesy of Hurricane Sandy. I told Big Mama that I'd be able to dig out the stumps, split the trunks, and we'd have at least two cords once they'd had some time to season. We would especially miss the two maples which used to frame our house. I planted both of them when we bought the place, and as we watched them grow they always made us think of Little Mama.

Now Little Mama was sitting in her own darkened home with Eurel, and our trees were gone as well. We talked about planting new ones, after all we were experts when it came to starting over. But what I really wanted to see standing upright was the thick wooden pole resting in our front yard. It held the downed power lines which once ran to our house. I would leave that job to the electric company, and they weren't promising any restoration of service for at least a week.

With our cell phones charging in our car, no television, and three hour waits at the few gas stations that were pumping, we'd commiserate with neighbors by day and sit by the fire at night. That was about all there was to do. I had to postpone a photo shoot for the book cover and reschedule an appearance at a small club. After a few days you adjust. A calm sets in as things which once seemed troublesome become less so. When life's basic needs become a challenge, things which are really unimportant are quickly forgotten. Neighbors pooled supplies, shared, and showed a level of concern that was heartening. We developed stocks of bottled water that will last for months as everyone who visited brought at least a half case. I'd use the cell-phone sparingly.

Sitting in the car I listened to a dozen messages with more than half from friends in Norfolk. We had multiple offers of round-trip transportation with unlimited room and board. I had to call back "Little Walter" and convince him that not only were we managing, but that Little Mama and Eurel were safe and well nourished. In my conversation with him I learned that Sandy had not spared Virginia's coastal regions, but their concern was for us.

My attempts to locate a generator were one disaster too late, and I found that every unit on the eastern seaboard was spoken for. Then Christmas came early, with Santa Claus dressed as a UPS driver dropping off a factory new unit on my front lawn. I don't know where my friend Mike Peter found one, but if you ask the neighbors, he's Santa, and we spent the morning filling gas cans so we could rig it up to power every refrigerator and hot water heater on the block.

Yank said he'd send a plane filled with drums of VitaPro to feed the entire county! I got calls from my band members who live in New Jersey, and I heard from musicians I hadn't performed with in years. Agents I had fired and promoters I swore I'd never work for checked in to see how we were managing. They weren't calling about the music, they were calling because of the music that brought us together, however briefly a very, very long time ago. Scott Barberino from New York's Iridium said he was prepared to reopen, and he was attempting to rebook all the cancelled shows. He was kind enough to offer the place to me for the photo shoot at my convenience. The Iridium is New York's best small room and I love playing there and going there when I am in town.

I do my best writing at night, and these powerless evenings have unleashed a lifetime of memories as I approach the completion of this manuscript. Big Mama and I sit close, our backs warmed by the fire, our eyes locked on the single red LED which tells us our memories are being recorded. We challenge one another to complete each other's recollections. Every sentence starts with, "I bet you don't remember the time," or, "Who appeared with us when we played that club in." I get about 10 years of memories between charges of the recorder, and tonight Big Mama and I, powerless, will push it to 20. I only wish the recollections came chronologically, because if they did I would already have this project buttoned up. I've also discovered that I have a pretty good hard drive between my ears, but sometimes it just needs a little coaxing, some hints from Big Mama, or another glass of merlot.

When the going gets tough, musicians make music. Melody and rhythm heal, and song helps you deal with adversity. I've got almost two songs completed that deal with Sandy, and commitments to do a bunch of shows where musicians will be raising funds to help those who have lost so much. There's talk of a video, a variation on "We Are the World," geared to help some of the devastated areas like Far Rockaway and Breezy Point where residents were facing years of rebuilding and dislocation. I sadly learned that some of my favorite clubs in Jersey did not survive and I can't believe we lost the Surf Club in Ortley Beach. We had such a great time there right before we left for China, and I would not bet against a new and improved Surf Club coming soon. It didn't take coaxing to convince Southside Johnny to do a show in Lakewood, New Jersey and I expect all his loyal fans will turn out as they always do so we can raise a few extra dollars to, "Restore the Shore." But the "once in a lifetime storm" will not stop rock and roll, just set it back a few days, and I am proud that the music community will help lead the recovery efforts.

I was anxious to get re-powered and move forward into my 54th year in the business. We were wrapping up 2012 with a bunch of new projects. In July we had finished work on my first Christmas album, *Christmas is On!* That album came about when we were talking about concepts for a winter release, a follow-up to *Let Them Talk*. We were considering another blues record when I looked back and saw that I had not recorded a Christmas song since 1964 (although it was released later). We were also working with a new publicist and the plan was to do a national push on the Christmas album and then go right into a U.S./UK book tour in the spring. I also needed to get back into the studio.

This autobiography may be the first book inspired by a song. Prior to starting the book, out of frustration from my inability to get it started, I thought I might have more success if I put my story into song. Given the choice of three minutes or three hundred pages, I went with three minutes. I thought I might be able to do in a song what I had been unable to do on paper. Starting with a title which became the subtitle for this book, "That's My Story," I wrote a couple of verses which told my story and I immersed it within a very recognizable Gary U.S. Bonds track. I included snippets of melodies from hits I recorded more than 20 years apart, but the more I listened the more I found a glaring omission.

In 1961, in that small, crowded, Legrand studio on Princess Anne Road, after singing two verses that I had added to an instrumental, I turned to the tenor-man behind me and invited him to start his solo. "Blow Daddy," I called and he responded with 12 bars which propelled "Quarter to Three," to the top of the charts. Some said I was referring to Daddy Grace, but most knew it was "Daddy G," Gene Barge that I wanted. To tell my story accurately, musically, I needed Daddy G, so I called him.

"Daddy, I got this song. It's about my life, and your life. Starts in Norfolk, I'm singing on the corner at Olney Road. It goes on to "New Orleans," and then the two of us driving to gigs in my Ford. I need a horn solo before I sing about the Springsteen record."

"What happened to the book?"

"It is the book, but I'm singin' it."

"You got something in mind, something written?"

"Yeah, you know it. You wrote it 50 years ago."

"Send me the track." And I did.

Two hours in a Chicago studio is all it took for Daddy G to nail a 12 bar solo that captures all we've ever done together professionally. He did it as effortlessly at 86 as he did at 35. For those too busy to read the book, I will suggest the record, and if they can't spare the three minutes, then they should listen to the solo. The tone, phrasing and intonation are flawless and timeless, a trap for every player who fails to see the genius embedded in his simple improvisation.

So again, I'll call, "Blow daddy," and again my friend will deliver. His horn speaks of the decades and married with my voice it proves that what we did was timeless, will survive us, and always take us to a happy place. And If my voice has ever lifted spirits or started a party, that is all I have ever wanted. I just wanted to sing.

Twenty

THAT'S MY STORY

For those who'd prefer my story in song:

That's My Story (I'm Sticking to It)
Music and Lyrics by: Gary Bonds

Well I was singing on a corner when a record store owner,
Came up in a shiny new car,
He said if you like to sing, I'll guarantee you by spring
I can make you a star.
So he gave me a song and I took it on home but
I changed it around just a bit,
And what-a-you know it, just a few months or so,
The damn thing was a hit.
Hey, hey, hey, yeah, I said, hey, hey, hey, yeah.

By U.S. Bonds — That's My Story

So I bought an old Ford and went out on the road,
Just me, Daddy G from the band,
We gassed up one day and drove to Phillie P.A. to appear on
American Bandstand.
Where we met Dick Clark, he was the King of the Hop,
He put us on his TV show,
I had hit after hit, it seemed I just couldn't miss,
Man I was raking in dough.

(Chorus)
Well that's my story, and I'm sticking to it.
My destiny, my life, my days of glory,
As I recall, that is just the way I know it.
That's the story of my life and I'm stickin' to it.

(Sax solo)
Yeah, blow, blow, daddy...

Well the sixties were tough, but the seventies got rougher,
When disco came into town,
No we couldn't compete, With that boogie-oogie beat,
Man it was beating us down.
Well the money got low and the gigs were slow,
I had lost everything but respect.
But I knew how to survive, I was staying alive,
Life kept me in check.

(Repeat Chorus)

Then I met a man from Jersey who said he had heard me,
Sing a song about a quarter to three.
And then he asked me to listen to some songs he had written,
He said they sounded a lot like me.
And then he gave me this song and I took it on home,
And I changed it around just a bit,
And what-a-you know, In just a few months or so,
The damn thing was a hit.
This little girl is mine, ooh, ooh

(Repeat Chorus)

That's my story and it ain't over, I'm stickin' to it.

Used with permission: G L A Worldwide Music (BMI)

DEDICATION

I SANG ABOUT DEDICATION IN 1981 and now I get a chance to dedicate this book and acknowledge those who helped me get my story down on paper.

First, my thanks go to those who sat with me and shared their recollection of times we shared:

Steven Ameche	Norm N. Nite
Gene ("Daddy G") Barge	Michael and T.C. Peter
Yank and Yvette Barry	Gene Pitt
Jerry Blavat	John Regna
Lou Christie	Bill Reid
Tony DeLauro	Tim Royster
Chuck Jackson	Hal B. Selzer
Bobby Jay	Paul Shaffer
Southside Johnny	Joey Stann
Ben E. King	Lance Hyland Stark
Mike Lancaster	Charlie Thomas
Albert Lee	Steven Van Zandt
Mark Leimbach	Steve Winwood
Darlene Love	Bill Wyman
Bruce Morrow	

To all my friends from Norfolk for welcoming me back to where my story began and for your love and friendship:
  Purcell Beale
  Frissell Coleman
  Mayor Paul D. Fraim
  Richard Gault-Page
  D.L. Haskins
  "Little Walter" Johnson
  Joyce Moore
  Councilman Paul Riddick
  Lucille Sealls
  Curtis Stewart
  Lawrence Westbrook
  Frank Wilson
  Vernon Wilson

For those who turned my words and pictures into this book:
  Samantha Brand – editor
  Tommy L. Bogger, Ph.D. (retired) and his staff at the library and archives of Norfolk State University
  John Cavanaugh – photographer
  Rafaella Golinucci – tour photographer
  Eason Jordan – photographer
  Eric Lusher – photographer
  Glen Mason – videographer
  Jeffrey Meyer – Apple Direct, distribution and fulfillment
  ron ring – photographer
  Karrie Ross – book cover and interior design
  Hampton University – staff of the library and archives
  Mark Weiss – photo editor, photographer
  Matt Ziegler – photographer

Dedication

This book would not be complete without thanking another group of very talented musicians, and the many others who are unnamed. You have helped me sing my songs over the past 50 plus years:

Tony Amato	Ed Manion
Elizabeth Ames	Carl Mignano
Steve Barlotta	Joe Napolitano
Joe Bellia	Bruce Natalie
Jimmy Bevin	Dave Nunez
Dave Biglin	Ron Pacaud
Hayward Bishop	Paul Page
Ivan Bodley	Nicole Powell
Billy Cioffi	Lucille Grace Ridges
Dan Cipriano	Allan Schwartzberg
Bobby Comstock	Steve "Muddy Shews" Shewchuk
Doug DeHays	Walter Smith
Dennis Dibrizzi	Jim Squirrell
John Digiulio	Mario Staiano
Steve DiMartino	Stan Tartas
Gordon Edwards	Billy Vera
Zerrick Foster	Jim Wacker
Jim Heady	Gary Weiss
Danny Kean	Terry "Tunes" Winkler
Bobby Kibbler	Paul Zunno
Bobby Lynch	

Most of all to my girls, Laurie and Laurie, for never saying no, believing in me and this project unconditionally, and for making this book a reality. My love to all our family and friends and to all who have listened and continue to listen to my songs.

INDEX

A

A 1960's Revival Tour, 169
A and R Studios, 160
A Hard Day's Night, 75, 155
"A Night with Daddy G", 60
A Night with Mr. C, 20
"Action in the Streets", 139
Adesso, Carmela "Millie", 45, 46
Air Force base shows, 131–135
album covers, 34
Ales, Barney, 127
Ali, Muhammad, 184–185, 198
Ameche, Steve, 132
American Bandstand
   first appearance on, 35, 63
   Freddy Cannon on, 70
   last appearance on, 163
   return to, 145–146
American Men, 163
Amicus Pictures, 76
Amsterdam, Morey, 46
Anderson, John Henry Gary (Pop)
   childhood visits to, 17
   first performance for, 69
   love for learning, 15
   memorial for, 169
   Mom's love for, 92
Anderson, Laurie Celese ("Little Mama"). *see* Little Mama
Anderson, Reverend Atkin and Savannah, 16
Apollo, Frank, 107
Apollo, the, 13, 72
Apostol, John
   on Bonds/Springsteen collaboration, 128
   financial dealings with, 156, 158–159
   management company creation, 110
   as manager to Gary, 144, 155
   mismanagement by, 167
Apostol Enterprises, 110
Appell, Dave, 67
Arden, Don, 96
Atco, 112
Atkins, Pat, 107
Atlantic City, 81
Atlantic Records
   Guida pitches "High School U.S.A." to, 48
   purchase of "C.C. Rider", 40
   Rhythm and Blues Foundation, 187
   Ruth Brown's contributions to, 41
   signing of the Sheiks, 47
Attucks Theater, 21, 23
audiences
   for *Cover Me* show, 176
   of Dick Clark, 57
   expectations of nostalgia-show, 115
   gratitude for, 117
   happiness of as priority, 68
   talking to, 13, 14, 15
   want the hits, 203
   white vs. black, 12, 58
Aurora, New York, 123
Avatar Studios, 137
AVN (Adult Video News) Hall of Fame, 163
Axton, Hoyt, 127
Azalea Gardens Club, 42–43

B

Bachelors' Club, 32
Bailey, Pearl, 18, 189
Baker, LaVern, 12, 13
Ball, Kenny, 76
Bamboo Club, 82
Bandiera, Bobby, 23, 195
Banner Talent Associates, 110
Barberino, Scott, 226
Barge, Gene "Daddy G"
   career help from, 165
   Chicago career of, 97
   collaborations with, 24
   early life of, 41
   film recording, 76
   first gigs with, 40
   first recording with, 59–60
   as inventor of Garage Rock, vi
   nod to at Clemons' memorial, 20
   on the Norfolk Recording Studio, 48
   Norfolk's honoring of, 177
   in song version of this book, 228–229
Barn, the, 101
Barrett, Richard, 90
Barry, Yank
   career of, 181
   at Gary's 70th birthday, 197
   Gary's meeting of, 160
   on Gary's voice, 186
   marriage of, 185–186
   salesmanship of, 182
   VitaPro proposal, 182–184
Barsalona, Frank, 57, 62, 74, 106
Beatles
   domination by the, 96
   films of the, 75
   "I Want to Hold Your Hand", 97
Belafonte, Harry, 46, 70
Bella Fleck and the Flecktones, 194
Berry, Chuck, vi, 12, 109, 114
Bessie, 28
"Best Comeback Blues Album", 192
Betts, Dickey, 191, 192
"Betty Davis Eyes", 148
Big Mama
   on Air Force base tour, 132, 135
   appearance and looks, 7, 82
   as backup singer for Gary, 132
   career decisions with, 167–168
   cooking of, 89
   courtship of, 83, 84
   family life in Williamsburg, 84–85
   Little Mama's engagement news, 206
   meets Gary, 81–82
   New Century Platters work, 104
   post-show Skype call with, 6–7
   pregnancy announcement of, 96
   summertime visits to, 20
   teen career of, 79–80, 82, 90
   wedding to Gary, 88
   work with VitaPro, 183–184
"Big Man of the Year Award", 162
Biggs, Noah, 55

Bilk, Acker, 76
Billboard Hot 100
   Beatles' domination of, 97
   British Invasion of, 107
   "Copy Cat", 78
   "Friend Don't Take Her (She's All I Got)", 113
   "High School U.S.A.", 49
   "If You Wanna Be Happy", 87
   "Limbo Rock", 87
   "New Orleans", 58
   "Not Me", 59
   "Out of Work", 155
   "Quarter to Three", 62, 63
   "Seven Day Weekend", 77
   "This Little Girl", 149
Bingham, Howard, 184
birthday celebrations
   Gary's, 197
   Springsteen's, 222–223
Bittan, Roy, 139
Blavat, Jerry, 62, 168
Blind Faith, 8
Blue Caps, 49
Blues Brothers 2000, 43, 187
Blues Foundation, 192
blues music, 191, 192
BMI, 98–99, 233
Bongiovi, Tony, 137
Booker T. Washington High School, 20, 40
Born in the U.S.A., 154
Born to Run, 128, 130
borrowing vs. infringement, 66–67, 70, 90
Bowen, J.T., 154
Brambleton, 36
Brandenburg, Ronnie, 169

Brecon, Wales, 2, 9
Brendan Byrne Arena, 147
"Bristol Stomp" (Dovells), v
British fans, 151, 171, 199
British Invasion
   adapting to, 100
   attempting to survive, 103
   casualties of, 161
   five years after, 107
   puts its heroes out of work, vi
   second wave of, 8
Broad, Graham, 199
Brooklyn
   of Big Mama's childhood, 84
   move to, 105
Brown, James, 22, 47
Brown, Ruth
   vs. Atlantic Records, 187
   contributions to Atlantic Records, 41
   early gigs with, 42
   Legends of Music Walk of Fame, 189
   package show with, 12
   on the "Wall of Fame", 18
Browne, Jackson, 156, 157
Brucie, Cousin, 213, 219–220
Bruno, George, 142
Bullet, 142
Burnell, Willie, 50
Burnette, Johnny, 75, 152
"Buy U.S. Bonds", 56
By U.S. Bonds
   inspiration for, 22, 24
   Paul Shaffer on, 43
   post-Hurricane Sandy work on, 227
   research with friends, 26

song version of, 228–229, 231–233
Byrd, Charlie, 189

C
Cafe Bar, 175
Cafferty, John, 23
Calypso music, 45, 70, 71, 86
Cameo Parkway, 67, 76, 87
Campbell, Jo Ann, 57
Cannon, Fabian, 57
Cannon, Freddy, 57, 70, 114
Canyon Records, 112
Capricorn Records, 112
Capris, 110
Caravan of Stars, 68, 69
career
    Act Two of, 138
    Ba-Bee on, 37
    Dick Clark's aid to, 57
    EMI's choices for Gary, 148–149
    family assessment of, 167
    financial innocence vs. responsibility, 71–72, 102–103
    first recording with Guida, 44–49
    Little Walter's contribution to, 34
    move to nostalgia circuit, 109–110
    1960s doldrums, 96, 100, 106
    Norfolk's pride in, 37
    partnership with Jerry Williams, 111–113
    "Quarter to Three" takes off, 63
    royalties from work with Guida, 177–178
    signing with EMI America, 144
    signing with Guida, 50, 58
    singing vs. recording, 127
    Springsteen's influence on, 130, 212–213
Carnes, Kim, 148
Carson, Wayne, 154
Cash, Johnny, 176
Cat, 47
Cavalcade of Stars, 57
"C.C. Rider", 40
Cedeño, Laurie. *see* Big Mama
Cedeño family, 85, 106
celebrity
    charity via, 184–185
    early-career image, 63
    Gary as unchanged by, 68
    pre-fame friends, 26
    pro-ams, 182
Cellar Door, 21
"Centerfold", 148
"Chain Gang" (Cooke), 58
Chairmen of the Board, 32
Champs, The, 87
Chance, Larry, 185
charity work
    for needy rockers, 188
    post-Hurricane Sandy, 227
    via celebrity, 184–185
Charles, Ray, 1
Checker, Chubby, vi, 34, 67, 87
Chedwick, Porky, 57
Chess Brothers, 95
Chess Records, 97
Chitlin' Circuit, 12
Christianson, Denny, 186

Index

Christie, Lou, 219
Christmas is On!, 228
Church Street Five, 60
"City Jail, City Farm", 94
Clanton, Jimmy, 62
Clark, Dick
    breaking of *Dedication*,
      145–146
    Caravan of Stars, 69
    first *American Bandstand*
      appearance, 36, 63
    first meeting with, 57
Class Reunion, 150
Clemente, John, 132, 142
Clemons, Clarence
    E Street Band collaborations,
      24
    memorial show, 20, 23
    on "This Little Girl", 138
Clemons, Nick, 23
Clemons family, 21
Cloud, Rusty, 142, 145
"Club Soul City", 154, 156, 158,
    176
Coasters, the, vi, 41, 114
Cochran, Eddie, 201
Cochran, Waye, 101–102
Codd, Elias, 56, 94
Cohen, Kalmann, 67
Cole, Natalie, 97
Coleman, Frissell. *see* Frissell
Collins, Leroy, 79
"Come On Let's Go", 162
Committee for Nuclear
    Disarmament, 156
Conn, Mervyn, 169, 170–171
Conte, Louie, 142
Cooke, Sam
    advice from, 13–14, 201

"Chain Gang", 58
"Cupid", 65
    package show tour with, 12
Cooper, Stephen, 9
"Copy Cat", 78
Cornell University, 123
country music
    as cousin to deep southern
      soul, 112
    "Friend Don't Take Her (She's
      All I Got)", 113
    "New Orleans" as, 98
Cover Me, 176
Cullinan, James F., 33, 171
Curtis, 19, 20, 83–84
Curtis, King, 41

D

"Daddy's Come Home", vii, 143
dancing, 32
Danelli, Dino, 162
David, Uncle, 17
Day, Margie, 41
D.C. Cab, 160
"Dear Lady Twist", 71
"Dedication"
    airing on *Bandstand*, 145–146
    recording of, 137–138
Dedication
    Clemons and Tallent on, 24
    as collaboration with
      Springsteen, 130
    fans on, 151–152
    finances of, 158–159
    first three songs, 138, 139
    growing popularity of, 147
    promotion of, 144–146
    tour supporting, 149–152
    "Way Back When", 141–142

Dee, Joey, 188
Dee-Dee, 31, 33
DeLauro, Tony, 193, 198, 203
Denlea, Jeff, 189, 192
Derby, Billy, 146
Diddley, Bo, vi, 114
digital downloads, 190
Dion, vi, 66
discrimination
    against Big Mama, 85, 91, 92
    in "dog-hitting" incident, 93–94
    in Green Hill Farms neighborhood, 95
    in Paris, 153–154
    see also racial issues
Dixieland jazz, 75
"Do the Limbo with Me", 86
Doherty, Denny, 170
Domino, Fats, vi
Dorothy, 80
Dorsey, Lee, vi
Dovells, The, v
"Dreams to Remember", 194, 202
dress
    Bonds' early-career, 34–35, 36
    of Daddy Grace, 49
    nostalgia-show expectations on, 116–117
    theft of Chuck Jackson's wardrobe, 73–74
Drifters, the
    as legends to Gary, 13
    package show tour with, 12
    "Save the Last Dance for Me", 58
    songwriting for, 74
    Van Zandt as producer for, vi
    work with Nader, 114
drivers, tour bus, 150
Dubsdread Golf Course shows, 123, 124–126
Duchess, 19, 32–33
Durham family, 16

E

E Street Band
    Clemons' work for, 20
    collaborations with, 24
    on *Dedication*, 143
    Gary's first recording with, 139
    Van Zandt as producer for, vii
    Wrecking Ball show with Gary, 216
Earl the Curl, 150
Earls, the, 185
early life
    dress during, 36
    first gigs with Sleepy King, 41–42
    first tour, 13–14
    musical education, 16
    side jobs, 28–29
    singing as a teen, 27–28
Eckstine, Billy, 30
Eddie and the Cruisers, 173
Edmunds, Dave, 176
education
    of Gary as a performer, 13–14
    of John Anderson, 15
Edward Waters College, 15
EF-N-DE, 47
Elektra, label, 112
Elmwood Cemetery, 99
EMI America
    Apostol's break with, 158–159

career choices for new artists, 148–149
delivery of *Dedication* to, 144
interest in Bonds/Springsteen collaborations, 140, 152
promotion of *Dedication*, 151
promotion of *On the Line*, 155
signing with, 144
waiting on payment from, 143
Ertegun, Ahmet, 95, 187
European tours
 A 1960's Revival Tour, 169
 with Ben E. King, 2–3, 203–204
 with Bill Wyman, 198
 for *Dedication*, 150, 153
 first, 74–75
 for *On the Line*, 156, 157
 with Roadhouse Rockers, 195
 second, 96

F

Facenda, Tommy "Bubba", 49
Fairley, Junior, 50, 60
Falovitch, Gerald Barry, 160
Fame, Georgie, 199, 200, 201–202
family
 Back in 20 record, 192
 Big Mama's, 82
 birthday celebrations, 197
 bomb-attempt on, 168–169
 financial management meeting, 167
 introducing Big Mama to Gary's, 81
 move from Sedgefield Drive, 100
 as priority, 27, 68
 Suffolk County home for, 120
 see also family members by name
"Fannie Mae", 192
fans
 British, 151, 171, 199
 Gary as Springsteen's, 212
 Grandma/Mom as, 172
 of Springsteen, 222
 Welsh, 196
 who requested "Jole Blon", 215
Fat Rat, 19, 26, 47
Faye, Lu, 98
Federici, Danny, 139, 141
Felt Forum, 114, 115
film
 Blues Brothers 2000, 187
 music videos, 155
 singing for Columbia Pictures, 74, 75
financial issues
 Apostol/EMI dealings, 156, 158–159
 early-career innocence, 71–72
 Guida's withholding, 95, 99
 in Jerry Williams partnership, 113
 pay for *A 1960s Revival Tour*, 170
 post-Sedgefield lows, 100–101, 103
 supporting a baby, 96
 supporting the Sedgefield house, 99
Fire and Fury Records, 112
Fitzgerald, Ella, 18, 189
Five Pearls, 46
Five Satins, vi, 110

Foreman, George, 136
Fort Dix, 83
Foundation for the Love of Rock and Roll, 188
Fraim, Mayor Paul, 21, 23, 37–38
Frank. *see* Guida, Francesco (Frank) Joseph
Frankie's Birdland
    Frankie's purchase of, 46
    promotes Springsteen-Bonds work, 148
    as start of Frankie's dream, 44
    success of, 52
Frazier, Smokin' Joe, 136, 185
Friday's, 151
"Friend Don't Take Her (She's All I Got)", 112
friends
    acceptance of Big Mama, 92
    autobiographical research with, 26
    celebrating difference among, 27
    on *Dedication*, 141
    at Gary's wedding, 89
    lifelong, 26–27
    Mark Leimbach, 173
    mutual protection by, 68–69
    post-Hurricane Sandy help from, 226
    as priority, 27
    relationships untouched by fame, 68
    Springsteen as, 131, 144, 210, 223
    supporting during tough financial times, 100
Frissell
    Air Force career, 33
    as life-long friend, 19, 26
    as a Turk, 31
    on a Turks reunion, 34

G

G L A Worldwide Music, 233
Garage Rock, vi
Gary Bonds and the Mallers, 136
Gault-Page, Richard (Ba-Bee), 36
General Artists, 62
Gersh, Gary, 140, 144, 152
"Gimme Some Loving" (Winwood), 8
Giordano, Charles, 215
"Give Me Just a Little More Time", 32
Global Village Champions, 184
Glover, Melvin, 69
golf
    celebrity pro-ams, 182
    at Dubsdread, 125
    Jeff Denlea, 189
    with Mark Leimbach, 173
    Yank Barry and, 161
    youthful hustling, 29–30
Good, Jack, 61–62
gospel music, 49
Grace, Bishop Charles Manuel "Sweet Daddy", 49, 60
Granby Street, 188–189
Grandma. *see* Newkirk, Mrs. Margaret (Grandma)
"Grandma's Washboard Band", 127
Granville Avenue, 80
Great American Soul Book tour, 1–5

greed, 106
Green Hill Farms house
   description, 89
   giving up, 100
   neighbors' discrimination, 93–94
   in a white neighborhood, 87, 91
Greenwich, Ellie, 142
Griffin Brothers, 41
Gross, Hermione, 31
Guida, Francesco (Frank) Joseph
   appearance and speech of, 52
   beginning of career end for, 78
   borrowing of others' sound, 67
   as co-inventor of Garage Rock, v
   death of, 196
   financial dealings with, 71–72
   first session with, 44–49
   infringement accusations by, 66–67, 70
   last hit by, 95, 96
   Legends of Music Walk of Fame, 189
   Norfolk Echo, 171
   Norfolk's honoring of, 177
   paranoia of, 77–78
   re-issuing of old material, 96, 148
   rise to fame of, 65–66
   royalties fight with, 177–178, 179
   third session with, 60
Guide label, 55
Gwendell (Ba-Bee's uncle), 37

H

hairstyle, 35
Haley, Bill, 35, 109, 110
Half Hollow Hills Country Club, 189
Half Hollow Hills School District, 120, 138
Hammersmith Odeon, 157, 170, 171
Hampton College, 15
Hanger, The, 129
Hazlet, NJ, 129
Hedwig, Ula, 142
"Hello Mary Lou", 115
Help!, 75
Hialeah Club, 82, 83
"High School U.S.A.", 49
Hispanic people, 91–92
Hitchings, Judge, 94
hits
   as audience draw, 203
   Guida's last, 95
   vs. misses, 11
   re-packaging, 96
   royalties from early, 178
   see also specific album/song name
Hogan's Heroes, 199
Holiday, Doc, 20
Holiday Inns, 126, 128
Hollies, the, 176
Holmes, "Daddy" Jack, 17, 55
Hong Kong Convention Center, 207
Hornsby, Bruce, 189
Hotel Talbot, 195
Howlin' Wolf, 97
Hughes, John, 150
hunger, fighting world, 184–185,

186–187
Hunter, Ivory Joe, 31, 127
Hurricane Sandy, 225, 227
"Hushabye", 32
Hyland, Brian, 207

I

"I Don't Want to Cry", 70
"I Want to Hold Your Hand", 97
"I Wish I Could Dance Like Fred Astaire", 162
"If You Wanna Be Happy", 86, 95
"I'm Gonna Sue", 66, 78
"Imagine" (Lennon), 9
incarceration, 93–94
Irene (Mom), Miss
   attention to Gary's dress, 36
   Ba-Bee on, 37
   death of, 127
   dislike of Big Mama, 85, 90, 92
   early life of, 16
   Gary as raised by, 15
   house parties with, 27
   moves in with Grandma, 100
   support of Gary, 51
Iridium, 226
Isley Brothers, 74
It's Trad Dad, 155
Ivy, Quin, 112
Izod Center, 147

J

Jackson, Bullmoose, 31, 127
Jackson, Chuck
   Global Village Champions, 184

"I Don't Want To Cry", 70
   at Nevele, 185
   New York shows with, 73
   work on *Dedication*, 141
Jacksonville, 17
Jacksonville Beach, 69
Jagger, Mick, 97
James, Tommy, 124
Jaro label, 55
Jay, Bobby, 35
Jay Geils Band, 148
jazz
   Dixieland, 75
   Frankie's Birdland, 46
   Georgie Fame's, 202
   Mark IV Lounge, 18–19
JB, 19
Jelly Belly, 51
Jerry Butler and the Impressions, 31
Jersey clubs, 227
Jersey Shore, 173, 175
Jersey Sound, 141, 173, 194
Jimmy and the Parrots, 195
Jimmy Soul. *see* McCleese, James ("The Wonder Boy")
Jive Five, 76
Joel, Billy, 34
John, Elton, 161
John, Little Willie, 197
Johnson, General Norman, 32, 33
Johnson, "Little Walter." *see* Walter Little
"Jole Blon"
   performed with Springsteen, 146, 147, 214, 220
   recording, 141
   UK performance of, 157

Jones, Tom, 69, 181
Joyce, 32, 169

K

Kamon, Karen, 160
Kent, Anne Guida, 179
King, B.B.
   advice from, 13, 14
   package show tour with, 12
King, Ben E.
   on *Dedication*, 141
   European tour with Gary, 2–4, 203–204
   Global Village Champions, 184
   on nostalgia circuit, vi
   "Save the Last Dance for Me", 58
   on signature songs, 116–117
   songwriting of, 25
King, Betty, 9
Kingsmen, 160, 181
"kiss curl" hairdo, 35
Klein, Larry, 145, 146
Knockouts, group 136
Kreisberg, Jack, 191
Kronfeld, Phil, 73

L

LaBelle, Pattie, 83
labels
   in the age of iPods, 190
   Atlantic Records, 40, 41
   Chess Records, 97
   EF-N-DE, 47
   EMI America, 140
   End Records, 90
   found with Jerry Williams, 112
   of Frankie Guida, 55
   King Records, 47
   Laurie Records, 48
   Legrand, 48, 49, 50
   Pheonix, 159, 162

   pitching Springsteen collaboration to, 140
   S.P.Q.R., 86
Lafferty, Tom, 132
Lakland Air Force, 133–135
Lambert, Lanny, 142
Lancaster, Mike, 151, 157
Las Vegas, v
"Last Time", 154
Late Show with David Letterman, 43
Laurie ("Big Mama"). *see* Big Mama
Laurie ("Little Mama"). *see* Little Mama
Laurie Records, 48, 55, 66
Lee, Albert, 199
legends, rock
   on the *Blues Brothers 2000* set, 188
   early tours with, 13
   Gary named as a, 187
   Nader negotiates among, 114
   Norfolk's Legends of Music Walk of Fame, 22, 188
Legends of Music Walk of Fame, 22, 188
Legrand
   beginning of end for, 78
   contract with, 50, 97
   fight over royalties with, 177–178, 179

Hot 100 hits, 48, 49
last record with, 105
as one of Frankie's labels, 55
re-issuing of old material, 148
rise to fame of, 65–66
Sewells Point Rd. studios, 70
UK distribution for, 62
Leimbach, Mark
   Back in 20 song, 192
   at Hong Kong show, 207
   long-time friendship with, 173
   loyalty of, 193, 196–197
   at the Springsteen show, 217
Lerner Shops, 29
Lester, Richard, 75, 76, 155
"Let Them Talk", 33
Let Them Talk, 197, 228
Levy, Harry, 96
Lewis, Gary, 127
Lewis, Jerry Lee, 114
Lincoln, Fred J., 162
Little Mama
   on Air Force base tour, 132, 135
   birth of, 99
   collaborations with, 24
   college graduation of, 169
   contributions to *Standing in the Line of Fire*, 162
   early schooling, 119
   entrance into the music business, 137
   godfather of, 141–142, 143
   Hong Kong honeymoon, 208
   as host at *Wrecking Ball* show, 210
   as in-home producer, 190–191
   leaving Norfolk to protect, 104
   lyric-writing by, 186
   marriage to Eurel, 205–206
   orchestrates performances with Springsteen, 211–214, 216, 220
   as tour manager, 4, 6–8
   on tour with Gary and Bill Wyman, 199
   weathering of Hurricane Sandy, 225, 226
   work with VitaPro, 184
Little Richard, vi, 41
"look," Gary's, 34–35
Lopez, Vini "Mad Dog", 23, 24
"Lose Your Inhibition Twist", 76
"Louie, Louie", 160, 181
Louis, Joe, 30
Louise, Aunt, 17, 172
LuLu, 19, 26
Love Notes, 90
Lowe, Bernie, 95
loyalty vs. responsibility, 158, 165, 167
Lucille, Miss
   creates re-union for Gary, 26
   on Gary's dancing, 33
   kick-start to Gary's career, 17
   Mark IV Lounge owner, 18–19
luck, 34
Lulu, 111
Lymon, Frankie, 36

M

Madison Square Garden, 35, 110
Mamas and Papas, 170
Mankind Records, 111
Mann, Kal, 95

Marco Label, 55
Maresca, Ernie, 66
Mark IV Lounge, 18–19, 26, 46
Marsh, Dave, 152
Martin, Joe, 146, 150, 154
Martin, Loretta, 57
Matilda, 46
"Matilda", 46
Matthews, Patricia, 77
Maynor, Dorothy, 189
M.C. Records, 192, 195
McCleese, James ("The Wonder Boy")
   duo show with, 42–44
   first recording with Guida, 54–55
   "If You Wanna Be Happy", 86, 87
   incarceration and death of, 172
   "Twistin' Matilda", 71
McDaniel, Gene
   British tour with, 77, 152
   film singing with, 74, 76
   musical talents of, 77
McEachin, Bonnie, 13
McFarlane, "Spanky", 170
McKenzie, Scott, 170
McPhatter, Clyde, 28, 31
Mead, Frank, 199, 201
Meisner, Randy, 114
Mello Kings, 110
Memories, club, 168
memory, imperfect, 11
"Men Without Women", 152
Miami, 101, 102
Miami Horns, 143
Micara, Mike, 142, 145
Milinder, Lucky, 31

Miller Beer, 155
Mimms, Eddie
   Big Mama's relationship with, 90
   Gary's busboy work with, 29
   at Green Hill Farms house, 88
   meeting of Mom (Irene), 17
   move in with Grandma, 100
MJ's New York Times, 126
Mom. *see* Irene (Mom), Miss
money. *see* financial issues
Moore, Joyce, 32, 69, 169
Moore, Sam, 1
Moose, 31
Morehouse College, 15
Morrison, Jim, 178
Motown
   Ales, Barney, 127
   "appropriation" of Guida's work, 70
   Guida's answer song to, 90
   songbook, 101, 107, 133
   taps into white market, 100
MTV, 155
Muddy Waters, 97
Mullican, Moon, 146
Murray, Juggy, 112
music videos, 155
Muso, Steve, 107

N

Nader, Richard, 35, 108, 114
name change, Gary's, 55–56
Nashboro Records, 112, 113
Nassau, Steve, 132
Nathan, Syd, 47, 95
The National, 21
Nebraska, 154
Nelson, Benjamin, 2

see Ben E. King
Nelson, Rick, 114–117
Nevele, 185
Neville, Aaron, 58
New Century Platters, 104
New Journal and Guide, 67, 93
New Musical Express, 151
"New Orleans"
  Bill Wyman on, 198
  Billboard Hot 100, 58
  with Neil Sedaka, 161
  promotion of, 56
  recording of, 53–54
New York, 72, 74
New York Institute of
  Technology, 169
Newkirk, Grandpa, 17, 172
Newkirk, Mrs. Margaret
  (Grandma)
  Ba-Bee on, 37
  death of, 172
  house parties with, 27
  move to Norfolk, 15, 16
Newsom, Tom, 189
Nightingales, 43
Nite, Norm N., 14
"No Nukes" Hollywood Bowl
  concert, 146, 149, 156
Norfolk
  Bill Reid's promotion of,
    21–22
  first record to break in, 60
  as Gary's hometown, 38
  Hispanics as absent from,
    91–92
  move from, 104
  Norfolk Sound. *see* Norfolk
    Sound
  racial issues, 27

  reasons to move to, 16–17
  return to, 177
Norfolk Community Golf
  Course, 29
Norfolk Echo, 33, 44, 171
Norfolk Recording Studio,
  47–48, 51–54
Norfolk Sound
  as foundation for Jersey
    Sound, 194
  honor ceremony for pioneers
    of, 189
  Laurie Records' interest in, 66
  Mayor Fraim on, 37–38
  Norfolk Echo for fans of, 171
  telling the story of, 22
Norfolk State University, 177,
  178
Norfolk's Legends of Music Walk
  of Fame, 22
North, Freddie, 112–113
Northern Soul, 40
Northwestern Senior High
  School, 15
Norva label, 55
The NorVa, 20, 21, 22, 23, 188
nostalgia circuit
  audience expectations at,
    116–117
  creation of, 108–109
  with Mark Leimbach,
    174–175
  as only available option, 8
  return to, 173
  work with Nader on, 114
"Not Me", 59, 95
Nothing Left to Lose, 186
Now Dig This, 151

O

Okeh Records, 40
Old Waldorf, 146
"oldies circuit, vi
On the Line
    players on, 24
    promotion of, 155
    recording of, 154
    slow sales of, 158–159, 160
    Van Zandt on, viii
"Once Around the Block Ophelia", 160
"One Broken Heart", 112
"One Million Tears", 55, 62
Orlando, 124, 126, 127
Orlons, 59
"Out of Work", 154, 156, 158

P

Pace, Babe, 132
Palmer, Sy, 34
Panico, Tony, 199
Paris, discrimination in, 153–154
Parisi, Rob, 142
Paycheck, Johnny, 113
Payn, Nick, 199, 201
Penn State University, 15
People, 149
Pepe, 132
"Perdido", 95
performing
    down time as part of, 68
    first by Little Mama, 132
    by imposters, 59
    for Pop, 69
    stage personality, 13–14, 33
    see also shows; tours

Peter, Mike
    career advice from, 127
    friendship with, 168
    Gary's meeting of, 123
    hosts Little Mama's wedding, 206, 207
    Orlando successes, 128
    partnership with, 165
    post-Hurricane Sandy help from, 226
Petite Ballroom, 32
P.G.A., 30
Phillips, John, 170
Phillips, Mackensie 170
Phillips, Reuben, 72
Phillips, Sam, 95
Pickett, Wilson, 1, 111
Pitt, Gene, 76
Platters, 73, 109
Plaza (Norfolk), 13
"Please Forgive Me", 54
Pointer Sisters, 176
Pomus, Doc, 74, 77, 187
Pop. *see* Anderson, John Henry Gary (Pop)
Powell, Clive, 201
    see also George Fane
Powell, Nicole, 198
The Power Station, 137, 140
Prater, Dave, 1
Premier Talent Associates, 106, 108
Price, Holly Cara, 197
Price, Lloyd, vi
pro-ams, celebrity, 182
"Promised Land" (Berry), 12
protest concerts, 156–157
Puerto Rican community, 85
Purcell, 26, 33

Q

"Quarter to Three"
  on *American Bandstand*, 35
  Barge on, 228
  Bill Wyman on, 198
  Bonds' gratitude for, 117
  chart-topping run of, 65
  influence of, 66
  Jack Good on, 61
  lawsuit, 76
  national airplay for, 62
  on *A Night with Mr. C*, 20
  at Norfolk honor ceremony, 178
  shows following success of, 12
  as sung by Springsteen, 128, 130, 176, 213
  thousand-person conga line to, 209
  writing of, 61
Queen's Lounge, 42

R

racial issues
  Attucks, Crispus, 21
  distrust of lawyers, 58
  divided seating, 12
  division of Williamsburg, 84
  education of African Americans in the 1920s, 15
  in golf, 29, 30
  in Guida's success, 46
  law enforcement prejudice, 42
  "non-racial" housing, 120
  in Norfolk, 16, 27
  restaurant segregation, 88
  see also discrimination
Ramone, Phil, 160

Rayle, Sally, 149
recording
  business in the age of iPods, 190
  "Dedication", 137–138
  failed records, 99
  first-record following, 58
  of the Five Pearls, 47
  Gary's first, 51, 54
  in-home, 190–191
  with Jerry Williams, 111–112
  last Gary/Guida, 105
  On the Line, 154
  luck of, 34
  with Mark Leimbach, 173
  Norfolk Recording Studio, 48
  "Not Me", 59
  Nothing Left to Lose, 186
  vs. singing shows, 127
  "This Little Girl", 138
  Twist/Calypso with Guida, 71
  by Yank Barry, 160, 185
Redding, Otis, 1, 194, 202
Reeves, Martha, 170
Regal, Chicago, 13, 14, 74, 82
Reid, Bill, 20, 34, 37, 188
"Rendezvous", 158
responsibility vs. loyalty, 158, 165, 167
Rhino, label, 176
Rhodes, Ted, 30
Rhythm and Blues Foundation, 187
Rhythm Kings
  meeting the, 200–201
  tour offer with, 198, 199
"Rhythm of the Rain", 161
Riverboat, 127
Roadhouse Rockers, 193

Rock and Roll Revival: Volume 7, 114–117
rock n' roll
   charity concert for needy rockers, 188
   extremes of, 11
   Las Vegas "oldies circuit", v
   nostalgia circuit creation, 108–110
   in one's 40s, 167
   post-show tragedies, 4–5
   in the seventies, v
   as what Bonds does, 5
Rock of Ages, 195
The Rock and Roll Revival: Volume 1, 110
Roker, Wally, 112
Rolling Stones, 198
romance, 80, 81–82
Rose Bowl, 156
Royal Peacock, 13
royalties
   Atlantic's inaccurate reporting of, 187
   from work with Guida, 177–178, 179
Royster, Joe
   death of, 99
   Gary's first recording with, 52
   on "High School U.S.A.", 49
   meets Frank Guida, 48
   move out of Norfolk, 97
   post-Norfolk life, 98–99
   on "Quarter to Three", 61
Rubell, Steve, 126
Ruiz, George, 145
"Rum and Coca Cola", 46
"Runaround Sue", 66
Rust label, 55

Rydell, Bobby, 57, 70, 114

S

Sam & Dave, 1
Sanchez, Mike, 199
Sands, Ida, 55
Saturday Night Live, 151
"Save the Last Dance for Me", 58, 74
"School Is In", 70, 198
"School Is Out", 62, 65, 198
Scotland Neck, NC, 41
Seals, Miss Lucille, 17, 18–19, 26
Sedaka, Neil, 161
Sedgefield Drive house. *see* Green Hill Farms house
Selzer, Hal B., 193, 195
"Seven Day Weekend", 77
Sewells Point Rd. studios, 70
Sha Na Na, 109
Shaffer, Paul, 43, 187–188
Shannon, Del, 76
Sheep Meadow, 157
Sheiks, the, 47
Shep and the Limelights, 110
Sheraton, New York, 73
Shields, Emmett ("Nabs"), 41, 50, 60
Shiloh Church, 28
Shindig, 62
Shirelles, vi, 96, 109, 114
shout bands, 49–50
Showmen, 32, 55
shows
   as a "black act", 107
   for the "door", 99
   driving the box truck to, 121–122

Dubsdread Golf Course,
  124–126
early Turks, 32
Hong Kong, 207
for inmates, 32
with Mark Leimbach,
  174–175
negotiating egos on nostalgia,
  114
prioritizing friendship over, 27
protest concerts, 156–157
putting out at, 13–14
small hotels and lounge, 126,
  128, 168
South Florida, 101
with Springsteen, 146–147,
  211–216
see also performing; tours
Shuman, Mort, 74, 77
Sifford, Charlie, 30
Silky Straight, 35
"Since I Met You Baby" (Hunter),
  31
singing
  Barry on Gary's, 186
  Big Mama's, 82
  for Columbia Pictures, 74, 75
  financial responsibility of,
    102–103
  Gary on Springsteen's,
    130–131
  Gary's joy in, 229
  Johnson, General Norman, 32
  luck of recording, 34
  natural ease of, 30–31
  vs. recording career, 127
  signature songs, 116–117
  as a teen, 27–28
  Van Zandt on Gary's, vii, 143

Sirius XM satellite radio,
  219–220
Skeete, Beverly, 199
Sledge, Percy, 112
Sleepy King, 39
Slow Drag
  Atlantic City shows with, 81
  on Big Mama, 80, 82
  Big Mama on, 84
  Gary meets, 52
  leaving Norfolk with, 12
  road trips with, 72, 74
  as session aid, 60
"Sneakin' Away", 163
Snow, Pheobe, 192
Snyder, Tom, 150
Songwriters Hall of Fame, 25
songwriting
  autobiographical, 231–233
  of Ben E. King, 25
  with Bruce Springsteen, 138
  of Doc Pomus and Mort
    Shuman, 74
  "Friend Don't Take Her (She's
    All I Got)", 113
  Gary as influencing
    Springsteen's, 130
  on *On the Line*, 154
  by Steven Van Zandt, vii–viii
  style and collaborations,
    24–25
Sonny and Cher, 69
Soul, Jimmy, 44
Soul Book tour, 1–5
"Soul Deep", 154, 158
soul music
  aging "fathers" of, 4
  deep southern, 111, 112
  of Sleepy King, 39–40

Theater Brycheinoig show
 of, 1
Sound Mixers Studio, 141, 142
South Florida, 101
Southside Johnny
 and the Ashbury Jukes, vi,
  142, 163
 on *Back in 20*, 191
 at Clemons memorial, 23
 on *Cover Me*, 176
 on *On the Line* and *Dedications*,
  24
 on money, 168
 post-Sandy charity work, 227
Spaniels, 110
Spector, Ronnie, vi
Spencer Davis Group, 8
sponsorship by Miller Beer, 155
S.P.Q.R., 86
Springsteen, Bruce
 on *Back in 20*, 191
 Gary meets, 129–130
 gift of a '57 Chevy to, 144
 invites Gary to *Wrecking Ball*
  tour stage, 211–212, 215
 On the Line contributions, 154
 Mike Peter meets, 128
 nuclear protest concerts,
  156–157
 number of performances with,
  24
 recording at The Power
  Station, 137
 re-introduces Clemons to
  Gary, 20
 repackaging collaborations
  with, 176
 songs written for Gary, viii
 surprises a Leimbach/Bonds
  show, 175
 West Coast shows with Gary,
  146–147
 work with Van Zandt, vi, vii,
  154
 Wrecking Ball Tour, 209
"Stand By Me" (King), 3, 25, 117
"Standing in the Line of Fire",
 viii, 162, 163
Standing in the Line of Fire album,
 165, 166
Stann, Joey
 on *Bandstand*, 145
 inability to provide work for,
  163
 with Roadhouse Rockers, 193
 on tour bus drivers, 150
 on "Way Back When", 142
Stark, Lance Hyland, 193
Story, Lloyd, 48
Strange, Billy, 87
Suma, Lenny, 107
Supremes, 69
Surf Club, 227
Swanson, Earl
 in "dog-hitting" incident,
  93–94
 in Gary's early career, 40
 on "High School U.S.A.", 49
 recording of "New Orleans",
  53, 54
 replacement by Barge, 59
 as a tenor sax, 41
 on "Tiger Rock", 50
"Sweet Soul Music" (Conley), 9

T

Tallent, Garry, 23, 24, 139
Taxi, 107

Taylor, Sam "The Man", 40
Taylor, Terry, 199
Teenagers, 36
Teenchord, 35
"That's My Story (I'm Sticking to It)", 228, 231–233
"The Last Time", viii
"The Music Goes Round and Round", 97
"The Pretender", 143, 157
"The Star", 112
Theater Brycheinoig, 1
"There Goes My Baby" (King), 25
"This Little Girl"
   Clarence Clemons on, 139
   on *Cover Me*, 176
   performed with Springsteen, 147, 214, 222
   released as a single, 145
   in the top 15, 149
   writing of, 138
"This Magic Moment", 74
Thomas, B.J., 207
Thorogood, George, 194
Tic Toc Diner, 217
"Tiger Rock", 49
Tim, Tiny, 136
Tobias, Eurel
   career of, 209, 210
   marriage to Little Mama, 205–206
Tomorrow Show, 150
"Too Good For Each Other", 142
Toomes, Leroy (Bunchy), 53
tours
   "Chitlin' Circuit", 12
   early-career, 12
   first international, 75
   first New York, 72
   as opening act, 13
   with the Rhythm Kings, 200–202
   with Roadhouse Rockers, 194–196
   Soul Book with Ben E. King, 1–5, 203–204
   to support *Dedication*, 144, 149–150, 153
   to support *On the Line*, 155–158
   U.S. Air Force base, 131–135
   William Morris Agency, 149
   see also shows
Towering Performance Award, 25
Towne Club, 31
Trad music, 75, 76
Traffic, 8
"Travellin' Man", 115
Trinidad, 45
Turks, the
   asking Frissell about, 26
   early gigs, 32
   formation of, 31
   free shows by, 18
"Turn the Music Down", 158
"Twist, Twist Señora", 71, 75, 198
Twist movies, 75
Twist records, 67, 70
"Twist Up Calypso", 71
Twist Up Calypso, 71
"Twistin' Matilda", 71
Tyrell, Soozie, 215

U

Uggams, Leslie, 79
Underwood, Clarence, 29–30

Index

"United", 90
United Church of Prayer for All People, 49, 60
United Golf Association, 30
Uptown (Philadelphia), 13, 74, 82
US magazine, 149
'U-Turn Bob, 150

V

Valli, Frankie, vi, 124
Van Zandt, Steven
    "Big Man of the Year Award", 162
    "Daddy's Come Home", 143
    dinner honoring, 66
    on Gary, v, viii
    on *On the Line*, 154
    "Men Without Women", 152
    recommendation to Bill Wyman, 199
    work on "Standing in the Line of Fire", 162
    work with Gary's friends, 24, 141
Vincent, Gene, 76, 201
Vinci, Frankie, 162
Virginian Pilot, 178
The Virginian-Pilot & The Ledger Star, 56
VitaPro, 183
vocals. *see* singing

W

W Hotel, 214
Wales, 195
Walsh, Brian, 44, 171
Walter, Little, 20, 92, 226
    contribution to Gary's career, 34, 35
    on Gary's appearance, 36
    as life-long friend, 19
Warwick, Dee Dee, 111
"Way Back When", 141–142, 143
W.C. Handy Awards, 192
wedding to Big Mama, 88
Wells, Mary, 127
West Coast label Canyon Records, 112
Westbrook, 19, 26, 38
Wexler, Jerry, 48, 95
"What a Crazy World", 105
"When a Man Loves a Woman", 112
whiskey running, 28
"White Knight of Soul", 102
WHOD radio station, 57
Wienberg, Max, 139, 215
Wild Dunes, 182
William Morris Agency, 144, 148
Williams, Jerry ("Swamp Dogg")
    early career of, 103
    recording with, 111–113
    reuniting with in Brooklyn, 105
Williams Jr., Jerry, 24
Williamsburg, 84–85
Willis, Chuck, 40
Wilson, Frank, 26, 191
Wilson, Jackie, 1, 3, 31, 73
Winwood, Steve, 8–9
Woods, Greg, 132, 133–135
work farm, Norfolk, 94
WRAP 850, 17, 55
Wrecking Ball CD, 210
Wrecking Ball Tour, 209,

211–212, 215
Wrecking Crew, 87
Wyman, Bill, 198, 202

Y

"You Can't Sit Down"
  (Dovells), v
"You Can't Teach an Old Dog
  New Tricks", 191, 196
"Your Love", 141
"Your Precious Love", 31
"You're the Best", 3
Yuro, Timi, 62

Z

"Zing Went the Strings of My
  Heart", 32